A CALL
TO CIVIC SERVICE

A CALL
TO CIVIC SERVICE

National Service for Country and Community

Charles C. Moskos

A Twentieth Century Fund Book

THE FREE PRESS
A Division of Macmillan, Inc.
NEW YORK

Collier Macmillan Publishers
LONDON

The Free Press
A Division of Macmillan, Inc.
866 Third Avenue, New York, N.Y. 10022

Collier Macmillan Canada, Inc.

Printed in the United States of America

printing number

1   2   3   4   5   6   7   8   9   10

Library of Congress Cataloging-in-Publication Data

Moskos, Charles C.
   A call to civic service: national service for country and community/Charles C. Moskos.
      p.   cm.
   "Twentieth Century Fund Book."
   Includes index.
   ISBN 0–02–921991–4
   1. Labor service—United States.   2. National service—United States.   3. Youth—Employment—United States.   4. Youth volunteers in community development—United States. I. Title.
HD4870.U6M67   1988
355.2'236'0973—dc19   88–16104
                                                  CIP

The Twentieth Century Fund is a research foundation undertaking timely analyses of economic, political, and social issues. Not-for-profit and non-partisan, the Fund was founded in 1919 and endowed by Edward A. Filene.

For
Morris Janowitz and Donald J. Eberly,
mentors and exemplars of national service

Contents

Foreword

Citizenship is a matter of rights—and of obligations. The advent of the all-volunteer army during a period in which Americans were focusing on ensuring individual rights and entitlements while neglecting the teaching of civic responsibility resulted in a loss of a sense of civic obligation. National service, the term used to describe short-term participation in public service jobs by young citizens for little pay, offers a way to instill a sense of civic responsibility in today's youth.

Falling rates of voter participation and the problems of the all-volunteer army led the Trustees and staff of the Twentieth Century Fund to consider the pressing need to instill the idea of civic responsibilities in young Americans. We decided that any worthwhile study of national service would have to examine not only the history of national service but broader questions of social policy. National service has many benefits—it can instill work habits, provide job training and basic education, serve unmet social and environmental needs—but unless it is considered principally as a means of enhancing citizenship, there is a danger that it will be viewed as make-work or welfare.

In Charles C. Moskos, professor of sociology at Northwestern University and author of *The American Enlisted Man* and *The Peace Soldiers*, we found a scholar who saw national service in a broad policy context. Moskos wanted to provide a historical and comparative look at the ideas and programs that have, over the years, been encompassed in the term national service, and then suggest a comprehensive national service program for youth that would both build on historical precedent and take into account current political trends.

Moskos has succeeded admirably, presenting a reasoned case for national service that will enlighten the debate over this difficult policy issue. We are grateful to him for his efforts.

M. J. Rossant, Director
The Twentieth Century Fund
April 1988

Acknowledgments

First, I would like to thank my draft board. My service in the peacetime army of the late 1950s led to my interest and, eventually, to a very satisfying academic career in military sociology (and a good living to boot). Although my initial concept of national service began as a draftee, over time it has come to include the civilian server as well as the citizen soldier. Indeed, the underlying commonality of military and civilian service is the unifying theme of this book. The civic service called for here thus presents a blueprint for a voluntary program of national service encompassing both military and civilian forms.

I want to extend my gratitude to Marcia Bystryn, whose letter from the Twentieth Century Fund about doing a book on national service came at precisely the time I was pondering such an undertaking. Also at the Twentieth Century Fund I am grateful to Murray J. Rossant, Nina Massen, and Beverly Goldberg, who stroked me when I needed stroking and prodded me when I needed prodding. My debt is enormous to Michael Massing, whose editing on behalf of the Twentieth Century Fund taught me to think as well as write more clearly.

Many people helped out in the collection of the materials covered in this paper, and I have departed from normal practice by acknowledging them in appropriate end notes in order to recognize their specific help. More generally, I have profited greatly from discussions (indeed, often debates) with many individuals, and I wish to single out Bernard Beck, Wendell Bell, Peter Braestrup, Richard Danzig, Edwin Dorn, Arnold S. Feldman, Richard Halloran, Thomas E. Kelly, John Kester, James

Kielsmeier, Roger Landrum, Richard Leopold, Marion J. Levy, Jr., Jane Mansbridge, Cynthia Parsons, Peter Szanton, Will Hill Tankersley, Samuel F. Wells, Jr., and George Wilson. For helping make the policies proposed in this book part of a larger political discourse on national service, I am indebted to John G. Campbell, John Cuadares, Alvin From, Antonia Handler Chayes, Barbara J. Kennelly, Pam Lalonde, Will Marshall, Paul N. McCloskey, Dave McCurdy, Sam Nunn, Charles S. Robb, Phillip P. Upschulte, and R. James Woolsey.

I would also like to express my appreciation to the Woodrow Wilson International Center for Scholars and the Rockefeller Humanities Fellowship Program, whose support at different times gave me the opportunity to develop many of the ideas that came to be included in this volume. James A. Davis and Paul B. Sheatsley of the National Opinion Research Center, that peerless survey organization, kindly made available attitude data on national service. I am grateful to Martha Roth for editing help in the early stages of the manuscript. John Whiteclay Chambers II gave the typescript an invaluable reading and came up with the title that heads this book. Joyce Seltzer, my editor, and other members of the Free Press staff performed superhuman labors to publish the manuscript in rapid time.

Much of my professional and intellectual life centers around the Inter-University Seminar on Armed Forces and Society, an "invisible college" of scholars which I am privileged to head. The Seminar served as the intellectual incubator for my thoughts on national service. I wish to thank especially the following Seminar colleagues: John S. Butler, John B. Keeley, W. Darryl Henderson, John J. Mearsheimer, Sam C. Sarkesian, David R. Segal, John Alden Williams, and Frank R. Wood. Most of all I want to acknowledge Morris Janowitz and Donald J. Eberly, whose professional and personal dedication to national service is an inspiration to all who know them.

All errors in fact or interpretation are, of course, my own sole responsibility.

ONE

Citizenship and National Service

In the upper reaches of the Rio Grande valley, farmers have faithfully performed a communal task every spring for more than three centuries. The annual cleaning of the *acequias*, or irrigation ditches, is required so that water can flow into the orchards and fields of the small farmers who work the harsh though beautiful land of northern New Mexico. Young men clear the debris that has gathered over the winter, older men supervise them, and women bring food for the men. The significance of the yearly repairs of the *acequias* is not only that it is the oldest continuously performed community task in the country, but that it stands as a kind of parable for the way shared civic duties become the social glue that holds a society together. In the face of urbanization, a changing economy, and social flux, how well the ditch duties are carried out reflects the social cohesion of the community.

There is no more powerful expression of such civic sharing than what is commonly called national service. This entails the full-time undertaking of public duties by young people—whether as citizen soldiers or civilian servers—who are paid subsistence wages. "National" is used here in the broadest sense. It encompasses youth service performed at the state, local, and community levels for both governmental agencies and nonprofit organizations. Common to all such service is the performance of socially needed tasks that the market cannot effectively handle and that would be too expensive for government employees to carry out.

1

From the beginning, it is important to understand that national service must not be seen as a magical talisman, a mystical means for transforming socially indifferent Americans into paragons of civic virtue. But national service does mean the performance of citizen duties that allow individuals to have a sense of the civic whole—a whole that is more important than any single person or category of persons. It is upon some such norm of fulfillment of a civic obligation, upon some concept of serving societal needs outside the marketplace, upon some sense of participation in a public life with other citizens that the idea of national service builds. We will refer to these notions hereafter, for purposes of shorthand, as *civic content*.

There has been some confusion among national-service supporters about who is supposed to benefit from the work performed—the server or society—which has produced two schools of thought about national service, what might be called the *instrumental* and the *civic*. The instrumental tradition justifies national service by the good done to the server. The civic tradition focuses on the value of the services performed. The first tradition provokes negative stereotypes by inviting speculation on deficiencies in the character of the server. The second tradition offers national service as an end in itself, thereby fostering positive images of servers. Only when national service is cast in terms of its civic content can its positive, but necessarily derivative, benefits for the server be achieved.

One other issue must be gotten out of the way early on. Because civic content is the lodestone of national service, whether the service performed is compulsory or voluntary is not an essential element of any definition of national service, however profound may be the policy implications of that question. This book will propose a form of comprehensive national service that would include a substantial number of youth—as many as one million in either military or civilian service—and would not be mandatory. By promoting a spirit of civic mindedness, national service will accomplish a range of much-needed national tasks, thus reshaping American life in fundamental ways.

WHY YOUTH?

For good reasons national service is almost always presented as a program for youth. Although arrangements can be made for older people to participate in national-service programs, the primary focus must be on teenagers and young adults. From a practical standpoint, young people are more flexible than adults and have fewer family obligations. Furthermore, since many have not yet entered the work force, young participants would prove less disruptive to the nation's economy; indeed, their value as workers may be enhanced by the service experience itself, thereby making America more competitive in the new realities of global economic interdependence. In addition, young adults can usually perform certain physical tasks—notably military and conservation work—more efficiently than older people. The growing tendency of American youth to postpone the responsibilities of adulthood makes national service potentially an attractive way station between school and work. But there is also an intangible: focusing national service on youth makes it a rite of passage toward adult citizenship, dramatizing its importance.

The preference for youth makes sense from a citizenship standpoint as well. Practically speaking, if one does not serve while young, one is not likely to serve at all. Certainly civic values are more effectively imparted at an earlier rather than a later age. Inasmuch as research indicates that schools are doing a poor job of inculcating civic values, national service offers an alternative vehicle for civic education. Common sense suggests that national service would have its maximum impact at the beginning of adult life. Young men and women who have completed a term of service in the Peace Corps or VISTA, as well as the peacetime military, typically describe their experience in special and positive terms. Those who have not done national service can never fully understand what it is like, and those who have are never quite the same afterward.[1]

The fact remains that national service is less likely to be experienced by the present generation of young Americans than by any other youth cohort in living memory. Yet there are numerous contemporary instances of youths voluntarily serving abroad, although far from the type of national service I envision. Each winter since 1984, for example, some five hundred young Americans, Sandinista sympathizers, have volunteered to pick cotton or help bring in the coffee harvest in Nicaragua. These volunteers pay their own travel expenses and work ten-hour days for subsistence wages. Similar leftist youth volunteers have been cutting sugar in Cuba almost every year since the Castro revolution. And there are other groups who serve voluntarily for very different reasons. Religiously motivated youth serve throughout Latin America, Africa, and the Pacific islands. No reliable statistics exist, but the number of young evangelists serving overseas far exceeds the number of Peace Corps volunteers. The Mormon Church alone has about 21,000 men and women serving "missions" abroad—twenty-four months for men, eighteen months for women. Supported by family funds and personal savings, these young missionaries have made the Mormon program one of the most successful youth outreach ventures in history.

To be sure, none of these activities contains civic content; quite the contrary. But the examples cited here—and they represent only a small sampling—refute the general characterization of American youth as irrevocably self-absorbed and apathetic. Clearly, if the proper opportunities were available, many more would serve. What ideology and religion have done to motivate a select group, national service could do for a broad sector of American youth.

EMERGING PUBLIC PHILOSOPHY AND NATIONAL SERVICE

Citizen rights and citizen duties have traditionally been at the center of Western political theory. Originally seen as complementary, the two doctrines have, over time, come to be viewed as conflicting. In modern times, theorists have tended to downplay the duty side of the equation. This is true of figures on both the left and right. Take, for example, the writings of two of our most eminent political philosophers, John Rawls and Robert Nozick.[2] Politically, the radical egalitarianism of Rawls and the conservative libertarianism of Nozick could not be more at odds. Yet both de-emphasize the role of citizen duties in favor of a highly individualist rights-based ethic. Whether political theorists favor an activist state handing out benefits, as liberals do, or a state that needs to be curbed, as conservatives do, the view of citizenship remains the same: individuals exist apart from one another, bound by no meaningful obligations.

But since ideas seem to run in cycles, a reaction against a rights-only concept of citizenship was bound to occur. Political theorists are showing a new appreciation of citizens' obligations

and the importance of shared values. The intellectual origins
of the new interest in the duties of citizens are not difficult to
locate. They are a result of both the inadequacies of Marxism,
with its materialist analysis and collectivist prescriptions, and
the inadequacies of libertarianism, which offers a similar materialist analysis but with an insistent stress on the individual. The
political center, so to speak, is reasserting itself against the right
and left.

The recovery of the civic in public philosophy is apparent
in a series of important works that have appeared in the past
few years. In *Liberalism and the Limits of Justice*, Michael J.
Sandel articulates the emerging disenchantment with the idea
of a social world made up of civically unencumbered individuals.[3] Sandel essentially supports the classical idea of the civic
republican tradition, in which private interests are subordinated
to the public good and in which community life takes precedence
over individual pursuits. Similarly, in *Reconstruction of Public
Philosophy*, philosopher William M. Sullivan asserts the need
to recover a sense of civic life, to develop those qualities of
social life that go beyond competitive success and economic
well-being.[4] For Sullivan civic responsibilities are necessary not
only for the public good but also for individual "self-fulfillment
and even the working out of personal identity."[5] Likewise, Sandel
holds that to imagine an individual incapable of attachments
and allegiances is "to imagine a person wholly without character,
without moral depth."[6] The renewed emphasis on civic participation in Sandel and Sullivan, among others, is often technical
and not always in a form accessible to the general reader. Nonetheless, such work in democratic political theory is laying the
philosophical foundation for the popularization of national
service.[7]

One of the most explicit connections between the emergent
civic theory and national service is found in Benjamin R. Barber's
Strong Democracy.[8] "National service is a vital constituent in
the relationship between rights and duties under a strong democratic regime," writes Barber.[9] The current problems in the body
politic—cynicism about voting, political alienation, privatism,
the growing distrust of public institutions—are symptoms of a
malaise that is inseparable from the diminution of civic obligations. Barber believes that a thriving democracy must be rooted
in active citizenship, involving direct participation and commu-

nal responsibilities. "Universal citizen service," as Barber calls it, means that young people would choose from among military service and a variety of civilian corps. Such service would answer a number of problems plaguing the all-volunteer military, job-training programs, and deteriorating public facilities.

The contemporary shift toward a reemphasis of citizen duties is nowhere better exemplified than in *Spheres of Justice* by Michael Walzer, one of the country's leading social thinkers.[10] Walzer starts by showing how each of the different "spheres" of community life—economic, political, social—generates its own distributive rules. Justice requires the autonomy of the spheres, preventing any group from dominating across all spheres. Thus, Walzer is less concerned with the distribution of money than with limiting the things money can buy. Injustice lies in money's power to dominate where it does not belong— for example, its use to purchase human beings, to control free expression, to buy political offices, and, especially important from our perspective, to purchase exemptions from national service, that is, from military service or communally imposed work. Certain public needs—military service in the past, perhaps national service in the future—cannot be obtained on a marketplace reckoning. Walzer goes as far as to describe the merits of obligatory and unpaid, but temporary, labor to do the necessary work of society that is dangerous, grueling, or dirty.

In the emerging political philosophy, national service is regarded as a form of civic education. This dimension is discussed most fully in *The Reconstruction of Patriotism* by sociologist Morris Janowitz.[11] He argues that not only have citizen rights become disconnected from citizen duties, but that formal educational institutions no longer seem capable of fostering a sense of civic consciousness. In his view, the national-service experience can itself provide a more effective dose of civics than the customary courses given in our schools. For Janowitz, a shared sense of civic participation creates civic consciousness, not the other way around.

A handful of books does not a movement make. But something is astir. Though the terminology may vary, the emerging public philosophy has certain basic precepts: the interdependence of citizens in a commonwealth, the need for active participation in civic life, and the sharing of a commitment to community values.[12] It would be silly to ascribe all of our social problems to an imbalance between citizen rights and duties. To refocus on citizenship duties is neither to postpone examination of systematic economic and social ills nor to deny the existence of competing interest groups. But the need for a more balanced and nuanced formulation of citizenship is becoming increasingly apparent. By insisting that citizenship has a moral dimension, the new theorists have helped bring attention to bear on an important question—whether one can be a good citizen without actively performing civic duties.

Discussion of civic obligations inevitably brings us to patriotism, a concept that is too frequently avoided when talking about national service. Patriotism as a social good has been an unfashionable perspective among most serious analysts of American society in recent decades. Certainly the ambiguities and anomalies of patriotism cannot be denied. Chauvinistic and even fascistic sentiments are often seen lurking behind that term. Patriotism without jingoism is no small trick. If this left us in a position of absolute relativism—believing that nothing is special or better about one's country—it would be morally unnerving. But insofar as this and the opposite absolute—that is, blind obedience to one's country—can be avoided, it is possible to think critically while maintaining our patriotic beliefs.

A civic-oriented national-service program must ultimately rest on some kind of enlightened patriotism. The critical step in making the case for such a patriotism is not so much to grasp why those in power deserve to be distrusted (seldom a difficult task), but to see that power can be fashioned so that it deserves trust and loyalty. There is no reason to be ashamed of a patriotism that reminds us of the enduring worth of America's civic institutions, even if many were long excluded from their benefits and still others do not yet have their fair share. Enlightened patriotism involves reason and criticism as well as emotional ties to the nation-state. Such self-critical patriotism is quite different from that which amounts to enthusiastic acceptance of the status quo. Patriotism, like other human virtues, must be tempered by balance and reflection.

National service points to a civic formulation of patriotism. The renaissance of American political culture that national service would bring about would entail a search for a new balance after an indiscriminate weakening of the sense of citizenship duty. It is not a case of my country right or wrong, or of what amounts to the same for ideologues, my country left or right, but more directly and simply, a case of who shall perform citizen duties.

A POLITICAL CULTURE IN CRISIS?

There is no need to retreat into the mists of a presumed golden age to feel that there is something lacking in the civic consciousness of the present. Political scientists point to the downward slide in voter turnout, despite the easing of such barriers to voting as poll taxes and obstructive registration rules.[13] No society has ever paid its taxes happily, but we Americans have prided ourselves on having one of the highest tax compliance rates in the world. In recent years, however, tax evasions have become widespread.[14] Education surveys show that today's college students are much more likely than earlier students to be preoccupied with making money and less interested and less prepared to exercise civic responsibilities than their predecessors.[15] Our national psyche is described in pathological terms—narcissistic, egoistic, possessive.[16]

The "crisis of legitimacy" has generated its own school of American political commentary. Conservative commentators decry the unsettling growth of popular expectations and the erosion of traditional moral values. Liberal observers rue the retreat into a mean-spirited privatism that has led to a widening gulf between haves and have-nots. And, in the center, there is concern with the unraveling of America's social consensus in which the pursuit of politics is based upon class, race, gender, or sexual preference, a veritable "democratic overload." This all dovetails with the school of the United States in decline, an almost autumnal reading of America's economic and hegemonic power.[17]

To speak of the American political system as being in deep trouble may be hyperbole, but there are disturbing signs nevertheless. Two of America's leading political scientists, Seymour Martin Lipset and William Schneider, have given us the most comprehensive analysis of the public mind in *The Confidence Gap*.[18] Political alienation and cynicism have grown rapidly in the wake of Vietnam and Watergate (not to mention the Iran-contra affair). The disaffection has not yet developed into a European-style *ressentiment,* a negativism toward authority so deeply rooted as to make violent upheaval possible. Nonetheless, Lipset and Schneider believe that the United States has a lower reserve of confidence in its political system than in times past. Our political institutions may not be as resilient as before and thus may not be able to withstand another severe shock on the order of the Great Depression or the Vietnam War.

The need for national service as a vehicle of civic education is especially strong now because of the relative weakness of other forms of community. In the United States, national community can only be grounded in citizenship because Americans really do not have a *patrie,* or fatherland. America does not claim solidarity and unity by virtue of a claimed common ancestry or some divine foundation myth. America is the immigrant society par excellence. Our cohesion depends upon a civic ideal rather than on primordial loyalties. At stake is the preservation in the United States of a shared citizenship that serves to knit this increasingly ethnically diverse society together as a nation.

MILITARY AND CIVILIAN SERVICE AND
THE LONG SHADOW OF WILLIAM JAMES

The idea of national service is conventionally traced to William James's 1910 essay, "The Moral Equivalent of War."[19] James coined the concept to contrast the noble human qualities evoked by war with the destructive purposes they served. Is it not possible, he asked, to call forth the same heroism without the shooting and the bloodshed? James held that many values of military life are worth preserving. "Intrepidity, contempt for softness, surrender of private interest, obedience to command, must still remain the rock upon which States are built," he wrote.[20] For James, national service presented a means by which a democratic nation could maintain social cohesion without having to go to war.

James's essay was an important work, setting the tone of discussion for decades to come. In retrospect, though, it is by no means clear whether James's effort was an important breakthrough or an unfortunate detour on the way to making national service a reality. Although he consciously tried to steer a middle road

between what he termed the "war-party" and the "peace-party,"
James was an avowed pacifist.[21] For him, civilian service was
clearly superior to military service. This is why neo-Jamesians
continue to portray civilian service as the most noble form of
national service, with a consequent belittlement (if not hatred)
of military service.[22]

The Jamesian formulation assumes an inherent conflict between military and civilian service. The conflict is a real one,
as I can perhaps illustrate with a personal experience. In the
course of my research travels, I went to locations like Honduras
and Micronesia, where Peace Corps volunteers and American
soldiers were assigned, often within walking distance of each
other. While not surprised that these two groups came from
different social backgrounds and held different political values,
I was surprised—and depressed—to find how much each group
held the other in contempt. The soldiers saw the Peace Corps
volunteers as confused "air-heads" who had gone native and
whose Americanism was suspect. The Peace Corps volunteers,
for their part, viewed the soldiers as boisterous louts whose
insensitivity to local ways was an embarrassment to the United
States. (It is a further commentary on the state of national service
that so few young Americans have served in both the armed
forces and civilian-service programs. I would be surprised if
their number exceeded several hundred.)

Despite such examples, I will here assiduously attempt to refute
the idea that the two forms of service are inherently in conflict.
Though we are accustomed to thinking of military and civilian
service as alternative ideals, even alternative character types,
the tough-minded and the high-minded, the split may be more
apparent than real. Contrary to James, the virtue of military service rests not in its martial values but in its character, in a democratic society, as one of the deepest forms of citizenship
obligation—a quality true of civilian service as well. Military
and civilian service, if not quite a seamless web, are, to the
degree they contain civic content, cut out of the same cloth.

Overall, the supporters of civilian and military service have
much more in common than they realize. Both parties agree
that national service must stand apart from marketplace considerations. Both call for the participation of a large cross section of
American youth. Both believe that society is served by fostering
in young people a commitment to citizen duties. Only by placing

such citizenship concerns at the core of the national-service debate can we begin to move out from under the shadow of William James. Only by drawing on both its tough-minded and high-minded wellsprings can national service ever hope to become a reality.

TWO

National Service
in American History

For all the debate over national service, its history in America remains obscure. In this and the following two chapters, I will chart the development of three forms of national service: military service by citizen soldiers, alternative service by conscientious objectors, and public service by civilian youth. Despite considerable organizational, functional, and emotive differences among these various forms of national service, some vision of citizenship is the property common to all of them.

Any chronicler of national service in America must avoid two temptations. One is to portray American history as a descent from a civic Eden, the view that all citizens in an earlier America gladly did their share to promote the common good. The other is to indulge in a form of Whiggish history, where attention is paid only to evidence that points to a supposedly inevitable consummation of civic behavior into national service. The real history of national service in America shows notions of civic obligation periodically expand and contract. At certain times, national service is held out as a civic ideal against which all other public activities can be measured; at other times, it is a marginal factor, dismissed as irrelevant or utopian.

Here I will attempt to show that our country has no greater exemplars of national service than those young people who have performed as citizen soldiers, as conscientious objectors, or as volunteers in conservation and human services. The central point is that, even though national service comes in many shapes and sizes, the unity of civic content is of more lasting consequence than the diversity.

THE CITIZEN SOLDIER

There is no more basic form of national service than military service. The citizen soldier is the only individual conscripted to perform a public task. And, from the very start, the role of citizen soldier has had a high degree of civic content. The citizen soldier is both a unique type and an archetype of national service.[1]

The first colonists came to these shores anticipating conflict, and they prepared for it. Each colony formed its own militia, marking the first appearance of the citizen soldier. The militia was founded on the principle that fundamental liberties entailed individual responsibilities. Building a citizens' army was thus one of the earliest imperatives in our country's history. As a governor of the Massachusetts colony put it, every male must consider "it his truest honor to be a soldier-citizen."[2]

The militia was not a voluntary force; every able-bodied man was obliged to possess arms and train periodically, and he was subject to call-up when military needs dictated. Aside from minor variations, the militias were similarly organized throughout the thirteen colonies. Service was for short periods at locations close to home. At the heart of the militia was the "muster"—a periodic, mandatory gathering of able-bodied free males. The militiamen not only brought their own weapons but also served without pay. Although legislative bodies issued some guidelines, the actual operations were left to locally elected militia officers.

By the early 1700s, as the Indian threat receded, the number of muster days decreased. Militia forces were increasingly used for local police functions, and militia companies took on more of a social character than a military one. Toward the middle of the eighteenth century, the militia system began to erode, only to be reinvigorated at the start of the War of Independence. Indeed, the militia experience highlighted the great cultural differences between the colonists and the British. The British army was marked by sharp class divisions between officers and troops;

by contrast, American militiamen served under officers who were neighbors and often friends or relatives. Furthermore, as historian Charles Royster has shown, revolutionary soldiers were motivated by a deeply religious and patriotic idealism that convinced them of their own moral superiority over the British.[3]

The military needs of the Revolutionary War also led to the creation of America's first professional army. It remained small, due to the early Americans' deep distrust of a standing army. Still, it marked the start of our country's dual-army tradition, combining the republican ideal of the citizen soldiery, on the one hand, with a permanent, well-trained army, on the other. Opponents of the militia system held, with some reason, that the militia was a less effective fighting force than were regular soldiers and that militia performance steadily deteriorated over the course of the Revolutionary War. Militia supporters countered that the militiamen played a vital role in the struggle for independence and that without them the civilian population would not have swung over to the revolutionary cause.

The debate over the militia system at the founding of the republic anticipated controversies over military manpower that have continued to this day. The citizen-soldier concept based on the notion of public virtue collides with the military need for professional soldiers, for which the realities of long-term recruitment rely heavily on self-interest. The proper balance of these two considerations has been a perennial dilemma. In later years, when the citizen-soldier concept would come to include draftees and those in reserve units, the shaping of programs to recruit soldiers was most often determined by military manpower requirements. The original militia concept, however, was based solely on citizen obligation: that as many men as were physically able to serve should serve. In this sense, the militia system was a most broadly based service (recognizing that in those times neither women nor most blacks were considered full citizens) and possessed an extraordinarily high level of civic content.

Following the War of Independence, Henry Knox, the first secretary of war, pushed hard to systematize the militia and make it congruent with military needs. He hoped to institute an age-graded militia in which young men would be called up before those who were older. Under Knox's scheme, young militiamen would receive military training in "Camps of Discipline" distant from their homes. These camps would not only teach recruits military skills, but also expose them to regular discourses on "the eminent advantages of free governments to the happiness of society."[4] Knox thus wanted to place civic education at the core of the militia experience. In the end, Knox's proposals were not accepted because they fed fears of a national rather than a state-based militia. However, they did constitute the earliest blueprint for a national-service ethic extending beyond mere military training.

What did come about was the Uniform Militia Act of 1792, which required the enrollment of all able-bodied freemen between the ages of eighteen and forty-five years. The citizen soldier was to be the mainstay of national defense. Implementation of the act, however, was left to the states themselves, and without sanctions for noncompliance, the law represented no more than a recommendation to the states. Still, the principle, if not the practice, of universal military service was the law of the land. (In fact, Title 10 of the U.S. Code as amended in 1983 reiterates the tenet that every physically sound and mentally fit male between eighteen and forty-five years of age is, formally at least, part of the unorganized militia of the United States.)

During the early decades of the new republic, a military division of labor evolved, with the small federal army posted against Indians on the frontier and the militia serving as both reserve force and preserver of domestic order. During the early nineteenth century, however, the militia system went into a precipitous decline. A turning point came in the War of 1812, when militiamen fled the defenses of Washington, allowing British troops to occupy the capital. After the conflict, Secretary of War James Monroe made the first proposal for a federal draft in which military service would be compulsory for all young men. Although Congress rejected the proposal in 1814, it did institute a system of cash bounties to attract recruits into the federal force. In the following years, as the federal government sought to build up a national army of volunteers, support for the militia concept withered.

By the time of the Mexican War in 1846, most of the country's fighting forces consisted of volunteers attracted by cash bounties, the chance for adventure, and promises of land. From the early days of our history, then, supporters of a professional army have acknowledged the role of material incentives in garnering recruits. Those favoring a citizen army were more inclined to emphasize civic responsibilities. By the middle of the nineteenth century, the citizen school had clearly been eclipsed by the professional one.

When the Civil War broke out in 1861, the idea of a volunteer force, though initially popular, faded as the war lengthened and the pool of volunteers dried up. To obtain more troops, Congress passed the Militia Act of 1862, which compelled the states to upgrade their militia systems and furnish troops to the Union cause; however, this soon proved ineffective. Enlistment bounties went up as the war went on, from $50 at the start to $200, $300, and eventually $1,000. (At the time, the average worker earned about $500 a year.) Cities and counties raised the money for bounty payments through voluntary contributions, real estate taxes, and special fund-raising events. Overall, the nation spent more than $700 million in bounties, a sum equal to the entire wartime pay for the Union army.

But even the growing bounties were not enough, and in 1863 Congress took the unprecedented step of instituting a military draft at the national level.[5] The Enrollment Act, as it was called, contained certain provisions intended to make the draft more acceptable. A drafted man could legally escape military service in two ways. A "commutation fee" was set that allowed a draftee to avoid the army by paying $300; or a draftee could purchase a substitute directly by offering a bounty at a market rate.

The near absence of civic content in the Civil War draft was its most distinguishing quality. "Bounty brokers" matched affluent would-be draftees with those seeking bounties. "Bounty jumpers" took the enlistment money and then disappeared, often to enlist in another locale and disappear again. Draft insurance societies arose in which eligible men contributed money to a common fund to be used to buy exemptions for any of its members who were drafted. The class bias of the system—"a rich man's war, a poor man's fight," in the slogan of the day—led to major antidraft riots in several cities. The worst erupted in New York City in July 1863, where four days of looting and lynching of blacks resulted in about 120 deaths. The antidraft disturbances caused Congress to end commutation (though not substitution) in February 1864.

Under Civil War conscription, each congressional district had a draft ("enrollment") board responsible for meeting quotas set by national draft calls. If the quota could not be met by volunteers, substitutes, or commutations, then additional men were selected by lot to meet the quota. The Civil War draft was actually designed to use the threat of conscription to spur voluntary enlistments. In this regard, it did what it was supposed to do. During the draft's two-year existence, about one million men entered the Union army. Altogether, draft boards examined 522,187 men. Of the 203,777 called to service, only 73,347 were actually drafted. The remainder either purchased substitutes or paid commutations. Still, we should not lose sight of the true story of the citizen soldier in the Civil War. On the Union side, certainly, the war was fought mainly by volunteers imbued with a sense of moral righteousness probably unprecedented in American military history.

In 1865, James Oakes, the head of the enrollment board in Illinois, issued an assessment of the Civil War conscription system. He recommended that every draftee personally serve in the military, that is, all commutations and substitutes be eliminated. He urged that federal bounties, too, be phased out. In addition, Oakes proposed that the responsibility for registering should rest with the draftee, not the board. Given the contemporary sound of these proposals, and the linkage of civic responsibility with conscription, it is little wonder that Oakes has been called the father of the modern Selective Service System.

In the aftermath of the Civil War, the militia system, indeed, any concept of the citizen soldier, atrophied. During the 1880s, however, militia units were revived and reformed into the emergent National Guard. By the 1890s, the Guard had about 100,000 members, volunteers all, whose primary task seemed to be quelling labor strife (a role that rests none too comfortably in the memory of the Guard). Guard leaders recognized, however, that if the militia aspect were to be brought to the forefront, antistrike duty had to be de-emphasized. Accordingly, various steps were taken to reorient the Guard toward being a reserve for the regular army, the most notable being the institution of summer camps where more professional military training could be undertaken.

In the years preceding World War I, various legislative enactments shifted more and more functions of the National Guard to the federal level. A real milestone came in 1916 with the National Defense Act, which established the federal government as the major source of funds for Guard training. It required guardsmen to take a dual oath—federal and state—and stipulated that

Guard units could be compelled to serve abroad for unlimited periods in the event of national emergency. Although the state-based units of the National Guard were organizationally descended from the colonial militia, when "federalized" under the terms of the 1916 act, the Guard was not all that distinguishable from regular soldiers. In point of fact, when America entered the two world wars, most guardsmen were taken from their home divisions and assigned as individuals wherever the army thought they would be most useful, thereby violating the territorial basis of the organized militia.

The years before World War I also saw the ideal of the citizen soldier come alive from two different directions. One was a concern for a citizen army based on universal military training (UMT) and the other a desire to create a trained citizen officer who could be rapidly mobilized in the event of war. Both movements were heavy in civic content.

The intellectual force behind the citizen army in the twentieth century was Brigadier General John McAuley Palmer (1870–1955), West Point graduate, historian, protegé of General John J. Pershing in World War I, and confidant of General George C. Marshall in World War II,[6] Palmer believed that only if the entire military were stocked with civilians, from raw recruits to high-ranking officers, could the nation be protected against adventurism or other abuse of military power. Palmer saw UMT as a form of liberal education. He was fond of quoting John Milton's precept: "I call, therefore, a complete and generous education, that which fits a man to perform justly, skillfully, and magnanimously, all the offices, both private and public, of peace and war."[7]

Palmer was the first to make the distinction between military *service*, or conscription into the regular army, and military *training*, which would require a soldier to serve less than a year before reverting to reserve status. For Palmer, and for most subsequent proponents of UMT, a citizen soldier could not be assigned to the regular army without the direction of the president and the concurrence of Congress. Although some consideration was given to UMT in Congress in the period just before the United States entered World War I, no legislative action was ever taken. Interestingly enough, advocates of UMT were opposed not only by antimilitarists but by powerful military groups as well, who saw UMT as diverting time and money from regular soldiers.

The notion of a citizen soldier appeared in yet another form in the pre-World War II period, this time with more concrete results. Under the forceful advocacy of General Leonard Wood, who served as army chief of staff from 1910 to 1914, and such political figures as former President Theodore Roosevelt, one of the most remarkable national-service concepts in American history came into being—the Citizens Military Camps.[8] The purpose of these summer camps was to train a force that would feed into the junior officer corps in the event of mass mobilization. The first camp was set up in 1915 in Plattsburg, New York, and it soon inspired similar camps throughout the nation. During its first year, the "Plattsburg movement" attracted about 4,000 young men willing to endure a spartan summer receiving military training. In 1916, the second year of the program, the number of Plattsburgers exceeded 16,000, and the figure was projected to increase to 50,000 in 1917. (Foreshadowing his later interest in national service, Franklin Delano Roosevelt, then assistant secretary of the navy, initiated "Naval Plattsburgs.") Most of these volunteers were college students or well-to-do young professionals. Even more impressive, the participants themselves bore the expenses of the camps: only the training cadre and equipment were furnished by the army.

In 1916 the leadership of the Plattsburg movement shifted to Grenville Clark, a young New York lawyer. Clark, heir to a banking and railroad fortune, was a major donor to the fledgling National Association for the Advancement of Colored People and a founder of the United World Federalists. He was also a leading proponent of UMT and remained so for half a century. Clark sought to broaden both the purpose and the social base of the movement. Under his direction the camps began to stress not only military training but also civic awareness. Military training was increasingly seen as a mechanism to reduce class, ethnic, and regional antagonisms in America. Clark consistently tried to expand recruitment by offering scholarship aid to promising youths who were unable to pay their own way. In the summer of 1916, a Plattsburg-like school for young women was set up in Chevy Chase, Maryland, offering courses in sanitation and first aid. Over the opposition of the army, Clark planned to open a camp for blacks in the summer of 1917.

With America's entry into the war in 1917, the Plattsburg experiment came to an end. The immediate impetus for the Plattsburg movement was the shift toward military preparedness. Indeed, 90 percent of the Plattsburgers saw military service during World War I, most as officers at the front. But the Plattsburgers also reflected a strong reaction against the materialism of the gilded age. The mood of the movement was captured in its advertising slogan: "Give your vacation to your country and still have the best vacation you ever had."[9] The Plattsburg movement represented an effort to spark a moral reawakening in America by promoting participation in national service at elite levels. Even though the Plattsburgers mainly came from privileged backgrounds, they did not shy away from the dangerous work of war, nor did they hesitate to mix with those of more plebeian origins.

Contemporaries clearly recognized the civic component of the military training camps. In 1915, *The New Republic*, in an editorial on "The Plattsburg Idea," stated the Plattsburgers "seek to attach soldiering to citizenship; and they do it in such a way as to make the soldier really a civilian." The article warned of a "real danger of national disintegration" and lamented that democracy in America was not sufficiently identified with "the responsibilities of citizenship."[10] For the leading progressive journal of the day to run such a favorable editorial shows how highly regarded the Plattsburg movement was in reform circles.

With the entry of America into World War I, Congress passed a Selective Service Act. Reflecting the lessons of the Civil War experience, the new draft law was founded more explicitly on civic principles; it allowed neither substitutes nor purchased exemptions. The burden of registration fell upon the individual, not on the draft board, and failure to register was cause for imprisonment. All conscripts would serve for the duration of the war. Local volunteer civilian boards were set up to administer the draft. The draft law eventually provided for the registration of all men between the ages of eighteen and thirty-five. (No one under twenty was ever drafted, however.) During the eighteen-month duration of the wartime draft, 24 million men were registered. Conscription brought some 2.8 million men into the military, about three-quarters of all those who saw service in World War I.

The relative efficiency of the conscription system in the First World War and the solid performance of the draftees constituted an important development in the evolution of military mobilization. In the future, whenever the nation needed to expand its armed forces, draftees would become the mainstay. But as in the aftermath of other American wars, the concept of the citizen soldier went into decline. At the end of the Great War, supporters of UMT were startled to find there was little support for any form of military requirement, even one limited to training. The opposition of the professional officer corps and National Guard to a federalized citizen army was predictable. But more significant was one of the most important changes in American intellectual thinking: peace came to be associated with disarmament rather than preparedness. Progressives who had supported the Plattsburg movement before World War I turned against the military in the wake of the horrors of world war. Liberal educators and pacifists, including John Dewey and Jane Addams, formed committees to reduce military influence in American society and found much more support for their view than before the war. (Later, on the eve of World War II, there was a reverse crossover: many liberals came to support conscription in the face of the rise of fascism in Europe, and many conservatives became anti-draft as a way to stay out of war.)

If the citizen soldier was generally a dormant concept in the 1920s and 1930s, it did revive in a special way on college campuses. The National Defense Act of 1916 had created the Reserve Officers Training Corps (ROTC), a program that trained officers for reserve duty in the federal army. ROTC replaced the Morrill Land Grant Act of 1862, which required military training for male students attending state agricultural colleges. World War I delayed the implementation of ROTC, but the program grew rapidly after 1920. By 1928, more than three hundred colleges and universities had ROTC detachments. Throughout the 1930s, about six thousand men a year were given ROTC commissions, most of whom were to see active service during World War II.

The question as to whether ROTC was to be compulsory never was absolutely settled. Negotiations between the War Department and the land-grant colleges stipulated that military training was required for all male students for at least two years. Fewer than 10 percent of ROTC cadets, however, took the complete four-year program that qualified them for commissions. When the University of Wisconsin in 1923, responding to student agitation, made ROTC elective, the War Department did not contest the decision. Only a handful of educational institutions, however, dropped mandatory ROTC during the interwar period. Opponents of mandatory ROTC suffered a severe blow when a 1934 Supreme Court ruling held that compulsory ROTC did not violate conscientious objectors' rights because the military instruction was "unaccompanied by any pledge of military service."[11] Thus a distinction was drawn between military training and service that would surface again in debates on UMT.

In September 1940, Congress passed the Selective Service and Training Act, the first peacetime draft legislation in the nation's history.[12] The new draft had strong UMT undertones and reflected the lobbying on Capitol Hill of John McAuley Palmer and Grenville Clark. The act required every male aged twenty-one to thirty-five to register and, if selected through a lottery and certified by a local civilian draft board, to enter the army. In its formal organization, notably the reliance on local civilian draft boards, the new draft act was a copy of the World War I law. In content, however, the act was strictly a peacetime measure, with the draftee's term being limited to one year of training and with inductees limited to service in the United States or its territories. Despite these palliatives, peacetime conscription was extremely unpopular among both the draftees and the population at large.

In December 1941, after Pearl Harbor, Congress passed a wartime draft act that extended the obligation to the duration of the war plus six months. Military manpower mobilization during World War II was awesome. Selective Service registered 36 million males.[13] In the four years following Pearl Harbor, 16.3 million Americans wore uniforms (including 260,000 women). Ten million of these were directly inducted. The draft legislation changed in bits and pieces over the course of the war, but conscription effectively applied to men between the ages of eighteen and thirty-eight. Seventy percent of all male Americans in that age range served in the military, making World War II the broadest national-service experience in this country's history.

By the spring of 1942, the situation on college campuses was chaotic. Draft calls and enlistments were reducing college enrollments. Student deferments were given mainly to those in science and engineering courses, to the detriment of the liberal arts. The colleges were rescued by the new army and navy educational programs geared toward the campus. Starting in 1943, the Army Specialized Training Program (ASTP) and the navy's V-12 program sent qualified college-age draftees to colleges—around 200,000 in total—to receive advanced education, most of it in the sciences and engineering.[14] ASTP and V-12 gave the colleges not only needed students and a role in the war effort but also a welcome subsidy. The World War II campus programs thus created a novel, if short-lived, national-service type—the citizen soldier-student.

Several months before his death in 1945, President Roosevelt, with the strong encouragement of Chief of Staff George Marshall, asked Congress to consider a program of UMT. When Harry Truman assumed the presidency, he took up the cause with even greater vigor. To move toward the goal of UMT, Truman appointed a commission, headed by Karl T. Compton, the president of MIT. In its report, issued in 1947, the Compton Commission strongly recommended the implementation of UMT.[15] Briefly, it proposed that all eighteen-year-old men be called for six months of military training with a reserve obligation to follow. The participants would not be part of the regular military but considered rather civilian trainees in uniform. Exemptions would be kept to a minimum, and even conscientious objectors would be required to fulfill some form of alternative training. The Compton plan would have eliminated all racial segregation; this at a time when the armed forces were still rigidly segregated. Even women would be required to enter some compulsory training, though what kind and how long was never specified. The Compton proposals were the clearest expression of civic obligation for youth ever voiced by a formal government commission.

UMT was seriously debated in 1947, and, for a while, its passage in Congress seemed likely. However, public support proved to be weak. The distinction between military training and military service was too fine for most people to grasp. Opponents at various points of the political spectrum—both the ultraconservative *Chicago Tribune* and the Communist *Daily Worker* came out against UMT—began to conduct an effective lobbying campaign against UMT. A contradictory grouping—anti-Cold War leftists, National Guard supporters of state militias, anti-big government conservatives, isolationists, and unions worried about the conscription of labor—coalesced to bring UMT down. With the 1948 elections approaching, congressional enthusiasm for this politically volatile issue faded. A UMT bill met a quiet death in a House committee.

UMT died for another reason: its proponents sent mixed messages. From the first serious proposal at the beginning of the century, UMT has been advanced as much for its character-building qualities as for its military worth. This detracts from the central premise of citizen obligation. The Compton Commission trumpeted the physical and mental benefits of UMT "whether or not such service is of a direct military character."[16] And, in his memoirs, Truman wrote: "This was not a military training program in the conventional sense. The military phase was incidental to what I had in mind. While the training was to offer every qualified young man a chance to perfect himself for the service of his country in some military capacity, I envisioned a program that would at the same time provide ample opportunity for self-improvement . . . to foster the moral and spiritual welfare of our young people."[17]

The moral to be drawn is that military service specifically, and, by implication, national service generically, really gains popular support only when the country at large is convinced that there is a civic obligation to meet a public need that would otherwise not be met. Character-building arguments are not sufficient grounds for national-service advocacy, even for an idea as ingrained in our history as the citizen soldiery.

In March 1947, the Selective Service Act expired. And with that, the era of the citizen soldier came to an end—for the time being.

CONSCIENTIOUS OBJECTORS

If the citizen soldier can be traced back to the very origins of America, so can the conscientious objector. Conscientious objection is an extraordinary freedom. For however defensible it might be on other grounds, conscientious objection frees certain select citizens from the most basic—and dangerous—of civic obligations: the duty to defend one's country. Yet, through time, the notion has grown that conscientious objection could not only be allowed, but that mandatory civic duties could be performed in other than a soldier's role. To the degree the state defines alternative service as a legitimate way of meeting citizenship obligations and to the degree the conscientious objector accepts that definition, we come to a profound expansion of the meaning of national service.

The first recorded instance of pacifist resistance to military service occurred in the province of Maryland in 1658, when one Richard Keene was fined and "abused by the sheriff" for "refusing to be trained as a soldier."[18] Yet, from the earliest times, the American colonies allowed certain exemptions to militia obligations for members of pacifist religious groups, the so-called peace churches—Mennonites and Brethren coming out of a rural German Anabaptist tradition and Quakers of English stock who were mainly well-educated city and town dwellers. No colony, it seems, ever forced religious objectors to bear arms if they were willing to pay for exemption.

During the Revolutionary War, Mennonites and Brethren frequently purchased exemptions from military service, while Quakers suffered fines or even confiscation of property for their refusal to enroll in the militia. Over the years, the obvious moral integrity of the conscientious objectors gained them grudging respect and toleration. In his original proposal for a bill of rights, James Madison included the following clause: "no person religiously scrupulous of bearing arms shall be compelled to render military service in person."[19] It is not clear why this clause was not adopted, but the evidence suggests that the framers of the Constitution favored leaving military exemptions to the jurisdiction of the states.

Conscientious objection first achieved legal recognition during the Civil War. As during the Revolutionary period, the objectors included the traditional peace sects—Quakers, Mennonites, and Brethren—plus the Seventh Day Adventists, who added an urban, working-class component to the pacifist population. During the war, treatment of objectors varied, from relative leniency in the North to harsher penalties in the South.

The 1864 revision of the draft had momentous implications for conscientious objection and, indirectly, for national service. Commutation was abolished for everyone except conscientious objectors—the first time that federal law made specific provision for religious objectors. The law also provided that objectors drafted into military service "be considered non-combatants." President Lincoln made it policy to assign such noncombatants to duty in hospitals or in educating freed slaves. The Lincoln administration, by creating a de facto mode of alternate civilian service, thus introduced civic content into conscientious objection. A watershed had been crossed in the meaning of national service in America.

The World War I draft law exempted from *combat* service, but not *military* service, those conscripts who came from traditional peace churches. Some 450 individuals would not cooperate with the conscription system in any way and went to federal prisons. Of the 65,000 drafted men who initially laid claim to conscientious-objector status, only 4,000 stayed the course. Most of these did medical work in the army, but some ended up doing menial labor in and around military encampments. Under pressure from the American Friends Service Committee (founded in response to World War I conscription), the military authorities eventually made some limited and local adjustments to alternative service, but no formal alternative-service program ever developed during World War I. The judgment is clear that the policies of the Wilson administration were retrograde from the alternative-service standards allowed by Lincoln during the Civil War.

The issue of conscientious objection was squarely faced in the peacetime conscription law of 1940 and reiterated in the draft legislation of World War II. New ground was broken when membership in a strictly pacifist group was no longer a requirement for objector status, although religious motives remained so. Conscientious objectors divided into three categories: non-combatant soldiers, who though unwilling to fight in combat are willing to serve in other military roles; absolutists, who refuse to cooperate in any way with the conscription system or to participate in alternative activities, even if unrelated to the war effort; and alternativists, who refuse any military identity but accept alternative civilian work as directed by the government.

The first category was the largest: an estimated 25,000 World War II draftees served in noncombatant roles. The military set up special basic training courses in which "1-A-O's," as they were known from their draft board designations (a simple "1-A" meant the draftee could be assigned anywhere), did not partake of weapons-handling or training. Most such unarmed soldiers served in the medical corps, where they often performed extremely hazardous work. Some were killed in combat areas, and one received the Congressional Medal of Honor. Conscientious objectors in uniform willing to perform noncombatant roles cause little problem for the system and easily meet the standards of the citizen soldier.

The absolutists went to jail. All told, some 6,000 men were

sentenced to prison terms for as long as five years. About three-quarters of these were Jehovah's Witnesses (whose claims for blanket exemption as ministers have never been recognized by the government).[20] The remainder consisted of hardcore religious objectors and some Black Muslims protesting the racism of American society in general and its military in particular.

Alternativists came under the provision of the draft law that allowed conscientious objectors to be assigned "to work of national importance under *civilian* direction." [Emphasis added.] Learning from the World War I experience, the authorities decided that no conscientious objectors willing to do alternative service would be forced into the army or confined in prison. This set in motion a novel national-service program called Civilian Public Service (CPS). Some 500 objectors volunteered to be guinea pigs in medical experiments. (Among them was Max M. Kampelman, later the Reagan administration's chief arms negotiator.) Another 2,000 or so worked in asylums and mental wards, thereby bringing an unprecedented humaneness into the handling of the mentally ill in this country. The great majority of alternativists—about 12,000—served in CPS camps located in rural areas, where participants performed conservation work. Alternativists worked without pay. For spending money, they had to rely on individual savings, family, or religious groups. Wives and children of conscientious objectors had to fend for themselves, a cause of great resentment among objectors.

The CPS camps came under the technical administration of the Selective Service, but they were run by a consortium of the traditional peace churches. Mennonites, Brethren, and Quakers (and later Methodists) ran their own camps. The sponsoring church provided food, clothing, and medical care, as well as camp staff for round-the-clock supervision. The actual conservation work was supervised by the Agriculture or Interior Department. The army loaned cots, bedding, utensils, and other camp equipment.

Most camps tended to be religiously homogeneous. Objectors from nontraditional peace churches were likely to go to the more tolerant Quaker camps; but it was also the Quaker camps, perhaps because of their social heterogeneity, that were the most likely to be demoralized by the harshness of the work and the absence of pay. Serious offenders against camp procedures were reported to the Selective Service and became liable for prosecution in civil courts. In 1943 the government set up several of its own camps for conscientious objectors who did not want to serve or could not adapt to the regimen of the church camps.

At first, most pacifist groups considered the CPS system a great triumph for conscientious objection; it certainly contrasted favorably with the repressive policies of World War I. By the end of the war, however, most religious objectors came to see the CPS experiment as a moral capitulation by the pacifist establishment to the state. The consortium of peace churches was also influenced by the growing rebelliousness of assignees, who increasingly came to view the CPS camps as penal institutions. Management of conscientious-objection camps by pacifist churches was an unhappy experience that future administrations would try to avoid.

Overall, the World War II experience helps to clarify the relation of conscientious objection to national service. Of the three categories of objector, the noncombatant soldier most clearly accords with the definition of the citizen soldier. And the absolutist most clearly falls short; however much he may be acting on the basis of high principle, the absolutist does not fulfill any civic obligations. It is the alternativist who poses the hardest case. World War II showed just how different from a civic standpoint the alternativist is from the draft evader, the deserter, and the absolutist. Indeed, the war demonstrated that conscientious objectors, by performing civilian work, can truly fulfill their civic obligations. Establishment of the principle of alternative service had lasting importance. The legitimacy of certain forms of civilian national service in lieu of military service was now accepted by the authorities, the public at large, and, importantly, the conscientious objectors themselves.

CIVILIAN SERVICE

An argument could probably be made that antecedents to civilian national service can be found in late nineteenth-century American developments that ran counter to the materialistic ethos of the time. Perhaps someday an intellectual historian will do so. For now we can say that there were idealistic eddies when the main current in American life was especially materialistic. Along with the dominant crassness of the Gilded Age, there coexisted a "muscular Christianity," with its message of middle-class manliness in Protestant service among the working class. It was also a time when character-building was the driving force in youth organizations, a force which gave new momentum to the YMCA and YWCA (whose establishment in the United States antedates the Civil War), and anticipated the subsequent founding of the Boy Scouts (1910) and Girl Scouts (1912) in this country.[21]

Also important on the cultural margins of American society of that time was socialist utopian thought. Edward Bellamy's *Looking Backward*, first published in 1888, exercised a far-reaching influence in this ideological school.[22] Bellamy's futuristic book described an "Industrial Army," based on compulsory youth service, as the cornerstone of his new social order. What gives *Looking Backward* more than an antiquarian interest for our purposes is that it not only first introduced the concept of civilian service by youth, but that it presented a military analogy to describe the organization of civilian service, a trademark of much subsequent national-service thought.

Whatever the precursors, the national discourse over civilian service in this country was to be permanently shaped by William James's 1910 essay, "The Moral Equivalent of War."[23] Curiously, James's statement makes no explicit mention of citizen duty, but it does make a general case for nonmilitary national service. As he put it: "If now—and this is my idea—there were, instead of military conscription a conscription of the whole youthful population to form for a certain number of years a part of the army enlisted against *Nature*, the injustice [of social inequality] would tend to even out, and numerous other goods to the commonwealth would follow. . . . To coal and iron mines, to freight trains, to fishing fleets in December, to dish-washing, clothes-washing, and window-washing, to road building and tunnel-making, to foundries and stoke-holes, and to the frames of skyscrapers, would our gilded youths be drafted off, according to their choice, to get the childishness knocked out of them, and to come back into society with healthier sympathies and soberer ideas."[24]

Today, James's proposal has an old-fashioned ring to it. He was clearly thinking only of young men, and it seems, Ivy Leaguers at that. Placed in its historical context, it is no coincidence that James's formulation struck a chord about the same time the Plattsburg and UMT movements were beginning to germinate. This is how we are to understand why such contemporaries as Herbert Croly and Walter Lippmann, writing in *The New Republic*, could find merit in both Grenville Clark's Plattsburg movement and William James's "war against nature."[25]

Much closer to James's original conception of national service was Randolph Bourne, the literary critic and polemical spokesman for young radicals opposed to World War I. In a remarkable essay published in 1916, entitled "A Moral Equivalent for Universal Military Service," Bourne described the Plattsburg camps as preparations for war albeit "sugar-coated" as a form of civic education.[26] Bourne's concept of national service was path-breaking in at least two respects. First, he envisioned two years of compulsory service for both young men *and women*, not wanting to omit the "feminine half of the nation's youth."[27] Also, Bourne, foreshadowing postindustrial society, specified national-service tasks that have a surprisingly modern ring: "organized relief, care of dependents, playground service, nursing in hospitals."[28] Where James described national service in terms of manual labor, Bourne discerned the emerging needs of a modern society. But like James, Bourne placed soldiers and civilian servers in opposite camps, an opposition that continues to plague neo-Jamesian thought to this very day.

National Service and the New Deal

The Depression placed national service on a different footing. The goal was no longer one of building the character of "gilded youths," but of providing jobs for desperate young people who were out of work. To address the problem, the New Deal created two major programs—the Civilian Conservation Corps (CCC) and the National Youth Administration (NYA). Both focused on unemployed youth and received substantial federal funding. The CCC and NYA permanently changed the class orientation of national-service programs to include poor youth.

The idea for the CCC originated with Franklin Delano Roosevelt himself. Even before becoming president, Roosevelt had displayed a strong interest in both youth service and conservation. He was also a strong supporter of the Plattsburg movement. As governor of New York, Roosevelt initiated a state reforestation program for unemployed young men, a kind of mini-CCC.

The Civilian Conservation Corps was created in 1933 to provide temporary work relief, but two years later it was converted into a standing program.[29] Some 1,500 camps were located in all parts of the nation, but mainly on public lands in the western states. The work varied with the location, but the main projects were soil conservation, tree planting, flood control, trailblazing, and road building. Great pains were taken to avoid projects that might compete with private enterprise or displace employed workers.

The camps drew on the services of numerous government agencies. The army administered the camps and was responsible for all aspects of CCC life except the work projects themselves. These were managed by the Interior Department and the Forest Service. Recruitment was handled by the Labor Department. While camp commanders came from the army, the ancillary staff—education directors, cooks, craftsmen—were all civilians.

In the original design (which changed slightly over the years), enrollees were unemployed, single males aged eighteen to twenty-five years with no criminal record. Enrollment was for a six-month period, renewable up to two years. Participants received food, shelter, uniforms, and a monthly payment of $30, two-thirds of which was sent directly to the enrollee's family. It was not much, but given the harshness of the times, the corps had few problems attracting applicants. In the early years of the program, five people applied for every opening. Enrollment peaked during the mid-1930s at 500,000 a year. The annual total dipped to between 250,000 and 300,000 by the late 1930s. By the time the program ended in 1942, nearly 3 million young men had participated.

Despite the large numbers, the CCC's requirement that only the unemployed could participate limited the program's social diversity. Only about 10 percent of CCC enrollees had high school diplomas, and most came from rural areas or backgrounds. Urban youth, particularly those of recent immigrant stock, seemed singularly unattracted by the program. In addition, the army, in accordance with the policy of the time, ran strictly segregated camps. Blacks made up about 8 percent of the total CCC enrollment, well under their share of the total number of unemployed youth.

From the very start, the CCC enjoyed widespread popularity. Public-opinion surveys consistently showed that support for the

CCC was broad and cut across political lines. Even the unions, which early on feared that the subsistence pay of the program would drive wages down, were mollified when Roosevelt selected a union leader as the CCC's first director. Moreover, given the desperate economic times, it was clear that anything reducing unemployment could only boost labor's bargaining power in the long run.

The CCC was not without problems. The daily routine was strict and the camps isolated. Many enrollees—especially from urban areas—were unable to adapt. Complaints about food were endemic and seemed more serious than the usual grousing over institutional meals. Fights in town with local youths were not uncommon, especially at dances. About one in four enrollees deserted or was administratively discharged. In addition, the army's role promoted concern that the CCC was being used to "militarize" youth. Yet it was only on the very eve of World War II that rudimentary military drills were introduced, and the army's involvement never really became an issue. On balance, the army's role probably gained the CCC more support than it lost.

The CCC would permanently change how the country perceived the concept of national service. Started as a means of providing temporary work relief, the corps had, by the mid-1930s, turned into something much deeper. The program's achievements in the area of conservation were very real, and many of them remain environmentally useful a half-century later. Also, the beneficial consequences in terms of personal development of enrollees had assumed greater importance in popular understanding and press coverage of the CCC. These features, more than the work-relief aspects, were most mentioned by CCC veterans in later years. In the glow of memory, the depth of the civic content of the CCC has probably become more pronounced than it actually was. Still, the CCC was a national-service program, the broadest civilian one this country has ever had.

If the CCC was Franklin Roosevelt's idea, the National Youth Administration was Eleanor Roosevelt's favorite project. Over the life span of the NYA, from 1935 to 1943, nearly five million young men and women participated. The NYA was aimed at young people between the ages of eighteen and twenty-four, initially those who were on relief, but later those who were merely unemployed, an administrative distinction that allowed for a wider recruiting pool. The NYA was an agency under the Works Progress Administration.

The NYA was as urban as the CCC was rural. The program's activities included work training programs, education classes for unemployed youth, upgrading of public facilities, and filling jobs in government agencies. Much of the work was part-time, and $15 monthly was a typical stipend. Ninety percent of the enrollees lived at home or at school. In a forerunner of what would later be called work-study programs, an estimated one in eight college students received part-time work from the NYA.

The NYA represented the left wing of the New Deal. Its director, Aubrey Williams, was closer to the Popular Front thinking of the time than any other New Deal administrator. The NYA had a special Office of Negro Affairs, whose head, Mary McLeod Bethune, served as a liaison between the Roosevelt administration and the black community. The NYA did not discriminate against blacks and resorted to segregation only in areas where doing otherwise would provoke violence. In contrast to the all-male CCC, women made up about half of NYA participants.

Yet there was a paradox in the NYA. Although its leadership was far more ideological than that of the CCC, the NYA always kept the work-relief dimension in the foreground and downplayed any service ethic. Director Williams went to great lengths to deny that the NYA was a "youth movement in any sense of the word." Much of the reason for this stance was to ward off any comparisons between the NYA and more sinister organizations like the Hitler Jugend and the Russian Komsomol—comparisons much favored by enemies of national service.

Although its civic content was shallow, the NYA set important organizational precedents in national service. It marked the first time that federal aid was offered to college students. The program was highly decentralized, with local community involvement in defining projects. Women were coequal participants, and the races were integrated as much as possible. Finally, the NYA showed that a nonresidential program was far more economical than a camp-based one. Freed from having to house and outfit enrollees, the NYA provided jobs for its participants at half the cost incurred by the CCC. Overall, the NYA model would have a strong effect on future national-service planning.

Both the CCC and NYA lacked one major quality: social breadth. As work-relief programs with a service patina, they were targeted toward the needy. One individual sought to overcome this limitation: Eugen Rosenstock-Huessy.[30] A German refugee who had arrived in the United States in 1933, Rosenstock-Huessy was deeply committed to the concept of youth service in an egalitarian setting. He had already done pioneering work in the German Weimar Republic on civilian-service camps drawing from youth from different social backgrounds. In the United States as a professor, first at Harvard, later at Dartmouth, Rosenstock-Huessy impressed his ideas on some of his students.

In 1939, Frank Davidson became the first college graduate to enter the CCC. A recent Harvard graduate and student of Rosenstock-Huessy, Davidson was originally refused entry as CCC regulations limited admission to youth who could not find work elsewhere. Davidson's desire to join the CCC attracted the attention of Eleanor Roosevelt, and eventually his case went all the way to President Roosevelt before an exemption was approved. About a score of other Ivy League graduates were to follow Davidson into the CCC.

Clearly, there was interest among at least a few idealistic college students for a form of civilian national service. So, in 1940, at the suggestion of Rosenstock-Huessy and with the endorsement of both Franklin and, especially, Eleanor Roosevelt, a special CCC camp was established in Tunbridge, Vermont.[31] Called Camp William James, the experimental facility differed from the standard CCC camp in a number of ways. William James was run by civilians rather than the military. It cooperated with local groups in devising work projects. Most important of all, the camp welcomed a mixture of university students and working-class youth. Of the forty or so members who lived in the camp at any one time, about two-thirds were college graduates. The stated purpose of Camp William James was to train a cadre who would staff a reoriented CCC geared to a more broad membership with a more explicit ethos of national service.

From the start, Camp William James was harassed by the CCC bureaucracy, who saw the facility as a competitor. By March 1941, the CCC hierarchy managed to bring the camp's management back under its control. A rump group from William James formed an independent work camp in a nearby rural community, but the experiment came to an end soon after the attack on Pearl Harbor, when camp members prepared to enter the military. Despite its short existence and small membership, Camp William

James marked the first time that a civilian-service program had achieved a mixed-class membership.

President Roosevelt gave some thought to putting national service on a more permanent footing. In 1940, he announced that he would recommend some form of compulsory service for all young men. He had three categories in mind—active service in the military, behind-the-lines service by uniformed military technicians, and civilian defense work.[32] That same year, Representative Jerry Voorhis of California introduced a bill expanding Roosevelt's proposal. It encompassed not only military-related national service but also agencies such as the CCC, NYA, the Public Health Service, and the Civil Aeronautics Authority. Voorhis's bill was soon overtaken by the enactment of the peacetime draft, but for the first time a bill had been introduced in Congress for compulsory national service. Also in 1940, the American Youth Commission (AYC), an arm of the American Council on Education, called for a universal youth program for both sexes and with nondiscriminatory treatment of the races. Such youth service was to be regarded not so much as work relief but as a way to give "citizenship training" to American youth.[33] The civic content of the AYC proposal was the clearest for any national-service concept up to that time.

President Roosevelt himself broached the topic of national service again in a 1943 news conference. Looking to the postwar future, Roosevelt said he objected to the term "compulsory military service" and preferred to speak instead of a "year's contribution of service to the Government."[34] Any program that develops, he said, "would be only partly military." In 1944, a year before his death, in another press conference, Roosevelt said that what he had in mind was closer to the CCC model than to military service.[35] It was never clear from the president's fragmentary remarks what exactly he thought about the relation between military and civilian service. But it would be a long time, if ever, before national service would again receive such high-level sponsorship.

LOOKING BACKWARD

The history of national service in the United States through World War II had been marked by many ups and downs, but a few important patterns emerge. One is that the nation has been inconsistent in its theory and practice of citizen soldiery. Although the nation essentially came into being through the services of the colonial militia—one of the purest embodiments of citizen obligation—the country never embraced a permanent citizen-soldier system similar to, say, the Swiss militia, which features universal military service, concentrated training, and a long period of obligation. Since the Civil War at least, however, the country has held firm to the principle that no one can buy his way out of serving in the military. Nonetheless, similar outcomes have been achieved indirectly through such practices as college deferrals, enlistment bonuses for volunteers, and market wages for recruits.

In another significant development, the definition of the conscientious objector has expanded over time. From the Revolutionary period, when the concept was limited to traditional "peace churches," conscientious objection gradually reached the point where, by World War II, it included all religious-based resistance to military service. In addition, the idea of alternative service in lieu of military duty has become increasingly accepted by the government, the public, and the objectors themselves.

On the social plane, civilian service has persistently suffered from class polarization. On the one hand, affluent youth enrolled in such idealistic programs as the Plattsburg movement and Camp William James (and later the Peace Corps). On the other, poor and unemployed young people flocked to the CCC and NYA (and "job-corps"-type programs later). Between the rarefied programs for the elite and the targeted offerings for the poor, American national service has had little to offer the broad middle class. Until now, it is only in the military that national service has achieved a class mix, and even there only imperfectly.

Another observable trend is that public interest in national service follows a cyclical pattern. A slow inflow of national-service support is followed by a rapid ebb. Actually, there is nothing like a war to knock down the concept of the citizen soldier. A sharp drop in support for the militia or universal military training followed both world wars as well as the Revolutionary War and Civil War in earlier times and the wars in Korea and Vietnam later. Support for civilian service underwent similar ups and downs. William James's "war against nature" never regained momentum after 1918. Similarly, the buildup of national-service sentiment coming out of the New Deal era dwindled after Pearl Harbor and did not revive in the immediate post-World War II period. But at each upswing in the cycle, the level of support for national service is established at a higher level.

Finally, and perhaps most important, support for military and civilian service, rather than being some kind of zero-sum relationship, tends to rise and fall in tandem. Contrary to the opposition usually seen by the respective supporters of either military or civilian service, history seems to say that tough-minded and high-minded approaches to national service are not only compatible, but even reinforcing.

As we shall see, these patterns hold into the contemporary period.

THREE

Contemporary National Service

If America astonished the world between 1941 and 1945 by our limitless resources and industrial might, we also astonished ourselves. Millions of Americans, who had spent their entire lives in isolated communities spread across the continent, whose youthful experience had been shaped by the Depression, were drawn together for the first time by the Second World War. By the war's end, the feeling of common purpose had produced a sort of national euphoria.

Alas, the sentiment was short-lived. The world war quickly gave way to the Cold War and then Korea. In the 1960s, the national fabric was ripped by assassinations, urban riots, and Vietnam. Watergate and the Iran-contra affair also took their toll. The much-heralded return of patriotism in the 1980s, moreover, was not accompanied by a renewal of national service in practice. The enthusiasm which the memory of the Second World War still invokes marks a significant emotional distance between the prevailing sensibilities of World War II Americans and those of our own time.

The national-service ideal in the contemporary era has been affected, mainly for the worse, by several trends. The citizen soldier has come under attack from both those who see the military best recruited (wages set) by the marketplace as well as those who resist anything that puts more Americans into uniform. Broadening definitions of conscience break the sectarian mold of earlier conscientious objection and introduce a political dimension into what was heretofore mainly a religious motivation. Civilian national service confronts the dilemma of being posed either as an answer to youth unemployment or as an idealistic expression for affluent youth, thus precluding any widespread appeal to the broad middle class.

For the concept of national service to escape the constraints of segmented appeals, the central point must be the specification of societal needs, military and civilian, that neither the market nor conventional governmental bureaucracies can meet. That this has not yet occurred is why those who come to the study of national service expecting to find a purposive spirit in American history, a *Geist* culminating in some sort of unity of citizenship and national service, are doomed to disappointment.

FROM CITIZEN SOLDIER TO ECONOMIC MAN

In the first few years after World War II, the draft was drastically cut back. A new Selective Service Act was passed in June 1948, but only 30,000 were inducted under it, and most of them were released after serving only fifteen months of their twenty-one-month tour. The outbreak of the Korean War quickly changed that. With the passage of the Universal Military Training and Service Act in 1951, a military manpower system was set up that extended conscription beyond the end of the war in Korea. The draft assumed a kind of permanency unprecedented in peacetime America.[1]

Support for the draft in the post-Korea era remained high, and few of the young men directly affected offered any resistance. In fact, a very high proportion of draft-age men ended up serving, the result of a combination of a small cohort (due to the low birthrates of the Depression) and the expansion of the U.S. military. Of all men in the eligible age group (eighteen to twenty-four years), 64 percent underwent some form of military service; 24 percent were judged to be unfit; and only 12 percent escaped being drafted or otherwise serving.[2] (The draft was also a major impetus for ROTC enrollments during the 1950s and early 1960s.) Military service became the typical experience of young men in the years between the wars in Korea and Vietnam. The very

ubiquity of military service accounted for the widespread acceptance of, if not enthusiasm for, peacetime conscription.

What is more, the peacetime army was characterized by an
impressive social mix. A full 75 percent of male high school
graduates served, as did 70 percent of all college graduates; for
those who had not completed high school the figure was 41
percent.[3] In contrast to World War II, the races mixed fairly
easily in this period, thanks to President Truman's executive
order requiring the integration of blacks in the armed forces. In
short order, the military was transformed from one of the most
rigidly segregated institutions in American society to one of the
most open. Although lacking the glamour and controversy of
war, the Cold War draft was one of the most remarkable, if least
remarked upon, episodes of national service in American history.

All this changed with Vietnam. At the high point of the war,
about 300,000 men a year were drafted; all told, about 9 million
entered the military between 1965 and 1972, of whom about 2
million served in Southeast Asia.[4] Interestingly enough, due to
a large youth cohort (the "baby boom" of the 1950s), a somewhat
smaller proportion of young men actually served than during
the peacetime draft. More noteworthy, though, was the class
bias of the draft. High school dropouts were twice as likely to
enter the service as college graduates. As a result, the draft army
of the Vietnam era had a narrower social base than at any time
since before World War II.

Escalation of the war in Vietnam was matched by the antiwar
movement at home, especially on college campuses. One person's
citizen soldier had become another's militarist. Antiwar faculty
and students demanded the closure of ROTC units. Such protests
did not prevent 101,882 men from receiving ROTC commissions
during the war, 40 percent of whom were assigned to combat
duty. ROTC became a convenient target of antiwar activists. Several score ROTC buildings were bombed or set on fire. The low
point was reached in May 1970, when Ohio National Guardsmen,
called to quell an anti-ROTC demonstration at Kent State University, let loose a fusillade that killed four students and wounded
nine others. The modern-day equivalent of militiamen, under
some provocation to be sure, had nevertheless shot American
college students.

As the antiwar movement gained momentum, the citizen-soldier concept was unraveling everywhere.[5] The reaction of some

part of American youth toward the Vietnam War was no doubt idealistic. But much more importantly, the war became a personal threat; to be drafted could mean to die in Vietnam. Draft dodging became a mass phenomenon. During the years of the war, more young men evaded the draft through legal and semilegal means than were conscripted. More starkly, more than 500,000 violated the draft laws, not counting the 50,000 who fled to Canada. Once the notion of the citizen soldier lost its political and social legitimacy, the days of the draft were numbered. Something became clear that had never quite been understood before: the draftee was ultimately a volunteer.

In 1973, military conscription officially came to an end. Moving to a voluntary military had the remarkable effect of simultaneously relieving the upper classes of military service, calming the campuses, disarming the leftists, and quieting antimilitary pacifists. Richard Nixon was later reported to express regret at his decision to end the draft, but it was one of the most popular acts of his presidency.

When the actual draft ended in 1973, draft registration lingered on. But in 1975, President Gerald Ford allowed registration to lapse as well. Following the Soviet invasion of Afghanistan in 1979, President Jimmy Carter asked for a reinstatement of draft registration. In a significant break with the past, Carter requested that women be included in the registration process. Congress authorized funds for registration but excluded women from the registration process. Thus a male-only draft registration was reinstated in 1980.[6]

The procedure was that all men must register within thirty days of their eighteenth birthday. Even men who could not or would not serve in the military, such as the handicapped or conscientious objectors, were required to register. The actual registration was accomplished by filling out a form the size of a large postcard available at the post office. The forms were then processed at the Selective Service headquarters in Washington, D.C. The registrant was also supposed to notify Selective Service by mail of any change in address. Refusal to register or to notify of change of address was a felony and carried a maximum penalty of five years in prison and a $10,000 fine.

The citizen soldier made somewhat of a comeback on the college campus. From a low of 60,000 in the early 1970s, ROTC enrollment by 1987 almost doubled to 110,000, with units on

more than 500 campuses. ROTC commissioned some 8,000 officers a year, accounting for about one-quarter of the annual total.
Increasing numbers of blacks entered the corps, so that by the
1980s their share of ROTC enrollments exceeded that in the
population at large. And, in 1972, women first gained admittance
to ROTC; within a decade they accounted for one in five candi-
dates. With little fanfare the social demography of the ROTC—
the citizen soldier of the campus—has undergone a change of
such proportions as would have been unthinkable a generation
ago.

In general, though, the advent of the all-volunteer force (AVF)
was at cross-purposes with the ideal of the citizen soldier. Leaving
aside how the social composition of the American military has
changed since the end of the draft, an issue we will look at
directly in a later chapter, we can say for now that the AVF is
based on a marketplace mentality of recruitment and retention.
The rationale for the AVF was contained in a 1970 report of a
presidential commission, named after its head, Thomas S. Gates,
a former secretary of defense and Morgan Trust executive.[7] The
main policy recommendations were to give hefty pay raises to
recruits to induce enlistments and to rely more on career soldiers
than on single termers. The Gates Commission was primarily
driven by conservative economists Milton Friedman and Martin
Anderson (who later became President Reagan's first chief domestic policy adviser).

The philosophy that underpinned the Gates Commission im-
plied a redefinition of military service away from an institutional
format to one more and more resembling that of an occupation.[8]
Such a redefinition of the military is based on a set of core
assumptions. First, there is no analytical distinction between
military systems and other systems, especially no difference between cost-effectiveness analyses of civilian enterprises and military services. Second, military compensation should as much
as possible be in cash (rather than kind) and be linked as much
as possible to skill differences of individual service members,
thereby allowing for a more efficient operation of the marketplace.
Finally, if end-strength targets are met in the AVF, concepts of
citizenship are incidental concerns.

Recruitment for the AVF has persistently stressed material
allures—the pay that could be earned, the skills that could be
learned. Primary reliance for providing an armed force was placed

on monetary inducements and supply and demand variables in the labor force. The high salaries offered low-level soldiers—in 1987, a private first class earned the equivalent of $16,000 a year—have drained the armed forces of much of their civic content. A symbolic threshold was crossed in 1983 when, for the first time in American history, military manpower was officially counted as part of the labor force. Military service can no longer be assumed to be national service. Economic man had replaced the citizen soldier.

CONSCIENTIOUS OBJECTION AND ALTERNATIVE SERVICE

When the draft was brought back in 1948, it included no provision for conscientious objectors to perform alternative service. Rather, because the reinstituted draft was so mild in its application, conscientious objectors were de facto exempt from any requirement. With the outbreak of the Korean War and the enactment of permanent conscription, the issue of conscientious objection could not be avoided. In 1951, an alternative-service option under civilian direction was allowed for conscientious objectors. It was not the civilian-camp program of World War II, however; instead, alternative service was defined as work "in the public interest" for civilian employers that met the guidelines of the Selective Service System.

Alternative service was limited to public employment by federal, state, or local governmental agencies or nonprofit organizations engaged in activities benefiting the public. Thus the appropriate work was defined by the nature of the employer rather than by the character of the work itself. The initial burden for finding appropriate service was the responsibility of the conscientious objector. If an objector did not find his own alternative service, then the draft board would assign him to a specific task. This system remained the same in all essentials through the Cold War and most of the Vietnam War years.

Between 1951 and America's full-scale entry into the Vietnam War in 1965, about 30,000 conscientious objectors performed alternative service.[9] Most were Mennonites and Brethren; the remainder included Quakers and a scattering from denominations other than traditional pacifist churches. The typical conscientious objector served two years performing menial tasks in a hospital or mental institution. A most significant departure from the World War II experience was that alternative servers were paid by their civilian employers at the same rate as regular workers performing equivalent tasks. In almost all cases, these were entry-level wages for common labor, but still the compensation of the conscientious objector did not compare unfavorably with that received by military draftees.

Any account of alternative service must mention the two leading organizations representing the interests of conscientious objectors. The National Interreligious Service Board for Conscientious Objectors (NISBCO) was originally formed in 1940 to coordinate the efforts of the Mennonites, Brethren, and Quakers in response to the first peacetime draft. When the United States entered World War II, this group managed the Civilian Service Camps. By the 1960s, NISBCO had grown into a broad coalition of national religious bodies and served as the principal liaison between individual conscientious objectors and the Selective Service System. The Central Committee for Conscientious Objectors (CCCO) was founded as a secular organization in 1948 in response to the new draft law enacted in that year. Both NISBCO and CCCO oppose mandatory civilian national service as well as military conscription. Both are inclined against comprehensive voluntary programs as well, seeing such proposals as a Trojan horse for a military draft.

The Vietnam period brought about an exponential increase in the number of conscientious objectors. Indeed, the war's unpopularity caused a major transformation in the concept of conscientious objection, offering an alternative form of service to many thousands of young men who, for both noble and selfish reasons, did not want to bear arms. Between 1965 and 1970, 170,000 men were classified as conscientious objectors. In proportion to the number of men drafted, this was sixty times greater than the number of commanding officers (COs) in World War II! During the last two years of the Vietnam War, for every three men drafted, two applied for objector status. The immense number of objectors simply overwhelmed a system that could not find enough alternative work for all of them. Altogether, only about half of those granted conscientious-objection status performed alternative service. What the experiences of these alternative servers were like, what impact they had on the hospitals and institutions in which they worked, has never been examined in a systematic fashion. Strangely enough, we know more about the alternative service performed by the conscientious objectors of World War II than by those of the Vietnam period.

The great increase in conscientious objection was made possible from two Supreme Court decisions that liberalized the standards of conscience. Selective Service legislation has always required that objectors believe in a "Supreme Being"; it excluded "political, sociological, or philosophical views or merely a personal code." In 1965, the Court, in *United States* v. *Seeger,* broadened the criterion to include those with a belief that occupies "a parallel place psychologically important to the believer as belief in God." In 1970, the Court went even further, ruling in *Welsh* v. *United States* that "ethical and moral beliefs" were as valid as religious convictions. Now even atheists could qualify for objector status if they demonstrated a deep moral aversion to war. Only on the issue of selective objection to particular wars has the Court so far held firm. Through widening definitions of conscientious objection, then, the Court effectively laid the groundwork for an expansion in the practice of alternative service.

Tying up the loose ends of the Vietnam War was not easy. In 1974, President Ford announced a program of "earned re-entry" for Vietnam-era draft evaders who would perform two years of civilian service of the kind performed by conscientious objectors. Only 6,000 men received pardons through the program—the average period of service was ten months—whose administration was so confused that few ever understood its provisions or could explain exactly what was to be done. In 1977, shortly after taking office, President Carter issued a pardon to all those who had violated Selective Service laws during the Vietnam era. The blanket pardons were assailed by mainstream veterans' organizations and others as demeaning the obligations of those who served in the military. Although helping heal the social wounds of the Vietnam War, the Carter pardons set a major precedent whereby men who had illegally dodged the draft had their full rights restored, with no pretense of having fulfilled any citizen obligation. Also, the presidential pardons probably confused the status of the conscientious objectors in the public mind. The presidential pardons were given to those who actually broke the law; in contrast, conscientious objectors who performed alternative service were always within the law.

Conscientious objectors did not disappear with the end of the draft. In the all-volunteer era, between one and two hundred military people are released annually from the armed forces for reasons of conscientious objection.[10] These numbers are somewhat remarkable as they come entirely from military volunteers who changed their minds after they entered the service. NISBCO and CCCO have extended their activities to include counseling of conscientious objectors in the military. Some time in the 1970s, the first female conscientious objector—a woman who had enlisted in the armed forces—undoubtedly appeared, though her name may be lost to history. Technically speaking, a military member who is discharged for conscientious objection has a liability to perform alternative service for the "remainder" of his "obligation." Apparently, this stipulation has never been invoked.

The current draft registration also has implications for conscientious objection. Although an estimated 400,000 young men had not registered during the first six years of the program, only eighteen nonregistrants were indicted during this same period. All of these were men who had "gone public" in their refusal to register as a matter of principle. For those cases that went to trial and resulted in conviction, the emerging pattern in sentencing was probation to community service. The nonregistrant willing to push his case to the extreme often ends up really performing a form of national service. It is ironic that a number of young men are doing a form of "alternative" service in lieu of a primary service that no one else is performing. An even higher irony is that one nonregistrant, David A. Wayte, was sentenced to six months of house arrest in 1985 and prohibited from performing community service during that period because he was already performing such service!

In the 1980s, the concepts of conscientious objection and alternative service have undergone some quiet but profound changes. In 1983, the Federal Register carried new regulations for an Alternative Service Program to be set up in the event of a renewed draft.[11] Conscientious objectors would be required to perform two years of civilian work in lieu of induction. To help place them in jobs, Alternative Service Offices (ASOs) would be established throughout the country. These would maintain a computerized list of acceptable civilian employers (limited to governmental agencies and nonprofit organizations). Approved areas of employment would include health care, education, environment, agriculture, and social and community work. An objector could appeal assignment to a particular employer, if such employment violated his conscience.

The ASO concept marks an important new development in the annals of national service. Though administratively a part of the Selective Service System, the new structure would be run by civilians. Participants in the program would be treated less like conscripts than ordinary members of the workforce. Servers would receive the same pay as other workers performing the same jobs. They could also be fired like other workers, in which case they would be returned to the ASO for reassignment. A conscientious objector would be free to seek his own alternative-service work, subject to review by the ASO. He could also appeal his assignment if it violated his conscience.

The ASO plan takes on a special significance in the context of the ever-broadening definition of conscientious objection. Long gone are the days when the typical objector was a rural youth raised in a traditional pacifist church. With the introduction of secular criteria for avoiding military service, CO status will no doubt attract more draft-age men than ever before if conscription comes back. And, given the emphasis now placed on the holding of well-articulated moral and ethical beliefs, conscientious objection will likely be argued by intellectually sophisticated, and more affluent, individuals. Consider, in addition, that a future judicial ruling may well accept the principle of selective conscientious objection, legitimating opposition to particular wars.[12] Such a decision would lead to a massive increase in the number of conscientious objectors.

One way or another, the prevalence of objector status is bound to increase. The public and, to an extent, the government itself are becoming more used to the idea. And the availability of meaningful alternative service will make that option increasingly popular. The absolutist position—an unwillingness to participate in any program—will diminish as the alternative-service position becomes more insulated from the armed forces. If the draft is ever reenacted, there will be tens of thousands—perhaps hundreds of thousands—of young men seeking alternative service. Thus we may be backing into a major civilian-service program without ever having quite legislated one.

THE RISE AND FALL OF CIVILIAN SERVICE

Peace Corps

The 1950s were the doldrums for the idea of civilian national service. Dwight Eisenhower never expressed any interest in national service during his presidency. But the climate changed with the ascent of John F. Kennedy. During his presidential campaign, Kennedy advocated the creation of an overseas youth corps.[13] The proposal met with an enthusiastic reception on college campuses. So, shortly after his election, Kennedy set up a task force under his brother-in-law, R. Sargent Shriver, Jr., to develop the idea of a Peace Corps. The agency was created by an executive order in March 1961, and later that year Congress passed a bill making it permanent. Shriver was named the first director.

The wellspring of the actual program was a concept paper written by Warren W. Wiggins and William Josephson of the International Cooperation Administration; from the start they defined the Peace Corps as something different from a standard government job—tenure, promotion, retirement schemes did not apply. The three goals of the Peace Corps were to provide trained people for developing countries, to promote a better understanding of Americans on the part of the host country, and to promote a better understanding of other peoples on the part of Americans.[14]

The Peace Corps was thus a pure type of service program from the very start. When it began, Third World peoples had seen few Americans who were not religious missionaries, soldiers, or affluent tourists. The Peace Corps volunteer showed the world a different kind of American—one who spoke the local language and lived under local conditions. It also showed that thousands of young Americans had enough of an adventurous spirit to go into strange lands and perform services that Americans had rarely attempted before.

Despite its many changes of fortune, the Peace Corps proved remarkably durable. In the first twenty-five years of the program, nearly 120,000 volunteers served in ninety-two countries. In 1987, about 5,200 volunteers were serving in some sixty countries, the major host countries being the Philippines, Kenya, Ecuador, Zaire, and Honduras. In the 1980s, about half of all volunteers worked in education projects: mainly classroom teaching of English, but also vocational training and education of the handicapped. About a quarter of the volunteers were employed in health-related projects, and a similar number worked in food-production projects (the Peace Corps is the largest agency working with freshwater-fish breeding in the world).

The Peace Corps is highly selective in choosing its participants. Only about one in five applicants is accepted. Most volunteers come from upper-middle-class backgrounds; nearly all are college graduates, many from elite institutions. The Peace Corps was the first major national-service program to welcome women, and they make up about 40 percent of all volunteers. As has often been observed, racial minorities are not proportionately represented in the Peace Corps. At least as significant, but rarely noted, is the marked underrepresentation of southern whites. Proportionate to Vietnam veterans, Peace Corps returnees have had much more political impact. By 1987, two returned Peace Corps volunteers—Paul E. Tsongas of Massachusetts and Christopher Dodd of Connecticut—had served in the United States Senate, and seven have been elected to the House of Representatives.

Although the Peace Corps has, inevitably, changed over the years, the basic terms of service have remained the same. Peace Corps volunteers generally have three months of training (foreign language and cultural training and intensive short-term technical training), followed by two years of service. Volunteers receive modest wages set at a "subsistence" rate—averaging around $300 monthly in 1987. Peace Corps members cannot use overseas military and embassy commissaries and must purchase all items on the local economy. The volunteers also receive medical coverage and a readjustment allowance—$4,200 in 1987—at the completion of their tour. The annual costs per volunteer were $22,000, a figure reflecting the overhead of an international agency, certainly not the penurious stipend received by Peace Corps volunteers.

For all its achievements, the Peace Corps has had a stormy passage. After the heady years of the Kennedy administration, the Corps entered a period of real decline. There is no denying that, during the Vietnam War, the Peace Corps was defensive about being considered a draft evader's haven. Peace Corps membership, however, never gave statutory exemption from conscription; local draft boards decided what to do with Peace Corps volunteers. A few men were drafted out of the Peace Corps, but most were granted deferments while serving in the Peace Corps, and some were drafted after Peace Corps service. In 1971, the formerly independent agency was folded into ACTION, an umbrella organization created by President Nixon to include all federal volunteer programs. The effect was to greatly reduce the Corps's autonomy and visibility.

When Jimmy Carter took office, many Corps enthusiasts expected a renaissance of the agency, inasmuch as the president's mother was herself a onetime volunteer in India. But such was not the case. To serve as the director of ACTION, Carter appointed Sam Brown, a leading anti-Vietnam War organizer. Brown had a penchant for radical rhetoric that painted Peace Corps volunteers as unwitting agents of the Cold War and props for right-wing dictatorships. Where the Peace Corps of the late 1960s was seen as a hideaway for crypto-leftists, a decade later it stood accused by its head of being the "vanguard of American cultural imperialism."[15]

The Peace Corps regained its position as an independent agency during the Reagan administration, but it did so almost by accident. In 1981, President Reagan nominated Thomas Pauken, who had served as a junior intelligence officer in Vietnam, to head ACTION.[16] This caused a furor, as the Peace Corps had always taken pains to distance itself from any hint of involvement with U.S. intelligence agencies. A political compromise was fashioned: in return for Pauken's confirmation as head of ACTION, the Peace Corps was once again established as an autonomous entity with its own director, Loret Miller Ruppe, a civic leader and prominent Republican from Michigan. Under Ruppe, the Peace Corps seemed to find some measure of equilibrium.

The Reagan years were marked by yet another turn in the long-simmering debate over the Peace Corps's main mission. The debate pitted the "generalists," who favored recruiting untrained youth, against the "specialists," who believed in sending experienced volunteers to perform specific tasks. In the early years, virtually all Corps members were generalists. Many of these youths provided badly needed services; others were ill-prepared and became angry at the local peoples, the American government, and themselves. During the 1970s, the emphasis shifted toward the specialists, but it proved difficult to recruit skilled personnel, especially those adept in agronomy, a skill in special demand. The new focus was reflected in the Peace Corps's shifting age composition. In 1965, almost 90 percent of all volunteers were twenty-six years or younger; fifteen years later, the figure was down to 40 percent. By the mid-1980s, the pendulum began swinging back again. The number of young people climbed back to half of the volunteers. It had become apparent that generalists—which really meant recent liberal arts graduates—were more adept than specialists at learning languages and fitting into strange societies. It may be a harbinger of the new mood that the Peace Corps signed up twenty-five graduates of the Yale class of 1985, making it the class's single-largest employer.

There is no way to express the diversity packed into the term "Peace Corps volunteers"; tasks and locales are too varied to allow easy characterizations. The next few paragraphs draw upon interviews with Peace Corps servers in Honduras and Micronesia as well as with former volunteers back home. The defining quality of Peace Corps volunteers is that they are on their own almost all of the time. Although few Peace Corps volunteers live in the proverbial "mud hut" in the remote back country, they do nevertheless fend for themselves in the everyday life of a Third World country, taking care of their own food, shelter, laundry, and transportation. Most will live in a town or city and have a life-style similar to that of the lower-middle class in the host country. Except for fellow Peace Corps volunteers, they avoid other Americans and think of themselves as a special breed. The Peace Corps, of course, has had its failures as well as successes. Over the years, substantial numbers of volunteers—between 10 and 30 percent—fail to complete their tours of service (an attrition rate lower, however, than that of military recruits in the all-volunteer era.) The personal foibles and peccadilloes of individual volunteers have caused occasional embarrassment, but the remarkable thing is how few such incidents have been.

In the course of their overseas tours, Peace Corps volunteers typically go through three phases. The initial period "in country" is one of idealism and eagerness. This gives way to a phase characterized by disenchantment with the local culture and society, along with a feeling that they are not accomplishing very much. The awareness comes quickly that the Third World's gargantuan developmental problems are rooted in cultural, social, and natural resource realities as well as international relations.

The final phase, and most volunteers reach it, is a realistic assessment of their personal impact at individual and local levels combined with a basic sense of individual accomplishment. Almost all volunteers who complete their tours look back at their time in the Peace Corps as one of immense personal growth. The inevitable periods of frustration and loneliness are compensated by the rewards of learning about one's self while helping people in another culture help themselves.

Although a new threshold in national service was crossed with the advent of the Peace Corps, the program is not without its ambiguities. One is that, even after a quarter-century, the contradiction exists that the Peace Corps is an agency of the United States government, a reality that many of its members wish to deny, especially when distancing themselves from American foreign policies in the Third World. The other is that the rationale for the Peace Corps has never been quite clear as to who is the major beneficiary of the program: the volunteer or the host country. Yet, when all is said and done, the Peace Corps represents the civilian national service program with the highest civic content of any we shall encounter.

VISTA

The controversies surrounding the Peace Corps pale beside those that engulfed VISTA (Volunteers in Service to America). The agency's beginnings were auspicious enough. The early success of the Peace Corps made a domestic equivalent seem a natural follow-up. President Kennedy appointed a study group, headed by his brother Robert, then the U.S. attorney general, to explore the idea of a civilian-service program.[17] It was not until 1964, however, that VISTA, a youth-service corps, was set up as part of President Johnson's Great Society program.[18]

The VISTA organization made federal grants to sponsoring agencies—local governmental agencies and nonprofit associations—which in turn hired the VISTA volunteers and oversaw their activities. In its original formulation, VISTA tasks were defined as delivery of human services to the mentally ill, the elderly, the physically handicapped, migratory workers, residents of urban slums and depressed rural areas, American Indians, and other deprived groups. The relevant agency would essentially use the VISTA volunteers as extra help. In practice, the guidelines were vague enough that some number of volunteers felt they were marking time.

The early VISTA was patterned after the Peace Corps. The 2,000 or so VISTA volunteers all received a six-week training course, then were given assignment away from their homes. Participants received a subsistence allowance plus free health insurance. Volunteers were also given an end-of-service payment; in 1987, $75 for each month served in VISTA. Most of the volunteers, like their Peace Corps counterparts, were liberal arts college graduates from well-to-do backgrounds. In fact, many VISTA volunteers were unsuccessful Peace Corps applicants.

Then, in 1969, Congress authorized the recruitment of low-income individuals to work in their home communities. One result was a rise in VISTA enrollees through the 1970s, peaking at 5,000 in 1980. But more significant was the change in social composition and age. By the late 1970s, low-income volunteers accounted for two-thirds of the VISTA membership. And, as more low-income persons joined, the average age of members rose. The proportion of those aged twenty-six and older—negligible in the 1960s—increased to more than half by the late 1970s.

VISTA became embroiled in acrimony during the Carter years. Until then, the program was primarily devoted to providing social services directly to those in need. When Sam Brown became director of ACTION, under which VISTA along with the Peace Corps had been placed, VISTA was charged with "empowering the poor."[19] VISTA volunteers began organizing tenant strikes and advocating welfare rights. That the agency also made grants to some organizations with strong New Left ties caused antagonism among moderate and conservative members of Congress. Put in its best light, VISTA during the Carter administration sought to promote democratic participation among poor citizens. Put in another way, VISTA was subsidizing radicalism. Either way, the VISTA of the Brown era found many of the program's projects in an adversarial relationship with local establishments.

When the Reagan administration started its term, it set out to do away with what it viewed as a leftist bastion. The newly appointed director of VISTA, James Burnley, stated that he was "working hard to be the last VISTA director."[20] In 1983, ACTION created what was widely seen as VISTA's replacement—the Young Volunteers in ACTION. The new program was conceived as part-time work performed by uncompensated youth who learn about community-service projects as possible places of future employment. But predictions of VISTA's demise proved premature, due largely to the efforts of a group called Friends of VISTA. Founded by Sargent Shriver in 1980, the organization mounted an effective grass-roots campaign that succeeded in keeping VISTA alive.

The VISTA program that remained, however, was barely recognizable. Membership was cut in half to about 2,000 volunteers. The training period of the early years had long since been replaced by a pro forma "orientation" session given by the sponsoring agencies. Worse, VISTA has not recruited on college campuses since 1980. To add insult to injury, the letterhead on ACTION stationery omits VISTA from its list of volunteer programs. A young person at large seeking to join VISTA in the 1980s would most likely be given the runaround. For all practical purposes, VISTA no longer exists as a nationally recruited youth volunteer program.

What does exist is a program that consists almost entirely of low-income volunteers, fewer than one in five below the age of twenty-six. (In 1987, this meant that fewer than 300 young people were serving in VISTA.) While it is true that VISTA is no longer the corps of white idealistic college students it once was, the civic spirit of present volunteers should not be dismissed simply because the social composition has changed. Although the steady-stipend and job features of VISTA most likely loom larger than in times past, the current membership also represents the self-help and localism that will characterize any decentralized national-service program of the future.

Conservation Corps

The Civilian Conservation Corps of the Depression years, so successful in carrying out its mission, left a strong imprint on the public mind. According to a 1961 Gallup poll, 80 percent of the American public supported the idea of reviving the CCC; even more remarkably, 59 percent said they believed such service should be required of all young men out of work and not in school.[21] During the late 1950s, bills creating a mini-CCC actually passed the Senate but, owing to opposition by the Eisenhower administration, died in the House. When John Kennedy assumed the presidency, the chances for a large-scale youth conservation program seemed excellent.

After Kennedy's death, however, the new Johnson administration, and later that of Nixon, moved away from notions of broadly based national service toward employment programs for poor and minority youth. As we shall see in a later chapter, programs such as the Neighborhood Youth Corps and Job Corps were devoid of any civic content but rather were jobs or job-training programs. What did evolve in the rationale of the conservation corps to be reviewed here was a conflict between those who viewed such programs mainly in terms of services performed (with perhaps some inculcation of work discipline among enrollees) and those who saw them simply as jobs programs. The former group favored open enrollment programs while the latter wanted corps targeted toward "at risk" youth. This dichotomy, another reflection of whether the emphasis should be on the service or the server, is a constant in civilian national-service proposals.

The largest and most successful of the civilian conservation programs was the Youth Conservation Corps (YCC).[22] The brainchild of Senator Henry "Scoop" Jackson and Congressman Lloyd Meeds, both of the state of Washington, the YCC was established in 1970—the first national conservation corps since the CCC. The YCC was a summer program for youths aged fifteen to eighteen years. Participants lived in residential camps, each accommodating about two hundred youngsters. Tasks included tree planting, erosion control, trail construction, and maintenance of recreation areas. Enrollees were paid a minimum wage for a thirty-hour week; in addition, they were required to spend ten (uncompensated) hours a week in environmental training. From 1970 to 1981, when the program was terminated, the YCC was host to about 30,000 teenagers a year.

Despite its relatively short existence, the YCC provided some useful lessons for future conservation and national-service programs. For one thing, the YCC introduced a new organizational model. No overarching single YCC organization existed as such; rather, funds were distributed approximately equally between three administrative groups: the Forest Service in the Department of Agriculture, the Department of the Interior (which in turn funneled the money to such constituent agencies as the Bureau of Indian Affairs, Fish and Wildlife Service, and National Park Service), and, most significantly, the individual states. All fifty states participated, each being required to contribute one-fifth of the total cost for the state. Despite its apparent cumbersomeness, this tripartite administrative structure and cost-sharing feature worked surprisingly well.

The YCC also showed how a youth-service program can avoid being labeled simply a jobs program, a common pitfall of youth-service programs. The legislation setting up the YCC did stipulate that "preference shall be given to disadvantaged youth." The clear intention of Congress, however, was that the YCC not be considered a poverty program, and thus membership was not restricted to the poor and unemployed. In point of fact, however, low-income youth did make up the bulk of YCC's enrollment. In 1981, the YCC's last full year, about half of all participants came from families earning less than $10,000 a year. About 20 percent of enrollees were blacks, Hispanics, and American Indians. The YCC experience demonstrated, however, that even when a program draws disproportionately from the poorer segments of society, it need not be defined as a holding operation for dead-end youth. The YCC avoided this label because it always reflected some class spread in its membership and consistently kept the service ethic in the forefront.

That the YCC was more than a simple jobs program is evident in the experience of those who enrolled. The corps had the lowest attrition rate—about one in nine—of any national-service program on record. Much of this is attributable to the corps' summer-only nature, but the attitudes of the participants were also a factor. A 1979 survey of YCC graduates by the University of Michigan reported that an astounding 91 percent found the program worthwhile, and a full 65 percent called it one of the most satisfying experiences of their lives.[23] The primary benefits, according to the study, were an increased awareness of environmental issues, a heightened ability to work with people from different backgrounds, and, in the case of low-income participants, "an increased persistence at studying and better relations with their families."

The YCC was a cost-effective civic program. At its high point, total annual costs came to $60 million a year, or $2,000 per participant. The value of the work performed under the program was computed at 94 cents on every dollar spent. Nonetheless, under the Reagan administration the program was essentially dismantled. By 1982, the YCC was no longer included as a line item in the federal budget. Both the Forest Service and the Department of the Interior deemed the program so valuable, however, that they asked for and received permission to use their own funds to keep the YCC from dying completely. In the summers of the mid-1980s, several thousand youths still served in YCC camps, but the future was unclear. For all intents and purposes, the YCC can be considered a part of history.

The successful YCC program was the direct precursor of the Young Adult Conservation Corps (YACC), which President Carter signed into law in 1977.[24] YACC was a year-round program in which enrollees, aged sixteen to twenty-three, served for twelve months. Like YCC enrollees, YACC participants received the minimum wage. Also like the YCC, the funds for YACC went in approximately equal shares to the Forest Service, the Department of the Interior, and the individual states.

Even though YACC was originally conceived as sort of an adult YCC, it did not turn out that way. The Department of Labor was the administering agency and fought for a targeted program. Eventually, a compromise went into the legislation; YACC enrollees had to be unemployed but not necessarily poor. With the Department of Labor in the picture, there was also constant pressure to define YACC simply as a jobs program, an interpretation resisted by the Forest Service and Interior Department and their counterparts in the states. An intra-agency agreement was signed between the Labor Department and all the parties, but because of continuous bureaucratic infighting the issue was never resolved.

YACC peaked at 25,000 enrollees in 1980. More than 200,000 young people participated at one time or another in the program, which had relatively high attrition and turnover. Forty percent of YACC enrollees were high school dropouts, and about a third were minorities, mostly black. About three-quarters of enrollees were commuters, and without the centrality of a residential system, YACC members developed little institutional identity. To make matters worse, a few of the YACC camps were marred by problems of enrollee indiscipline. (One of the crueler characterizations of YACC was "hoods in the woods.") Moreover, leaders of environmentalist and conservation movements never seemed to connect with black leadership, and vice versa. Little wonder that YACC did not survive the first budget cuts of the Reagan administration.

Still, despite definitional and sociological problems, YACC had a cost-effectiveness ratio more favorable than YCC's and similar to that of the old CCC. YACC volunteers accomplished $1.20 of work for each dollar expended. Also impressive was YACC's "outplacement rate"—74 percent left the program to resume their education, to take employment, or to enter the armed services. All in all, YACC was a successful conservation program, but it was a shallow form of national service with a civic content somewhere between the old CCC and a straight jobs program.

Between YCC and YACC some 450,000 young people performed conservation work from 1970 to 1982. The two programs received high marks from dispassionate evaluators for completing valuable conservation work throughout the nation. Yet, most Americans have never heard of either YCC or YACC. The two conservation programs of the 1970s never enjoyed the visibility or widespread support given to the CCC of the 1930s. No president ever visited the camps; nobody of importance was ever in charge, and no one ever seemed especially interested in telling the stories of YCC and YACC to the public. When the programs were ended in the early 1980s, there was little outcry from the hustings.

Still, the idea of a youth conservation corps persisted. The CCC precedent became particularly salient in the early 1980s when the youth unemployment rate reached levels not seen since the Depression. Unemployment rates for minority youth especially seemed impervious to recovery in the general economy. The logic of linking youth unemployment to conservation became more persuasive. A common political constituency developed consisting of those concerned with chronic youth unemployment and those worried about environmental issues. The movement to establish a modern form of the old CCC was gaining ground.

A bill to introduce an American Conservation Corps (ACC) was introduced in the House in 1981 by John F. Seiberling, an Ohio Democrat and a senior member of the Interior Committee. The Seiberling proposal, combining features of YCC and YACC, would become the 1980s model for a youth conservation corps. The original Seiberling bill called for $300 million a year for six years to provide summer work for 50,000 youth, aged fifteen to twenty-one, and year-round employment for 56,000 others, aged sixteen to twenty-five. ACC enrollees would receive the minimum wage and would have a mix of residential and nonresidential programs.

In order to attract urban youth, the ACC would locate as many camps as practical near metropolitan areas. Thus, in addition to conventional conservation tasks—soil protection and improvement of forests, rangelands, and national parks—ACC participants would undertake pest control, renovation of neighborhood parks and waterfront areas, and weatherization of poor housing. Although special efforts would be made to recruit the economically disadvantaged, the program would be open to all unemployed young people, including middle-class ones. The CCC analogy gave the ACC bill a distinctly civic aura. The national-service aspect of the proposal was evident in favorable newspaper editorials across the country, and the New York Times explicitly related the ACC to William James's essay on "The Moral Equivalent of War."[25]

The Seiberling bill passed the House in 1982 and again in 1983, the second time by a lopsided 301-to-87 vote. Companion bills were introduced in the Senate, and a scaled-down version passed both houses in 1984. Proponents of the ACC were confident that the compromise version would become law. In a historic decision, however, President Reagan vetoed the ACC, saying the program would be too costly, that it would inevitably grow, and that the work would not prepare participants for jobs in the private sector. ACC bills would be reintroduced in subsequent Congresses, but the momentum had been lost. It seemed that the ACC was an idea that had taken hold, but a program whose time was yet to come.

THE NADIR OF NATIONAL SERVICE?

By the late 1980s, a young person seeking national service would find it very difficult if not impossible to enter a federal program whose premise was performance of civic duty. The citizen soldier had given way to an all-volunteer force based on market principles. A handful of conscientious objectors who refused draft registration were performing national service at the community level—as part of their sentences. Fewer than 2,500 young people were in the Peace Corps and VISTA combined. No civilian conservation corps existed. Ironically, as the concept of national service was attracting increased attention in public discussion, national service had reached one of its lowest points in this century.

FOUR

Youth Service at State and Local Levels

From the ashes of national service at the federal level, youth service was to arise phoenix-like at state and local levels. By 1987, from Connecticut to California, from New York City to San Francisco, some 7,000 young men and women were enrolled in state and local corps. In both numbers of participants and range of activities, the nonfederal corps far outweighed the federal programs. Although few Americans have heard of these local ventures, they have, in a low-profile way, shown a remarkable capacity for innovation. Examining their successes and failures can tell us a lot about such national-service matters as cost, administrative structure, social composition, and staffing. On the key issue of civic content, too, local programs are rich in both example and caveat.

To try to cover each of the twenty or so year-round youth corps that came into being during the 1980s would be to risk turning this chapter into a kind of numbing Baedeker.[1] Rather, I have categorized the youth corps into three broad groups— state conservation corps, county and city programs, and social service programs—and look at some examples in each. Also, some commentary is given on the special case of the Guardian Angels. Throughout I will emphasize those features that might apply beyond the particular locality in question. In their scope and variety, these local ventures indicate the contours of a successful national program.

STATE CONSERVATION CORPS

In 1987, six states—California, Illinois, Pennsylvania, Texas, Washington, and Wisconsin—had year-round conservation programs with at least several hundred enrollees each. Alaska, Connecticut, Minnesota, and New Jersey had smaller programs. All were aimed at younger people—mostly between eighteen and twenty-five years of age—and usually compensated participants at minimum-wage rates. Many were targeted at economically disadvantaged youth.

The flagship program of the state youth corps is the California Conservation Corps (California CC). The California CC had a modest origin. In 1971, Governor Ronald Reagan established the California Ecology Corps as an alternative-service program for conscientious objectors. The corps remained small, consisting of about one hundred conscientious objectors from the state plus several hundred other people hired locally to stand watch for forest fires. In 1976, Governor Edmund G. Brown, Jr., replaced the Ecology Corps with an expanded California Conservation Corps. Initially, the program foundered under inept leadership, a "hippie" image, and drug-abuse scandals. By the spring of 1979, the state legislature was ready to shut down the entire program.

Then Governor Brown appointed B. T. Collins director of the corps. Collins, an ex-Beret who had lost an arm and a leg in Vietnam, has been described as "candid, irreverent, blustery, perceptive, foul-mouthed, and devastatingly charming."[2] He was also a superb manager, and he shaped the California CC into a program that gained the support of the public and legislature alike. He coined the corps's motto—"Hard work, low pay, miserable conditions"—and established five succinct rules. "No booze. No dope. No violence. No destruction of state property. No refusal to work." Collins also set some clear civic obligations: all corps members had to register to vote, give blood, and, if male, register for the draft.

The California CC has determinedly avoided becoming a targeted program aimed specifically at poor youth. Aside from age and California residency, the sole requirement is that applicants not be on parole or probation. The program is certainly popular; at any given moment, the waiting list is as long as the actual enrollment. Nonetheless, the California CC, like virtually all other nontargeted youth corps programs, draws disproportionately from minorities and the poor. Only 40 percent of all corps members have high school diplomas, and, even among those, only about a third took an academic curriculum. Although one of every ten enrollees has had some college, virtually none is a college graduate. About a third of the enrollees come from households receiving public assistance or food stamps. About three out of every five members are white, with the remainder almost equally divided between blacks and other minorities. Sixty percent report their fathers' occupations as blue-collar, 32 percent as nonprofessional white-collar, and only 8 percent as managerial or professional.[3]

Corps members enroll for one year and are paid the minimum wage, about one-third of which is subtracted for room, board, and medical insurance. All participants must complete a two-week course at a training academy, which, in true boot-camp fashion, features rigorous physical exercise, lectures on the work ethic, and instruction in first aid, water safety, fire training, and the use of tools. The California CC is mainly a residential program, with most members living in fairly isolated camps. Starting in 1986, though, the corps has set up nonresidential satellite centers in urban areas, to which enrollees commute daily.

Participants work in crews of a dozen or so, directed by an adult supervisor. Some of their tasks are rather mundane—planting trees, growing seedlings, removing log jams in streams, renovating fish hatcheries, repairing storm damage, trail-building, and developing park areas. The corps also engages in more dramatic activities, such as fighting fires, cleaning oil spills, and, in 1981, halting the infestation of the Mediterranean fruit fly. Weekends are usually free, but many weekday evenings are devoted to formal education courses expected to lead to a high school diploma.

One innovative element of the California CC is its writing requirement. It was introduced by Robert Burkhardt, Jr., then deputy director of the program, in 1980. "Everyone writes every day," he decreed. Starting at the training academy, each corps member writes a page a day—letters, work memoranda, resumes, project reports, and, most commonly, daily journals. Burkhardt convincingly argues to a visitor that the writing program improves morale and develops character. And from a practical standpoint, writing boosts the chances an enrollee has in later finding a job. Most importantly, the writing requirement adds a time for reflection to the corps's physical experience. To be sure, some grouse about the writing requirement, but few fail to fulfill it—a phenomenon all the more noteworthy, given the generally low educational levels of corps members.

There is no denying that the California CC has a high attrition rate. Only half of all entrants complete six months—the informal benchmark of success—and only about a third complete the full one-year term. (By way of perspective, the average six-month tour of the California CC member is slightly longer than the average term of enrollees in the Depression-era CCC and twice as long as that of the federal YACC program in the 1970s.) Most of those who leave the corps in the first months are expelled for violating the rules—failing to report for work, indiscipline, drug or alcohol use. Those who leave later do so mostly of their own volition. About half do so for positive reasons—to take a job, enter the military, or return to school. Those who voluntarily quit the corps are not allowed to reenter. Expellees, interestingly enough, are given a second chance, though they must retake the training-academy program without pay.

Camp conditions are functional but stark, with fewer creature comforts than most military barracks. Each camp has an average of sixty residents. There are no haircut or beard regulations, but there is a general understanding that anyone with too outlandish a personal appearance will not be promoted. The typical day starts with a 5:00 A.M. reveille, followed by physical training, breakfast in the dining hall, and cleanup. Work begins at 8:00 A.M., when the crews leave with bag lunches for their work sites. They return around 5:00 P.M., eat dinner, and spend the evening writing, talking, and relaxing. Quiet hour starts at 10:00 P.M., and lights are out at 11:00 P.M. The quiet hour and early lights-out prevent extensive music playing or carousing, and, in any event, most corps members are physically tired after a day's work.

Comparing a visit to a California CC camp with those I have made to army units, I believe the work ethic of conservation corps members equals, when not surpassing, the work ethic found in the enlisted ranks of the contemporary military. Although the California CC is not recruiting large numbers of youth who have stable employment backgrounds or who possess college educations, a youth with middle-class sensibilities would not feel uncomfortable in the corps environment. Race relations, though by no means perfect, seem generally smooth. The isolated nature of the camps promotes easy social mixing. In addition, the high proportion of minority members in the staff has minimized perceptions of discrimination on the part of minority corps members.

Women make up about 25 percent of the California CC, and sex roles seem egalitarian. Women perform all tasks save those requiring the heaviest labor. There are few complaints among the men that the women do not pull their share of the work. For their part, women members generally believe they are treated fairly, and sexual harassment is not a common complaint. There is some dating among corps members and, inevitably, some sexual hanky-panky, although persons caught flagrante delicto are dismissed from the program. In general, male-female relations are attenuated due to the program's high turnover rate.

From the start of the Collins era, the California CC has been marked by a heavy brew of pragmatism and idealism, and that has helped win it bipartisan support. This was confirmed when Republican Governor George Deukmejian, elected in 1982, continued to fund the program at about the same level as his Democratic predecessor. Although organizational changes were occurring in the late 1980s—more nonresidential centers, a shortened training-academy cycle, plans for a summer-only program, some assignment of corps members to individual rather than crew work—the initial civic spirit continued to pervade into the corps's second decade. The California Conservation Corps stands as a preeminent example of how a comprehensive national-service program might operate at the state level.

Although the California program dwarfs all the rest, other state corps have some distinctive features worth mentioning. On the matter of cost, for instance, the Ohio Civilian Conservation Corps (Ohio CCC) offers a less expensive alternative to the higher-cost California CC. California's high staff ratio, its training academy, and residential character boost annual per capita costs (about $19,000 in 1986). By contrast, per capita costs for the Ohio CCC, with about four hundred members, come to $16,000 for each residential member and $9,000 for each nonresidential one.

Ohio's program typifies a no-frills approach. The staff is relatively small, and there is virtually no education or vocational training. Originally, the Ohio corps had a mandatory training academy similar to California's, but this was dropped in 1986 due to budgetary cutbacks. In its camps, the Ohio CCC has consciously attempted to replicate the military atmosphere of the New Deal CCC. Bugle calls punctuate the daily routine at the residential camps, from reveille to taps; meals are referred to as "chow," and uniforms resemble the garb more of soldiers than forest rangers.

The Ohio CCC bears down heavily on the proposition that its mission is to instill a work ethic in participants while they perform needed conservation work. All applicants are personally interviewed by the head of the corps or a high-level staffer, a time-consuming task that pays off with what is probably the lowest attrition rate of any conservation program; about three out of every four entering corps members complete the initial six-month term. The black proportion has gone from almost nothing in the program's early days to about one-quarter of the membership in 1987, an outcome of the establishment of satellite centers in metropolitan areas.

A new wrinkle in state programs was introduced by the Michigan Civilian Conservation Corps (Michigan CCC). With about five hundred members, the Michigan CCC is part of a broader program called "Project Self-Reliance," an experiment in workfare. Admittance to the Michigan CCC is limited to youth on general assistance, which makes the program one of the most highly targeted in the country. Participants forego their welfare checks and food stamps in return for a minimum-wage job. In theory, only volunteers sign up with the Michigan CCC; in practice, many of the youth report strong informal pressures from the state employment offices to take Michigan CCC jobs when openings appear.

The Michigan CCC has no training academy, no vocational or counseling staff, and, most importantly, all supervisory staff are regular workers in state conservation agencies. Costs are correspondingly low, the lowest of any youth corps in the nation: $13,000 per person per year for residential camps and $6,000 in the nonresidential program. The Michigan CCC is much more a jobs program than an activity with high civic content. Still, it rests on a promising idea: that welfare recipients can become contributing citizens by participating in work for the public good.

The state experience offers some insights for service programs on a national basis. For one thing, nonresidential programs encounter a very common everyday problem—the unreliability of teenagers' automobiles and the resultant epidemic of absences and tardiness. The problem can be overcome in part by locating centers at sites accessible to public transportation or by setting up some kind of shared van system. Residential programs in rural areas have their own problems. They are generally unattractive to urban young people, especially minority youth. It is important to remember, moreover, that even in the Depression, white city youth were least likely to join the CCC. The situation of women in traditional conservation corps appears anomalous. Women perform as well as men and often occupy leader positions in work crews. Yet, the proportion of women in rural corps seems to hit a ceiling of around 30 percent, and even this figure is probably somewhat inflated, as special efforts are made to recruit females.

A visitor to a state conservation corps will encounter a disproportionate number of young men from hardscrabble rural backgrounds. Not a few are seminomadic, with no place to call home. Most conservation corps members (a major exception being the California CC) will identify themselves to outsiders as employees of the state's department of natural resources rather than as corps members. This is partly because state conservation corps have low visibility, but mainly because working for the state sounds more like "a real job" than does being a corps member. In other words, many corps members *resist* identification with the corps because it may be stigmatized as welfare in disguise. The general rule is that the less civic content a program has, the less likely participants want to be identified with it.

CITY AND COUNTY PROGRAMS

The growing number of youth-corps programs at the city and county levels has opened up a new dimension in national-service prototypes. They have a much higher proportion of minority males, and women commonly make up half or more of the enrollees. Perhaps the most significant generalization is that none of the local programs is more than a few years old.

The first local youth service program was the Marin Conservation Corps (Marin CC) located in Marin County, California. The county, located just north of San Francisco, has a strong conservation constituency, combining both conservative farmers and liberal environmentalists. Begun as a summer experiment in 1982, the program was made permanent and year-round in 1984. The Marin CC is open to youth aged eighteen to twenty-six who are selected on the basis of interviews. In 1987, the Marin CC had about forty members in the year-round program, along with a summer program of about 150 enrollees. The program is formally open to all youth but unofficially aims toward economically disadvantaged youth.

The Marin CC set a possible example for national-service entities by incorporating itself as an independent nonprofit organization, with a board reflecting the diversity of the community. In contrast to government agencies, such a structure allows for a minimum of red tape and flexibility in the hiring and firing of staff. On the negative side, Marin's nonprofit arrangement makes for a less secure funding arrangement than would be the case in a publicly supported program. The corps's budget of about $1 million a year must be pieced together from various grants and from contracts with local governmental agencies and park groups. Whenever anticipated contracts do not materialize, the Marin CC undergoes a financial crisis.

The Marin program has a strong vocational orientation. In addition to featuring the usual conservation projects, the corps has specialized crews to teach enrollees such job skills as tree surgery, landscaping, carpentry, and weatherization.[4] The Marin CC has a high per capita cost, owing mainly to the salaries of the skilled craftspersons needed to lead the specialty crews, and in part to what some say is an overstaffed operation. Although nonresidential, the per-slot costs are about $21,000 per year.

In point of fact, the Marin CC is sort of a hybrid job-training program and a service corps. Enrollees receive $3.50 an hour, a sum deliberately set higher than the minimum wage to avoid the stigma of a jobs program. Raises are given to good workers. The relatively high pay of the corps makes the civic content of the Marin CC somewhat problematic. Still, the delivery of conservation services is emphasized in the image projected to the public at large. And, in a departure from a straight job-training program, corps members are required to devote time to community service.

The first youth service corps in a city was established in the spring of 1984 in San Francisco. The San Francisco Conservation Corps (San Francisco CC) was designed to test the idea of a conservation program in a strictly urban setting. It is entirely nonresidential and includes both year-round and summer programs, with about seventy young adults enrolled in each. The San Francisco CC seeks to instill a work ethic via service to the community; there is little stress on job training per se, though some of it occurs in the actual work.

The San Francisco CC, like its Marin counterpart, is set up as an independent nonprofit corporation and receives basic funding from community development grants, but private foundations and corporations also contribute substantial funds. Additional money is raised through small contracts negotiated with nonprofit and public agencies that receive the services of the San Francisco CC. Altogether the annual budget is about $1.5 million. In 1986, costs per corps member were calculated at about $14,000 for the year-round program and $2,500 for the summer corps.

All participants start the day at corps headquarters with calisthenics, then move out in work crews by van to their job sites. Projects include such activities as reforestation of the Twin Peaks recreation area, renovation of senior citizen housing in the Tenderloin district, and landscaping work at Alcatraz. The enrollees work a thirty-two-hour week at the minimum wage and spend one unpaid day a week in the classroom. The director is Robert Burkhardt, Jr., the man who introduced the daily writing requirement into the California CC. He has done the same in San Francisco. Burkhardt occasionally reads poetry, with generally happy results, to corps members during the classroom time.

The San Francisco CC has its own motto: "Service, Friendship, Competence, Character." And it has an earthy code of conduct: "Booze it, lose it; get high, goodbye; throw a punch, gone before lunch; steal, no appeal; noncooperation, unpaid vacation." Punctuality is strictly enforced; coming to work late by even a minute or two is cause for immediate dismissal. (Some offenders are given second chances, however.) Such rules have produced a high attrition rate—about 40 percent during the first month. But the enrollees who remain develop an identity with the corps unusual in local programs. The civic content of the San Francisco CC is high.

By far the most ambitious of the local service programs is the New York City Volunteer Corps, started in 1984. The initial inspiration for the New York CVC came from Herbert Sturz, former head of the Vera Institute of Justice and later chairman of the City Planning Commission. But it was only with the advocacy of Mayor Edward Koch, perhaps the most forceful exponent of national service among elected officials in the country, that the New York CVC came into being. The program was launched, in Koch's words, with the explicit purpose of "people working to help others, not just for a paycheck." The project, he added, "will provide a basis of experience in an urban setting that could serve as a model for a nationwide service program which I believe should be and will be enacted by Congress."[5] As proof of his support, Koch arranged for the city to put up 90 percent of the CVC's initial $30 million, three-year budget. (Private foundations were to provide the rest.)

Carl Weisbrod, the corps's first director, designed the project to serve both pragmatic and idealistic ends. It would provide needed low-cost labor that would not otherwise be available; it would enable participants to acquire valuable job skills; and it would give young people a genuine sense of contributing to their communities. The corps intentionally avoided being defined as a jobs program. As Weisbrod told this writer: "Our volunteers are providers, not recipients of service."

CVs, as City Volunteers are known, serve for one year. At its peak in 1986, about 800 enrollees were in the corps. The tour of duty begins with a two-week training period in a camp in upstate New York. Once the training period is completed, the CVC is entirely nonresidential. Compensation, in the manner of the Peace Corps and VISTA, is defined as a subsistence allowance rather than wages. A CV receives a weekly stipend of $80 plus medical insurance; after completion of a year's service each is awarded a $5,000 college scholarship or a $2,500 cash payment. When work projects demand long hours, there is no overtime compensation. In addition to full-time service work, the New York CVC requires participants with educational deficiencies to rectify the situation. To that end, arrangements have been made with the City University of New York, among other institutions, to provide special classes in adult education, high school equivalency, and college preparatory courses. Annual costs per enrollee came to about $13,500, not counting cash-out and scholarship benefits.

Proposals for work projects can be submitted by public agencies or private nonprofit organizations. The New York CVC is built around the work team, consisting of ten to twelve members. Projects must be suitable for team activities, and it is expected that individuals or groups smaller than teams will not be assigned to particular projects. Ideally, over the course of the year, each CV will serve on several different teams and will take part in different types of projects in different neighborhoods throughout the city. All projects must be designed so as not to displace regular workers.

Corps members, among other activities, have repaired park furniture and planted trees in Roy Wilkins Southern Queens Park, tutored fourth-graders in reading in the Bronx, painted the St. George Ferry Terminal on Staten Island, performed play therapy with chronically and terminally ill children at Woodhull Hospital in Brooklyn, and completely renovated the oldest settlement house in America on Manhattan's Lower East Side. Periodically, the CVC calls all its members together to perform a "signature service" in one concentrated time period, such as delivering USDA surplus food to housebound persons or giving disaster relief during a hurricane.

The original concept of the New York CVC was to attract a cross section of New York's youth. This has not come to pass. In late 1986, 70 percent of the enrollees were high school dropouts and less than 5 percent were white. The failure to make any inroads into middle-class youth was a major disappointment. By 1987 the CVC was in a period of retrenchment. Enrollment was down to 700, and future plans were to have a solid base of 300 year-round CVs augmented by 150 part-timers. Annual budget projections were set at about half that of the original period. Nevertheless, the CVC appears to have moved from a demonstration project to a permanent presence in New York City.

The corps concept is catching on in many other communities, varying widely in local circumstances. The East Bay Conservation Corps, headquartered in Oakland, California, serves an array of counties, from suburbs to ghetto, from farmland to industrial areas. The Blue Knob Conservation Corps is a summer program serving a four-county area in central Pennsylvania. The Dutchess County Youth Community Service Corps operates in the exurbia of New York City. The Greater Atlanta Conservation Corps set up in 1986 is the first youth corps in the South. In 1987 Public/Private Ventures, a nonprofit research group that has been studying youth programs, announced it had received sufficient foundation support to start up a Philadelphia Youth Service Corps.

The local youth corps that came into existence in the 1980s tend to have high staff overhead and correspondingly high per-enrollee costs, at least in comparison with conventional state or federal conservation corps. Much of this is in the nature of the crew or team organization that requires continuous supervision by relatively well paid and full-time staff. The crew format, coupled with the nonresidential feature of local programs, also makes maintaining an overall corps identity a challenge. Some of the programs overcome this by having a residential training period, corps uniforms, headgear and other insignia, and a periodic bringing together of the whole corps either for work, training, or ceremonial purposes. It seems that some kind of harking to the institutional heartland is a requisite for corps cohesion.

SOCIAL SERVICE PROGRAMS

Contemporary state and local youth corps are miniatures for an expanded, yet decentralized, national program of youth service. Along with the models of conservation programs, there is another significant tendency in local programs, one geared toward delivery of human or social services. In time, it may be that these social-service programs will be the key element in building political support for national service. Two early experiments in community-based programs were mounted in Seattle and Syracuse. The contrast between them tells a lot about what to strive for, and what to avoid, in formulating national-service programs.

Seattle's Program for Local Service (PLS), established in 1973, was a path-breaking initiative.[6] PLS established three major precedents. First, PLS introduced the delivery of social services as a mode for youth corps. Second, PLS pioneered the concept of a federally funded but locally controlled youth service program. And third, PLS adopted a principle whereby the sponsoring agencies—local governmental agencies and nonprofit organizations—that used youth enrollees would contribute a sum for each enrollee, thus establishing an earnest-money precedent. PLS is as significant in its own way for shaping the patterns of delivery of human services for youth corps as the Civilian Conservation Corps was for influencing subsequent conservation programs.

The program got its start, in a sense, at the 1968 Republican convention. The keynote address was given by Washington Governor Daniel J. Evans, who spent much of the speech extolling the virtues of national service. The next step came in 1972, when ACTION head Joseph H. Blatchford, Jr., a national-service enthusiast, requested $4 million from the Office of Management and Budget (OMB) to start a nationwide program. OMB turned him down, but it did authorize the use of $1 million in ACTION funds to underwrite a small pilot project. The project was drawn up by Donald J. Eberly, an ACTION staffer, who selected Seattle as the locale because of Evans's support and who went on to become the program's director. In a curious proviso, however, OMB insisted that the program not be called national service, hence the name Program for Local Service.

Inevitably, PLS experienced considerable pressure to serve as a jobs program, but it nonetheless managed to retain considerable civic content. Community service always remained at the program's core. Seattle residents between the ages of eighteen and twenty-five were invited to volunteer for a year of full-time community service. Regulations specified that the work performed had to be antipoverty in nature, and participants could not replace regular employees. Although compensation was set at less than the minimum wage (plus medical coverage), the program was swamped with applicants—1,700 for 372 places— a response that surprised skeptics and pleased advocates.

PLS solicited both local government agencies and nonprofit organizations as potential sponsoring agencies, each of which was required to contribute $150 for each volunteer used. Eventually, two hundred sponsors came on board, generating a pool of twelve hundred positions. Few of the sponsors created new projects for the volunteers; rather, PLS enabled understaffed day-care centers, tutoring programs, old-age and nursing homes, and recreational centers to bring themselves up to full strength. PLS compiled a directory of available positions and then helped match applicants with sponsors. Eventually about half of the enrollees worked for public agencies and about half with a wide variety of private nonprofit organizations.

As PLS got started, some observers predicted it would turn into an elitist youth program like the Peace Corps or early VISTA; others insisted that it would attract only the poor. In the end, PLS proved both groups wrong. Like most open-enrollment programs, it drew heavily from the pool of unemployed youth, but an unusually large proportion—about half—had some college education. More significant, perhaps, PLS was the first service program to draw more women than men—six out of ten participants, thus reversing the usual male predominance found in conservation corps. The attrition rate for PLS was surprisingly low, with about two-thirds of all volunteers remaining for the full year of service. PLS sponsors estimated the value of work performed by volunteers at more than $2 million, or more than double the amount of the ACTION grant. Less than 10 percent of the public funding was spent on administering the programs; the great bulk went to pay enrollees.

PLS was phased out in 1977, a victim of federal cutbacks. Nonetheless, by showing that local programs could use young people to deliver social services, and could do so at low cost, PLS set a standard for future programs. The experience of PLS in human services also showed that there are a variety of projects well within the capacity of inexperienced young people, and that intergeneration projects that involve enrollees with older adults or with elementary school pupils seem especially valuable for all parties concerned.

The Youth Community Service, which operated in Syracuse, New York, from 1977 to 1981, had a less happy experience.[7] On the surface, YCS bore many similarities to the Seattle program. Volunteers were matched with sponsoring agencies and were paid less than the minimum wage. But the differences were substantial. The U.S. Department of Labor, which paid for the program, required that YCS volunteers be limited to unemployed and out-of-school youth, thereby undercutting YCS's value as a national-service experience. Simultaneously, ACTION, which administered the program, ruled that failure to report for work could not be considered grounds for withholding pay, thereby making it difficult to discipline enrollees.

As a result, YCS had problems from the start. Drawing almost exclusively from high school dropouts and minorities, it had difficulty finding positions for applicants. Furthermore, only one in four enrollees completed the full year. Overall, the program's long-term benefits were unclear. As a YCS evaluation put it, "almost without exception," enrollees showed "little interest in volunteerism."[8] Considering the persistent efforts by the Labor Department to steer YCS away from any concept of a service ethic, it is no surprise that the civic content of the Syracuse program was practically nil. The surprise is that the YCS volunteers performed as well as they did.

Ironically, ACTION defined the Syracuse program as an experiment in national service, something it was not. PLS in Seattle was explicitly told not to call itself a national-service program, but it turned out to set a historic precedent for national service. Everything went right with PLS, and just about everything went wrong with YCS (though some of its problems were straightened out in its late stages). YCS tarnished the idea of national service at the local level. PLS, by contrast, represented the first successful demonstration that community services could be delivered in a low-overhead, locally determined program of youth service.

Washington Service Corps

The state of Washington has one of the most innovative youth programs in the country—the Washington Service Corps (Washington SC). In many ways, the Washington SC is a resurrection of the Seattle PLS, except that funds come from the state rather than federal government. Since its founding in 1983, the Washington SC has been operating on a budget of about $1 million annually. Because the Washington SC sets some important precedents on how a decentralized program of national service that provides human services might operate, I will describe it in some detail.

The Washington SC is an entity of the state's employment department. Its director since its inception, William C. Basl, a former VISTA volunteer, sees service as the essential ingredient of the program. The corps's goal is to offer youth a training and work experience while they perform community service. The number of enrollees averages about 160 at any given time. The requirements for qualifying are broad: applicants must be state residents between eighteen and twenty-five years old and must be unemployed for at least two weeks; in effect, this means open enrollment. As usual, the program is heavy in low-income enrollees, but overall it represents a wider spectrum than almost any other local program; about one in eight enrollees has spent time in college. Roughly two-thirds of all corps members are white, with the remainder divided more or less evenly among blacks, Hispanics, and American Indians.

Unique among state programs, members in the Washington SC receive less than the minimum wage. The "stipend" is explicitly intended to be at subsistence level. In 1987, the monthly rate was $450, which, after deductions for income tax, Social Security, medical and life insurance, and workers' compensation, came to about $165 every two weeks. Plans were being made to have a postservice educational benefit starting in 1988. As a recruiting pamphlet states: "The pay is a mere pittance. The money you receive is only a small subsidy to help you meet some of your expenses during your commitment to serve. Personal satisfaction is the big payoff."

The Washington SC, like its PLS forerunner, is based on the sponsor system. The program is entirely nonresidential. Potential sponsoring agencies—federal, state, or local government agencies or nonprofit organizations—periodically receive circulars requesting proposals for use of corps members. Sponsors desiring the services of corps members submit requests along with project proposals. The requests are evaluated on the basis of community service and the skill training provided to enrollees. Projects are limited to six months. To insure there is a genuine need, more than to increase overall program funding, each sponsor is required to pay a cash match of $750 for each corps member per six-month project. No enrollee can be used for work that involves political or sectarian activities, or that displaces regularly employed workers.

The number of applicants is about four times the number of openings. Washington SC staff reviews the applicants' qualifications and usually refers several applicants for each opening requested by a potential sponsoring agency. Applicants are interviewed by the sponsor, and, if both seem amenable, a work agreement is drawn up and reviewed by the Washington SC. If either the enrollee or the sponsoring agency is incapable of completing the work agreement, notice is given by one of the parties. When there is disagreement, the Washington SC adjudicates. Basically, the arrangements are a three-sided pact between the enrollee, the sponsor, and the Washington SC. In the program's first four years, some three hundred agencies used volunteers. If the Washington SC's experience is any guide, nonprofit organizations are more likely than government agencies—whether state, local, or federal—to participate. About 60 percent of sponsoring agencies fell into the former category and only 25 percent into the latter. (The remainder consisted of school districts and Indian tribal groups.)

In general, small nonprofits seek Washington SC enrollees more than public agencies. The roster of participating agencies runs the gamut: Senior Rights Assistance, Food Oversight Operation, Library for the Blind, Metrocenter YMCA, Neighborhood Health Center, Catholic Family Services, Home Health Care, Nooksack Tribal Center, Raymond Chamber of Commerce, Noxious Weed Control, American Red Cross, and Skagit Rape Relief, among many others. One service with nationwide applicability is a program of home-chore service for the elderly; partially incapacitated old people who otherwise would be institutionalized can be helped to stay in their homes. Washington SC enrollees have also increasingly become part of the nonprofessional staff in shelters for victims of rape or home violence.

Because the Washington SC has no job-placement component (though 20 percent of enrollees are eventually hired by their sponsors) and because much of the overhead is absorbed by sponsoring agencies, the per capita cost to the state is very low—$4,200 per six-month term. With low costs and satisfied sponsors, the Washington SC has developed a strong political constituency. In 1987 the program was extended for another six years by unanimous vote in the state legislature.

THE SPECIAL CASE OF
THE GUARDIAN ANGELS

There are few more striking examples of civic-minded youth volunteers than the Guardian Angels. Since the organization was founded in 1979 to patrol New York City's crime-ridden subways, some 15,000 young people have passed through the organization. After stalling in the period from 1982 to 1985, the Guardian Angels gained a second wind, and by 1987 its membership was up to 5,000, 2,000 of them active. With fifty-one chapters, including three in Canada, the Guardian Angels has grown into a nationwide organization; nonetheless, it remains deeply local in character.[9]

The Angels are led by Curtis Sliwa, an articulate, charismatic young man, and his wife, Lisa, a professional model. With a knack for attracting media coverage, the Sliwas have been accused of fostering a cult of personality. Yet, the fact remains that, through their speaking engagements, the Sliwas have raised a lot of money for the organization while living what all observers agree is a threadbare existence.

The Guardian Angels has a very loose structure. The organization, which is incorporated as a nonprofit, has a national headquarters in New York. No Angel, however, including the Sliwas, receives a salary. Members are responsible for their own uniforms (red berets and T-shirts with angel-wing emblems), and expenses are not reimbursed. Chapter expenses average about $200 monthly, mostly for telephones, postage, and local transportation. Money is raised through mail solicitation, the selling of buttons and stickers, and local fund-raisers such as car washes and bake sales. Total expenses for the organization come to an astoundingly low $80,000 a year, or about $40 per active member. The Guardian Angels refuses all foundation grants or public funds on the grounds that to accept such would compromise the organization's autonomy.

Applicants must be at least sixteen years old and be either attending school, employed, or actively seeking work. Membership is predominantly inner-city and East Coast, with New York remaining the hub. Members tend to be black and Hispanic but include a number of working-class whites as well. In other words, Guardian Angels tend to reflect the population makeup of the high-crime areas in which they live. About a quarter of the membership is female.

Typically, a newly organized chapter starts off with high enthusiasm and then enters a period of dormancy. If the chapter can last through this letdown phase, it will usually stabilize at between twenty and forty active members. Although generalizations are risky, it might be accurate to say that about half the members of a chapter become inactive after a few months of patrolling. Most of the remaining half will stay active for about a year. Only a handful remain in the group continuously over several years.

Each recruit is required to take a training course that includes instruction in self-defense, legal aspects of citizen's arrest, and first aid. The instructors volunteer their own time and are often not Guardian Angels themselves; thus a lawyer may talk about citizen's arrest, or a Red Cross worker may teach first aid. The training is organized by the local chapter and typically involves two evenings a week for about eight weeks.

Guardian Angels work through patrols, normally consisting of riding public transit systems and walking through crime-prone neighborhoods. The whiff of danger that accompanies the patrolling experience accounts for the strong bonds among Guardian Angels, bonds that cut across racial and ethnic lines. Everyone is searched before going on patrol, and anyone possessing weapons or drugs is immediately dismissed from the organization. Patrols generally begin in mid-evening and end sometime after midnight. A guiding principle is that physical force is the very last resort, to be used only when protecting a citizen from physical attack. Guardian Angels patrols can be dangerous—three members have been killed on duty. Yet, although Angels have made hundreds of citizen's arrests over the years, the organization claims not a single volunteer has ever hurt another person while on patrol.

It would seem that the Guardian Angels fits in with the ongoing "community policing" movement, in which police departments reach out to citizens to form a partnership in the face of rising crime rates and decreasing budgets. Such was not to be the case. Although local communities are generally receptive to them, how effective the Guardian Angels are in deterring crime is unclear. Skepticism if not outright hostility toward the Guardian Angels has been the common reaction of big city police and mayors. Still, even while their opponents tend to dismiss their contribution, there is no denying that the Guardian Angels provide a comforting sight in public transit systems and areas of high crime, especially for old people.

Young people join the organization for a variety of reasons. For some, no doubt, there is the lure of smashing heads, but most Guardian Angels attach great importance to citizenship duties, a sentiment that is eloquently articulated by individual Guardian Angels. The organization is civically motivated but conspicuously nonpartisan. The conservative tilt one might expect from an anticrime organization is balanced by its proletarian makeup. Guardian Angels are neither fascistic nor revolutionary; their political philosophy centers on citizenship involvement.

The Bernhard Goetz incident in December 1984, and the intense reaction it provoked, point up the high level of public frustration over danger in public areas. In a sense, the Guardian

Angels represents a response to that despair. The accusation that the Guardian Angels are modern-day vigilantes misses the point. Unlike vigilantes, the Guardian Angels do not seek to punish those they apprehend. Why, then, demean the public-spirited impulse of some of society's least-advantaged young people? It is not the vigilante experience but the militia tradition of American history the Guardian Angels most fully exemplifies.

LOCAL LESSONS FOR NATIONAL SERVICE

The national-service experience has been marked by a great paradox. Originally conceived in grandiose, even cosmic terms—the moral equivalent of war—national service has, in practice, taken root on a much smaller scale. As the accompanying chart shows, the service concept is catching on in localities across the country. At first glance, these very diverse experiments might seem to defy generalization, but in fact some clear patterns emerge. Given that these state and local endeavors are de facto pilot programs for a more national approach, their implications are very much worth examining.

First off, there is the matter of cost. The simplest way of computing costs is the most valid. Add all expenses—staff salaries, enrollee compensation, administrative overhead—and divide by the number of enrollee slots. For residential programs, costs range from $13,000 per participant (Michigan) to $19,000 (California); for nonresidential programs, costs range from $6,000 (Michigan) to $21,000 (Marin County). Where a program falls within the spectrum depends largely on staff-enrollee ratios. The level of enrollee compensation—below or above minimum wage—is a relatively small factor (though workers' compensation and medical insurance are not). In addition, the use of sponsoring agencies can substantially reduce layouts. Judging from current operations, it seems that a well-run residential program could be had for about $16,000 per individual (what the Ohio corps costs), and a nonresidential program based on the sponsor system would probably cost $9,000 per slot-year (as it does in the Washington corps).

A truly accurate assessment, of course, should factor in the value of the work performed. But such valuation is not an exact science, although the consensus is fairly firm that the worth of

TABLE 4.1 YEAR-ROUND NATIONAL-SERVICE PROGRAMS AT STATE AND LOCAL LEVELS

Program (year founded)	Number of Positions in 1987	Compensation	Membership Criteria	Civic Content	Special Features
California Conservation Corps (1982)	2,000	minimum wage	nontargeted	high	mainly residential; training academy; writing requirement
Connecticut Conservation Corps (1981)	70	higher than minimum wage	nontargeted	moderate	nonresidential
Dutchess County Youth Community Service Corps, N.Y. (1983)	60	minimum wage	targeted	low	20 hours work, 20 hours school
East Bay Conservation Corps (1983)	80	minimum wage	semitargeted	moderate	strong education component
Greater Atlanta Conservation Corps (1986)	36	minimum wage	targeted	low	four-day work week, one unpaid day for education
Guardian Angels (1979)	2,500 part-time	none	nontargeted	very high	crime prevention; local chapters nonresidential
Illinois Conservation Corps (1986)	100	minimum wage	semitargeted	low	nonresidential
Marin Conservation Corps, Calif. (1982)	40	higher than minimum wage	semitargeted	moderate	job-training component
Michigan Civilian Conservation Corps (1984)	500	minimum wage	targeted	low	corpsmember on welfare when hired; "workfare" aspect

(continued)

Program (year founded)	Number of Positions in 1987	Compensation	Membership Criteria	Civic Content	Special Features
Minnesota Conservation Corps (1983)	60	minimum wage	semitargeted	moderate	may be basis for broad state program
Montgomery County Conservation Corps, Md. (1984)	20	minimum wage	semitargeted	moderate	administered by Montgomery College
New Jersey Youth Corps (1985)	300	minimum wage	targeted	moderate	high school dropouts only; 20 hours work, 20 hours school
New York City Volunteer Corps (1984)	700	stipend less than minimum wage	nontargeted	high	training academy; strong education component; college scholarship upon completion
Ohio Civilian Conservation Corps (1977)	400	minimum wage	semitargeted	moderate	residential and nonresidential; "no frills"
Pennsylvania Conservation Corps (1984)	450	minimum wage	targeted	low	includes urban as well as rural areas
Sacramento Local Conservation Corps, Calif. (1985)	60	minimum wage	nontargeted	moderate	four-day work week, one unpaid day for education
San Francisco Conservation Corps (1983)	60	minimum wage	nontargeted	high	strict discipline; daily journal; one unpaid day for education

Program	Size	Wage	Targeting	Level	Description
Texas Conservation Corps (1984)	300	minimum wage	targeted	low	residential; training academy; federal and private funds
Washington Conservation Corps (1983)	250	minimum wage	semitargeted	low	administered by six state agencies
Washington Service Corps (1983)	160	stipend less than minimum wage	semitargeted	high	delivery of social services; sponsor system with matching funds
Wisconsin Conservation Corps (1983)	350	minimum wage	semitargeted	moderate	public and nonprofit agencies submit proposals to state board
Youth Energy Corps (1981)	50	minimum wage for 20 hours weekly	very targeted	moderate	provides weatherization for low-income housing in New York City; 20 hours weekly mandatory education
Defunct					
Seattle Program for Local Service (1974–77)	370 (at peak)	stipend less than minimum wage	nontargeted	high	prototype of delivery of social services; ACTION funds
Syracuse Youth Community Service (1978–80)	2,000 (at peak)	stipend less than minimum wage	targeted	low	Department of Labor funds

work completed by conservation corps is at least equal to, and probably greater than, the total costs of the program.[10] It is much harder to quantify other types of longer-term social benefits— reduced unemployment, well-being of recipients of social services, lower crime rates, shrunken welfare rolls—but in all these cases, the level of savings would seem to be large indeed.

On the sociological front, the state and local programs provide further evidence for the iron law that even nontargeted programs draw disproportionately from poor and minority youth. At the same time, such programs, especially to the degree they emphasize civic content, are far less likely than targeted programs to be stigmatized as a last resort for dead-end youth. We also know that traditional rural conservation corps are often not attractive to many urban youth, especially blacks. Nor do they draw a proportional number of women. One way conservation corps can rectify this is by establishing satellite centers near urban areas or by having programs geared specifically toward urban conservation projects.

At times there is almost a hairline difference between a job program and national service, and, in reality, most state and local youth corps are a blend of both. More often than not, enrollees have difficulty finding steady work. Many come from troubled (though not necessarily poor) homes. The service corps can serve as an employer of transition, or even a refuge, providing young adults a chance to get through difficult patches in their lives. The service experience gives them the opportunity to have some structure in their lives while working with others for a public good. Put in their own words, local programs give young corps members a chance to get their "heads straight." Not to be dismissed is that quite a few conservation corps members take great satisfaction in working outdoors and learning about nature, while many enrollees in service corps find helping disadvantaged people a boon to their own personal growth.

Inasmuch as many of the corps members seemed to be the same kind of young people who join the armed forces, I was curious as to why they chose civilian service over the military. My original supposition that the corps members would be antimilitary or in some way influenced by the Vietnam War legacy was not borne out in discussions. Some wanted to enter the military but simply could not meet the entrance standards. But by far the most common reason for not joining the armed forces was that a military enlistment was seen as too long and definite a commitment. Unlike a civilian service corps, the military was viewed as too hard to get out of once one was in. The enrollees saw civilian programs as an option worth trying, while the military represented a closing of options.

Youth programs at the state and local levels have shown that national service can take many more diverse forms than originally envisioned. The Reagan budget cutbacks in domestic programs have thus had a silver lining: without them, it is unlikely that so many programs would have sprung up with such surprising speed. Their examples, positive and otherwise, provide many clues as to what to seek and to avoid in a larger program. In sum, the local operations point to the creation of a decentralized national system based on community organizations. Indeed, as Alexis de Tocqueville observed 150 years ago, Americans often satisfy the requirements of citizenship and desires for civic identity within subnational groups, like community, neighborhood, and voluntary associations.

But what the state and local programs offer in variety and innovation, they lack in scale. Few of the programs have much visibility, even in their home areas. Clearly, only the federal government can provide the resources and public attention necessary to make national service a real option for the youth of America.

FIVE

Youth and Poverty

The concept of national service offers a special hope for one of America's most disturbing and intractable trends: the solidification of a youth underclass, most visibly among racial minorities in our major cities. The societal and human costs of an underclass are incalculable—deprivation, crime, despair, alcohol and drug addiction. Whatever the prerequisites for a healthy liberal democracy, it is obvious that inability to integrate poor racial minorities into the mainstream augurs ill for the future.

The cause of the youth underclass is hard-core unemployment.[1] On top of general trends working against youth employability—increased participation of adult women and old people in the labor force, increasing mechanization of unskilled and semiskilled labor, and increasing movement of jobs outside the United States entirely—there are factors that weigh especially heavily on minority youth, namely, a pattern of racism that aggravates the effects of the decline of manufacturing in inner cities with its accompanying loss of unskilled and semiskilled jobs. Even this is not the complete story. Many of the young poor lack the basic capacities—literacy, knowledge of workplace expectations, and basic job skills—needed to obtain and keep almost any job. What characterizes American society today is that both good and bad economic times coexist to an extent not found since the abolition of slavery. A seemingly permanent underclass of youth has become restlessly juxtaposed with youth enjoying unprecedented material affluence.

The underclass crisis has absorbed the energies of a legion of social scientists and politicians. They have turned out learned treatises on the causes and implemented policies on the treatment of the phenomenon; however, they have not had much success in doing anything about it. Indeed, the problem of the underclass has more and more seemed immune to solution, causing widespread frustration, and, perhaps in the not-so-distant future, even hardhearted avoidance of the whole issue.

One key reason for our national malaise derives from a major fallacy on the part of the social engineers—the disconnection between jobs programs and citizen responsibilities. Thus, beginning with the Great Society, we have had one jobs program after another, each one costing significant amounts of tax dollars. Yet, for all the billions of dollars spent, the problem has only become worse. In fact, the record of futility is so great that jobs programs in general have come close to falling into disrepute among the public at large.

To tackle this constellation of woes, employment and job-training ventures for youth need a supplement—what I have called civic content. In structuring jobs programs, policymakers have paid insufficient attention to the types of service performed. Only when training programs involve young adults in the delivery of vital services to the community can they hope to inculcate the values that make for good citizenship. A youth program transfers a moral value to its members when its premise is the civic motivation of those members. This principle is rarely understood by the architects of jobs programs. In short, if job ventures for youth were structured as national-service programs, they might prove more successful in tackling the underclass problem.

An even more complicated matter is who benefits from jobs programs. Experience indicates that, even in targeted programs, resources tend to shift toward those young people who are better prepared and more motivated to begin with. This "creaming" phenomenon appears so often as to seem to be an iron law. Nonetheless, even in the most disadvantaged social strata, there are many young people seeking opportunities to improve their status. In what follows, I will attempt to describe the major jobs programs since the New Deal and indicate what they lack. I will also point to small experimental programs with civic content and discuss their promise. The working hypothesis is that national service can reach more deeply and more effectively into these lower strata than unvarnished jobs programs.

YOUTH UNEMPLOYMENT
AND JOB TRAINING

The Depression permanently transformed the way people think about civilian national service. From William James's original idea of building character in elite youth to providing jobs for poor youth, there was a sea change in national-service thinking. Such programs as the Civilian Conservation Corps and the National Youth Administration were created largely in response to the desperately high unemployment rates of the 1930s. Nonetheless, the New Deal programs, especially the CCC, never lost sight of the service that inspired them.

The same cannot be said for more recent federal jobs programs.[2] In every case, there has been an almost total absence of civic content. Consider the Manpower Development Training Act of 1963, the first post-New Deal youth-employment program. The MDTA's original goal was to provide jobs to adult workers displaced by broad technological and economic changes. However, with climbing youth unemployment rates, Congress decided in 1964 to earmark 25 percent of MDTA funds for young people aged sixteen to nineteen. These funds underwrote the Neighborhood Youth Corps (NYC), which ran from 1965 to 1973. The NYC, which operated in inner cities, offered part-time work in public agencies for high-school-age youth. The program's reach was substantial. Average annual enrollment was 130,000 for the in-school program, 360,000 for the school vacation period, and 80,000 for a school dropout program. During the peak enrollment period of 1972, more than one million young people passed through the NYC.

Considering its size, it is somewhat remarkable that the NYC left little institutional memory, much less any models for emulation.[3] The NYC suffered from the ambiguity of its mission; it remained unclear whether the program was set up to train youth for more permanent work or simply to give enrollees a temporary job. And though the work created by the NYC was supposed to be of value to the community, the program was often described as creating "dead-end" and "make-work" jobs. Indeed, critics contend the program was so poorly conceived that it actually had a negative impact on young people, teaching them how to be paid for work that they did not perform well or at all. When the corps was quietly killed in 1973, few voices were raised in protest. Despite its high-sounding name, the Neighborhood Youth Corps never developed a genuine service ethic among either its staff or its participants.

Even more ambitious was the Comprehensive Employment and Training Act (CETA), which lasted from 1973 to 1983.[4] CETA was created by the Nixon administration with the purpose of consolidating existing Great Society programs under one umbrella within the Department of Labor. CETA was a mammoth program, spending some $55 billion over its decade-long existence. It created summer jobs for as many as one million young people a year; it also funded short-term positions and training programs for hundreds of thousands more. As the program progressed, however, its emphasis shifted from offering job training to providing local public-service employment. Although evaluation studies showed that CETA provided many important services for localities and scored some achievements in training participants, the program was plagued by charges of local waste, muddle, padded payrolls, and outright fraud. By the time of its demise, CETA had a clouded reputation, to say the least.

The Reagan administration replaced CETA with the Job Training Partnership Act (JTPA) of 1983.[5] It was funded at about one-third the level of CETA, and, reflecting the president's economic philosophy, JTPA concentrates on offering the jobless short-term training for quick placement in the private sector. JTPA stipulates that funds for job training could be allocated only to profit-making enterprises. Placement of enrollees in public-service employment is prohibited except in the case of summer youth jobs. Because it must deliver employable youth to private businesses, JTPA, even more than other programs, passes over those most in need of help while aiding young people who are the most trainable and might well find jobs on their own. As a result of such selectivity, JTPA has not had much impact on the youth unemployment rate.

The Durability of the Job Corps

The Job Corps, a centerpiece of Lyndon Johnson's Great Society, has had more staying power than any other youth training program.[6] It was set up under the Economic Opportunity Act of 1964 and, five years later, was brought under the control of the Department of Labor. The corps's budget was halved by Presidents Nixon and Ford, but it rebounded under President Carter and, since 1981, has withstood the efforts of the Reagan administration to eliminate it.

The Job Corps is organized to help the most needy youth. Enrollees are given work clothes, room and board, medical and dental care, counseling, a modest living stipend (about $20 a week), and a readjustment allowance of several hundred dollars upon successful completion of the program. The typical one-year course begins with an emphasis on classroom education, then shifts to vocational training. In the 1980s, many Job Corps centers established ties with local businesses and labor unions, helping with both the upgrading of training programs and the placement of graduates.

In the early years, all Job Corps enrollees were assigned to residential centers, usually located in rural areas and operated by the Interior and Agriculture Departments. Later, more centers were set up in metropolitan areas, and private contractors were brought in to run them. In 1986, of 106 centers, 68 were managed by private contractors, 30 run by Agriculture or Interior, and 6 operated by nonprofit associations (including two Indian tribes). At any one time, there are approximately 40,000 enrollees, 90 percent of them in residential centers.

During the debates preceding its establishment, the Job Corps was portrayed as following the model of the Civilian Conservation Corps. However, aside from youth membership and residential centers, the two programs turned out to have little in common. The CCC was a jobs program with an aura of national service. The Job Corps is exclusively a job-training program with no civic content. In eight years of operation, the CCC accommodated 3 million young men; in its first twenty-three years, the Job Corps trained 900,000.

In addition to contrasts in civic content and scale, the two programs have been marked by very different social compositions. Whereas CCC enrollees represented a rough cross section of male youth, three-quarters of all Job Corps enrollees have not completed high school; about half are black, and one in three has an arrest record. And while the CCC was exclusively

male, the Job Corps is about one-third female (expulsion of preg-
nant enrollees was dropped in 1971). Most women enroll in
traditional female vocational courses: clerical, food service, cos-
metology, and health service. The initial Job Corps residential
centers were single-sex, but over time these have given way to
mixed-sex centers, except in isolated rural areas.

The problem of the centers in the early years—indiscipline,
vandalism, racial discord—gave the Job Corps a blemished name
from which it has never fully recovered. The Job Corps experience
shows location is important for residential programs. Morale
and discipline problems for inner-city youth, especially blacks,
are severe in residential camps located in white, rural areas.
Moreover, rural centers have difficulty attracting qualified staff
with the street savvy to handle inner-city youth. With the shift
toward metropolitan areas, the discipline problems of the Job
Corps have greatly receded.

The Job Corps has also been given low marks for its high
dropout rate—about one in three in recent years. Yet, the program
has consistently received positive evaluations from independent
researchers. A major study that followed graduates for four years
found significant benefits—higher earnings, lower unemployment, reduced welfare.[7] Of course, since the motivated participants are the ones most likely to join and graduate, it is hard
to separate neatly the effects of training from the initial predispo-
sition of enrollees. Still, the consensus of informed observers
is that the Job Corps has had a good long-term cost/benefit ratio
for society.

When it comes to direct costs, the Job Corps seems more efficient than other training programs. In 1985, the annual cost per
enrollee was about $15,000—several thousand dollars less than
for comparable residential youth programs. The difference is
due to the use of private contractors and nonprofit associations,
which seem able to manage the centers for less than the government can. Some of the high costs of the federal centers were
due to the simple fact that civil service personnel cost more
than comparable private workers. Considering the staff intensity
and training requirements of the Job Corps centers, the relatively
low costs are impressive and an object lesson for the organization of residential components of any future national-service
plan.

HIGHLY TARGETED PROGRAMS
WITH CIVIC CONTENT

The common thread in all jobs and job-training programs since the New Deal is that they are devoid of civic content. The principle is clear that only the enrollees are to be beneficiaries of the program. By way of contrast, we now turn to two programs that purposely introduce a service ethic into their job training. These are the Youth Energy Corps (YEC) and the alternative sentencing program of the Vera Institute of Justice, both in New York City. That a service ethic can have practical as well as moral consequences among the most disadvantaged youth is a consideration of immense significance.

YEC is directed exclusively at youth in their late teens who are likely to get into or already have been in serious trouble.[8] Most of the enrollees are black or Puerto Rican males; almost all are high school dropouts, and quite a number have criminal records. YEC was conceived by a group of foundations collaborating with the private sector and with state, city, and community agencies.

Enrollees are put to work weatherizing low-income apartments (primarily installing storm windows). The work setting is very tightly organized with one staff member for every six participants. Each youth's work is regularly assessed and documented, thus providing him with a clear sense of his progress. The basic principle is "No School, No Work."[9] YEC participants work twenty hours a week (for which they receive the minimum wage) and spend another twenty in school. Enrollees are permitted to stay in the program until they graduate from high school or earn an equivalency diploma.

Besides "hands-on" experience, the young people develop and apply computing and reasoning skills in the solution of practical problems, and they exercise writing abilities by keeping records of work procedures and results. The principle is that achievement in a nonschool situation can enhance the student's capacity to learn in the classroom. In turn, weatherization involves a number of skills learned in the classroom, such as making arithmetic computations and interpreting graphs. Members are thus led to make connections between their schoolwork and real work. But overarching all of this, enrollees know they are providing a valuable service to residents of run-down neighbor-hoods.

YEC has some clear limitations. For one thing, it is very small. Since 1981, it has graduated only 500 youth; in 1987 enrollment shrank to 50, a result of budgetary constraints. YEC is also expensive, costing about $15,000 per member per year, a fairly high cost for a program that is entirely nonresidential. Nevertheless, YEC is a rare example of a program that simultaneously targets poor youth and contains civic content.

Another model of community service comes out of the criminal justice system. While for many years some middle-class offenders have been sentenced to perform community service in lieu of a jail term, a recent development has been the use of similar sentencing for poor and minority criminals. One of the most highly regarded programs of alternative sentencing is operated by the Vera Institute of Justice. Under the Vera program, a thousand offenders a year, mainly young people, are assigned to work a number of hours in social-care agencies or other approved service programs.[10]

Offenders in the community service program are assigned to supervised eight-member crews, to work seven-hour days in centers for the elderly, housing projects, and similar places; jobs range from painting and maintenance work to staffing recreational programs for retarded children. Ninety percent of the offenders complete their work sentences. According to Michael E. Smith, director of Vera, the key to the program's success is close supervision and stress on the service performed. The Vera program requires offenders to clock in and out of the work assignments; should one fail to appear, an arrest warrant is immediately issued. Without close monitoring, community service sentences easily lead to widespread abuses. The major social good, besides the service performed, is that a community service sentence costs about one-tenth as much as keeping the prisoner in jail for the same amount of time.

Both YEC and the Vera program are rare examples of programs that simultaneously target "at-risk" youths and are based on the premise of community service. As such, they can serve as models for more comprehensive programs with specially targeted membership. The understanding is that only when national or community service is couched in terms of young citizens delivering vital services can its positive, but necessarily second-order, consequences of doing good for those who serve best be accomplished.

AVOIDING STIGMA BY NATIONAL SERVICE

It should now be apparent that, with the exception of a few experimental private initiatives, contemporary jobs programs offer little in the way of civic sensibility. Policymakers almost always focus on the employment and training aspects of the program rather than on the services, if any, provided to the community. The moral importance of the work for the enrollee is effectively scuttled. Whereas national service stresses that a youth corps position should be more than just a job, the Department of Labor seems intent on making sure it remains only a job.

This brings us to the perennial question of labeling. If programs are constructed for, targeted on, the most disadvantaged, they create an image of being designed only for failures, thereby stigmatizing the programs and their clientele. In many cases, the target population itself comes to share the prejudice that others project onto it. National service offers a way out of this dilemma. By adding a civic component to jobs programs, it can help instill a sense of pride and satisfaction in those who participate. These qualities make the YEC and the Vera programs models, albeit small and expensive ones, for an important component within a more general and comprehensive national service.

Only by dealing with young people as citizens, rather than as wards or clients, can derogatory stereotypes be avoided. Not to put too fine a point on it, many Americans view job-training programs as "giveaways" to unworthy recipients. This may be deplorable, but it is nevertheless a real and widespread sentiment. How much better it would be to create social definitions whereby job-training enrollees were cast in the role of civic-minded deliverers of services to the community. It would thus seem sensible to require that youth participants in a jobs program be required to undertake a stint of national or community service.

Such a recommendation is consistent with the social theory laid out in Lawrence M. Mead's provocative *Beyond Entitlement: The Social Obligations of Citizenship*.[11] It postulates that government should require people to earn their benefits by fulfilling certain fundamental obligations of citizenship. By failing to require those on public assistance to do anything in return for aid, the poor are prevented from attaining the civic competence necessary to be integrated into mainstream society. Any system that bestows entitlements without corresponding obligations is bound to create suspicions that recipients are not pulling their fair share. As Mead puts it, "Those who *only* make claims can never be equal, in the nature of things, with those on whom the claims are made."[12]

Finally, national-service programs could do well to emulate the military in placing the emphasis on the service performed, rather than on those who perform it. After all, we do not have an army to help young people mature or give them jobs (though these can certainly be important consequences). Whatever successes the military has had for turning dead-end youth into responsible citizens have largely been due to the discipline of the armed forces being legitimated on the principles of citizen obligation and patriotism.[13] Those very conditions peculiar to the armed forces that serve to resocialize poor youth toward productive ends depend directly upon the military not being defined as an employer of last resort or welfare in disguise. This is no less true for civilian programs.

The most extravagant expectations for national service, of course, will never be fulfilled. National service is not a panacea for all of society's problems, not even those directly associated with youth. The tangle of macroeconomic change, social pathologies, and racial marginalization that have produced an underclass youth will not magically heal and straighten with the introduction of national service. Nonetheless, compared to many other solutions that have been advanced, the service concept seems the most promising.[14] As a federal country, the United States is in an excellent position to try out decentralized programs of national service and expand upon the most promising. Especially important, there already exists within the black community a strong network of local organizations with a record and reputation for service. The energies of the voluntary organizations that achieved prominence in the struggle for civil rights may now be employed to confront the difficulties that beset the black underclass.

While being careful not to succumb to the seduction of national service as a cure-all for America's social ills, we should accept the powerful transformational aspects of concentrated performance of civic duty on the part of the youth involved. A comprehensive program of national service would call upon all of our country's races and classes to take part in a common civic enterprise. If this possibility is ignored and time is allowed to slide by, the richest country in the world will enter the twenty-first century crippled by an unemployed, unassimilated, and embittered underclass.

SIX

Education and National Service

A little-known but telling incident occurred at the American Legion convention of 1919. The gathering was controlled by Plattsburgers, men who had participated in the voluntary training camps of the prewar period before being called into the military during the Great War. Highly imbued with a sense of service, the former officers rejected the idea of giving cash bonuses to veterans, which they felt put a "price on patriotism."[1] Instead, the convention called for the awarding of scholarship aid. This was seen not as a reward for past service but a stipend for work to be performed—in this case, as a student. Although this display of civic idealism did not get very far at the time, it did anticipate a major transformation of American education following another world war. It also presaged the current discussion of linking student aid with national service.

The connection between national service and education has been tenuous. But national service and related concepts are beginning to be pushed by certain educators. Federal student aid was initially linked with military service; it then entered a period—that has not yet been left behind—where no service was expected, but now student aid seems to be moving into a third phase of linkage with civilian service. At the same time, there are service stirrings in high schools and on college campuses, a development that corresponds with an ascendant pedagogical viewpoint that formal education needs to be complemented by an experiential civic activity. All in all, omens are that national service and education will increasingly overlap.

STUDENT AID AND NATIONAL SERVICE

The GI Bill and ROTC Scholarships

The first major program for providing aid to college students was set up toward the end of World War II. The Servicemen's Readjustment Act of 1944, popularly known as the GI Bill, represented a compromise between officials who wanted to stave off unemployment and veterans' organizations that wanted a good package for returning servicemen.[2] The bill offered a federal subsidy to those veterans interested in continuing their schooling. All tuition, fees, and books were covered, and beneficiaries received a monthly stipend of $75 (the equivalent of $450 today). The outlays were immense; at the peak, in 1949, they came to $2.7 billion—almost one percent of the gross national product.[3] The GI Bill was the most sweeping venture in mass higher education ever in America.

The bill made some educators leery. James B. Conant of Harvard feared that the measure would undermine standards and distort curricula. Robert Hutchins of the University of Chicago predicted in 1944 that idle veterans would turn American universities into "hobo jungles."[4] Instead, the veterans turned out to be the most mature and self-disciplined group of college students in the nation's history. In the end, most university officials welcomed these new students and praised the bill for expanding access to higher education.

Everyone was surprised by the levels of enrollment. It was initially predicted that 150,000 at most would sign up. In fact, altogether, 2.2 million veterans crowded the nation's campuses with the bill's support; another 3.5 million attended schools below the college level. When on-the-job and farm-related training is added, the GI Bill reached more than 7 million people— almost half of all veterans. The measure's long-term consequences were profound. Prior service, not financial need or academic merit, was the sole condition of eligibility. And, for the first time, federal educational benefits were extended to a mass student population.

The World War II bill served as a model for subsequent programs. After the Korean War, a GI Bill enabled about 1.2 million veterans to attend college. Another bill was passed during the Vietnam era. The Vietnam bill was considerably less generous than its World War II predecessor, providing only a monthly stipend of $311 and no tuition. The calculations are that the typical Vietnam veteran received one-third the benefits his World War II counterpart did.[5] Nonetheless, an impressive 3.8 million servicemen and -women went to college on the Vietnam bill.

Because the Defense Department opposed it, the GI Bill lapsed in the all-volunteer force that came after Vietnam. The Pentagon manpower planners preferred to use available funds for enlistment bonuses rather than postservice education benefits. That a trial GI Bill for the all-volunteer force came into being in 1985 was due to the actions of Representative G.V. "Sonny" Montgomery, a Mississippi Democrat who chaired the House Veterans Committee. The basic provision of the new GI Bill was to offer all three-year enlistees a postservice educational stipend of $300 a month for thirty-six months of college. More or less generous benefits could be received under different options.[6] To qualify for the educational benefits, service members must contribute $100 monthly from their salaries for one year. As with the Vietnam bill, tuition costs were excluded. Still, the attractiveness of the GI Bill for quality recruits was unassailable. The case for the bill was also helped in an intangible way by the strong positive symbolism associated with the landmark GI Bill of World War II. The new GI Bill became permanent in 1987 and was named the Montgomery GI Bill in recognition of the man who was the guiding force behind the legislation.

The second major federal program of aid to college students was also related to military service: the Reserve Officer Training Corps (ROTC) scholarship program. In contrast to the GI bills, which gave educational benefits for military service already performed, ROTC offers benefits on the presumption of future service. The origins of ROTC can be traced back to land-grant colleges in the post-Civil War period that required military training for male students. These military departments were absorbed into the formally created army ROTC in 1916. The navy started its program in 1926, and the air force, which became a separate service after World War II, established its own ROTC in 1947.

The notion of student aid, making ROTC truly competitive with the service academies, was late in coming, however. The first scholarship program was instituted by the navy ROTC in 1947. "Midshipmen" on civilian campuses who met standards similar to those of the Naval Academy in Annapolis were given scholarships (the Marine Corps is part of the navy's program). Not until 1964, however, were similar army and air force scholarships made available for "cadets" at civilian campuses. Of the slightly more than 100,000 ROTC students enrolled in 1987, some 27,000 had ROTC scholarships. Such scholarships paid full tuition, books, and provided a $100 monthly stipend for up to four years of college study. In return, each scholarship holder is obligated to serve four years as a commissioned officer on active duty.

The GI bills and the ROTC scholarships set basic patterns for associating educational aid and military service: postservice benefits in the GI Bill and preservice aid in the ROTC program. Their costs were not inconsequential: steady state expenditures for the new GI Bill and other veterans' educational benefits were calculated at around $440 million annually, and about $130 million was expended each year on ROTC scholarships. Still, even these sums were dwarfed by the federal funds allocated to civilian student aid programs.

Scholarships and Civilian Service

The Soviet Union's launch of the world's first artificial satellite in 1957 prompted the first effort to link educational benefits to civilian, as opposed to military, service. In the post-Sputnik mood, Congress was determined to meet the Russian technological challenge by strengthening American education. The National Defense Education Act of 1958 set up a National Defense Student Loan program. The key provision was to allow recipients to cancel the amount of half of their loans after graduation by teaching science, mathematics, or foreign languages. Over the program's fourteen-year life, about 1.1 million borrowers had their loans forgiven in this way.

In 1972 the National Direct Student Loan (NDSL) program replaced the National Defense Student Loan program. In addition to the name change, the new NDSL restricted the kind of teaching that would count toward loan forgiveness. Renamed Perkins Loans in 1987 (after Carl D. Perkins, the late chairman of the

House Committee on Education and Labor), the program contains a provision that forgives loans of college graduates who teach in either elementary or secondary schools in low-income areas or in schools serving handicapped children. In the twelve-year period after 1972, some 350,000 graduates had parts of their loans canceled for such designated teaching.[7]

Even more public-spirited was the National Teacher Corps. Scholarships were awarded to idealistic young people willing to supplement their normal course of study with certain education courses. Participants agreed that, after graduating, they would teach for at least two years in urban ghettos, migrant communities, or impoverished rural areas, or, in some cases, Peace Corps assignments overseas. In the program's early years, about 1,500 people participated annually; by the mid-1970s, the number had dropped to several hundred. The program was finally terminated in 1981. The story of the National Teacher Corps— its impact on the teachers and those whom they taught—remains to be written.

Nonetheless, the idea of a Teacher Corps lives on. It has been embraced by both the Carnegie Foundation for the Advancement of Teaching and the American Federation of Teachers. In contrast to the original program, which sought to place teachers in impoverished areas, current concerns center on a pending general shortage of teachers across the country, a shortage already acute in mathematics, sciences, and special education. In 1982 only three states offered scholarships and forgivable loans to students agreeing to teach after graduation; five years later, thirty-eight states had such programs.

One of the more imaginative programs for connecting education aid and public service is the Police Corps proposed for New York State. Law enforcement experts Adam Walinsky and Jonathan Rubinstein have proposed a plan whereby the state would finance college educations for students who agree to serve in the police force for three years after graduation.[8] Their salaries would be half that of starting officers, and they would not be eligible for pension benefits unless they joined the regular force after their initial three-year obligation. The Police Corps encountered the opposition of entrenched interests. A substitute idea was implemented in 1985—a Police Cadet Corps in New York City. Cadets receive some scholarship aid, and those meeting qualifications will be hired into the police force at graduation.

But unlike the Police Corps, which was based on a citizen-service model, the Cadet Corps simply aims to recruit career police officers.

One of the most ambitious service programs is the National Health Service Corps.[9] It was created in 1970 to recruit doctors and other health professionals to serve in designated "Health Manpower Shortage Areas," mainly isolated rural communities. As inducements, Congress in 1972 set up the National Health Service Scholarship Training Program, which provided one year of full tuition to medical students for every year they agreed to serve in understaffed areas. In the program's early years, most enrollees served in rural areas; over time, though, increasing numbers were assigned to inner cities or prisons. During the Health Service Corps's peak years, the late 1970s, about 1,700 students annually were selected for fellowships. By 1985, fewer than fifty fellowships were awarded, and the program seemed to be on its last legs.

Although the Health Service Corps has successfully delivered medical care to needy areas, the program has provoked something of a scandal. Senate hearings in 1984 revealed that about 20 percent of all those who had completed their medical training had violated their scholarship contracts.[10] A similar scandal occurred in another federal education program. In 1979, the Department of Health and Human Services established a loan program to help students pursue careers in medicine, dentistry, and public health. In the program's first six years, $560 million was loaned to 41,000 students. By the mid-1980s, the default rate had climbed to between 10 and 15 percent—a figure that would cost the government $20 million a year.[11]

In the abstract, the idea of giving student aid to those who will serve in specialized corps seems an excellent means of encouraging young adults to serve their communities. But any appraisal of preservice scholarship programs in the civilian sphere shows that defaults in either services or payments are frequent enough to be serious concerns. The exception is ROTC, where reneging on commitments is minimal; any cadet not fulfilling his or her contract can, by law, be inducted into the enlisted ranks of the military. Without real sanctions, educational-benefits programs based on the promise of future national service will face the predictable problem of contract avoidance.

Student Aid without Service

Despite the original linkup with a national-service requirement of some sort in the development of student aid, federal programs took a dramatically different turn during the Vietnam era and afterward. Not only did federal support for college students experience an explosive growth, but citizen obligation became disconnected from such support. The amount of college aid appropriated by Congress for nonveterans rose from $120 million in 1964 to $1.6 billion in 1972 to a stunning $8 billion in 1986—about 9 percent of the total $85 billion budget for America's colleges and universities. Of 12 million college students, about 4 million received some form of federal assistance in 1986.[12]

One of the oldest and largest of the aid programs is the Guaranteed Student Loan (GSL), introduced in 1965. In 1986 this program cost the government about $3.2 billion and generated almost $8 billion in loans. Under GSL, the federal government subsidizes local banks and other lenders to make low-interest loans to students; if a student defaults, the U.S. Treasury reimburses the bank for money lost. Banks lending money to students thus find the GSL program a lucrative and risk-free enterprise. The big problem with GSL is the default rate. In 1986 alone, the government spent $1.3 billion to make up for unpaid student loans. Not only is the default rate in student loans growing out of control, but the effects of the loan program on student indebtedness and distortions in education and career choices have come into policy discussion.[13]

Other major student-aid programs were also started and expanded in the post-Vietnam era. In 1972, Congress established a student grant program, since renamed Pell Grants after their principal sponsor, Senator Claiborne Pell, Democrat of Rhode Island. Pell Grants are intended to provide financial assistance to the country's poorest families. In 1986 Pell Grants cost $3.6 billion and provided awards to some 2.8 million students. Other student aid programs and their approximate federal expenditures in 1986 included the College Work-Study Program, $600 million; Supplemental Educational Opportunity Grants, $400 million; and Perkins Loans, $200 million.

Under the Reagan administration there has been a major policy change to shift student aid away from grants to loans. Loans accounted for half of student-aid expenditures in 1987 compared to only 20 percent a decade earlier. There is good reason to suspect that the growing reliance on loan programs to underwrite college education explains the declining proportion of the working class and blacks entering college since 1980. By 1986, the average borrower attending four years of a public college owed $6,700; for private colleges, the figure was $9,000.[14] This not only resulted in increased defaults but caused distortions in undergraduate majors. Loan indebtedness likely pushes young people away from careers in public-service fields, such as teaching, and into fields where the fixation is on the bottom line.

The new civilian student-aid programs grew like Topsy, but, more importantly, they never had any civic content. In contrast to the GI Bill and ROTC scholarships, which were linked directly to military service, or the financial support given for civilian teaching or health-delivery service, the student-aid explosion of the 1960s and 1970s created an incentive not to perform national service of any kind. It seemed almost as if the country wanted to reward those who did not serve their country rather than those who did. In a perverse way, we have created a GI Bill without the GI.

The Significance of the Solomon Amendment

An amendment to the Defense Authorization Act of 1983 sponsored by Representative Gerald Solomon, Republican of New York, denies federal student aid to all men between the ages of eighteen and twenty-six who fail to register for the draft. The passage of this bill marked a signpost in the effort to restore civic obligations to those receiving student aid. Opposition to the Solomon Amendment, as the new law was called, was immediate and vehement. Opponents included pacifists, critics of draft registration, university presidents, and civil libertarians. The nation's three traditional peace churches—Brethren, Mennonite, and Quaker—offered to make up any federal funds denied students for their refusal to register. Colleges like Yale, Dartmouth, and Oberlin vowed to follow suit.

These opponents charged that the Solomon Amendment discriminated against males (since women did not have to register) and poor students (since the rich did not require aid). They further argued that the new law provided for judgment and punishment of supposed offenders without a trial. On the basis of this last point, a Minnesota district court issued an injunction against the amendment. The Supreme Court reviewed the case and, in 1984, by a six-to-two vote, upheld the law. The Court decided that the Solomon Amendment was not punitive because it was drafted to promote compliance with draft legislation and that no one was required to seek student aid. The Court also stated that the law was not discriminatory on the basis of class because all male nonregistrants were treated alike (the female issue was not addressed).

The Solomon Amendment set an important precedent.[15] In a related measure known as Solomon II, young men who wanted to participate in federal job-training programs had to prove they had registered with the Selective Service. In 1985, a law was passed that prohibited civil-service employment for any young man who had not registered. By 1986, four states—Massachusetts, Mississippi, Illinois, and Virginia—had enacted laws linking state college aid to compliance with draft registration. A Tennessee law went so far as to prohibit the enrollment of nonregistrants in state colleges and universities. The Solomon Amendment indicated a strong tremor, if not quite a full turn of the tide, in the notion that student aid and other entitlements were unconnected with civic duty.

SCHOOLS, STUDENTS, AND SERVICE

In the mid-1980s, no less than eight separate studies appeared on the state of high school education. Their recommendations were, for the most part, predictable—upgrade the caliber of teachers, tighten requirements for graduation, and a back-to-basics stress on mathematics, science, and English.[16] Certain pro forma nods were made in the direction of character development and moral values, but citizen duty has yet to hit mainstream thinking in high school criticism.

There was one exception, however—*High School*, issued in 1983 by the Carnegie Foundation for the Advancement of Teaching.[17] Written by Ernest L. Boyer, *High School* made a brief but strong recommendation that all students be required to meet their "social and civic obligations" by undertaking volunteer work in the school or community. This was followed in 1987 by another Carnegie Foundation report, *Student Service,* that assessed existing high school service experiments and summarized the essential ingredients for a successful program.[18] Both reports, however, stopped short of recommending a full-blown national-service program. Rather, they envisioned high school students performing part-time community service during evenings, weekends, or school vacations. In contrast to the approach advocated here, which conceives of national service as meeting important societal needs, the Carnegie proposals emphasized the beneficial effects for the individual. Still, in their rare recognition of civic service as an important ingredient of the education process, the Carnegie reports stand out.

While the notion of civic responsibility is only beginning to filter into the educational establishment, another pedagogical trend has served to push educators in the direction of national service. The notion of experiential education goes back to John Dewey's insight many decades ago about the enormity of the historic change whereby schools had replaced home and workplace as the dominant socializing force for adolescents. Dewey recognized that conventional classroom education suffered when it became separated from the realities of life. For Dewey, the key ingredient missing in formal education was "experience." From this wellspring, the notion of experiential education has come to have a strong impact on contemporary national-service thought.

The links between experiential education and national service figure strongly in a 1972 report issued by the Panel on Youth of the President's Science Advisory Committee, chaired by James S. Coleman, a leading sociologist of education. The report, titled *Youth: Transition to Adulthood,* concluded that, whereas young people's lives at the turn of the century were "action-rich" and "education-poor," the reverse is true today.[19] The report found contemporary youth culture to be excessively inward-looking and insulated from adult responsibilities and the world of work. The panel called for the creation of "new environments" in which young people could partake of civic roles. Among other recommendations, the panel proposed massive expansion of youth service corps to foster more "opportunities for public service."[20]

In 1980, another panel of distinguished Americans, the National Commission on Youth (sponsored by the Kettering Foundation) issued its report, *The Transition of Youth to Adulthood.*[21] The commission, also chaired by James Coleman, reiterated the theme that education was too important to leave exclusively to schools, but this time, in place of a bland mention of "public service," it explicitly referred to "national service" as a means to bridge the gap between youth and adulthood. The key recommendation was establishing a "National Youth Service guaranteeing all American youth the opportunity for at least one year of full-time service to their community or to the nation."[22] A whole chapter was devoted to specific policies for registration of youth, creation of service programs, making youth service a condition of employment, and educational entitlements for youth completing service. This was the strongest statement supporting national service by any recognized group up to that time.

An emerging idea is to treat national service as an extension of compulsory education. Indeed, more and more high schools are adopting community service as an elective—and, in some cases, a requirement—for graduation. In 1984, almost 5 percent of all high schools in the country had a community-service requirement; an additional 9 percent awarded academic credit for elective service. Another one in six schools encouraged community service as a voluntary activity to be performed by high school clubs. An estimated 900,000 students, or 6 percent of the nation's total, participated in such programs in 1984.[23] The activities included tutoring and working in hospitals, recreation centers, and social welfare agencies. Girl volunteers outnumbered boys three to two, apparently because boys are more reluctant to volunteer in human-service settings. Community service is most likely to be a direct part of the curriculum in Catholic and private schools and in public schools with predominantly black enrollments.

Atlanta is the largest school system in the United States with such a program. Every student must perform seventy-five hours of community service outside of school hours. Students can choose from a list of community organizations, compiled by the Atlanta school system, that includes local government agencies, hospitals, nursing homes, and more than forty nonprofit organizations. Each student must also write an acceptable composition about his or her service. Importantly, under the Atlanta program, community service adds to the graduation requirement and is not treated as a substitute for academic studies.

On college campuses, too, voluntarism is gaining ground. There has been a strong push for national service among key policy-shapers and presidents of elite universities. A threshold of sorts was crossed in 1985 with the recommendations contained in *Higher Education and the American Resurgence,* another report of the Carnegie Foundation for the Advancement of Teaching.[24] Written by Frank Newman, president of the Education Commission of the States (a national consortium created to help state leaders improve the quality of education), the report posed the issue in unusually strong terms: "If there is a crisis in education in the United States today, it is less that test scores have declined than it is that we have failed to provide the education for citizenship that is still the most significant responsibility of the nation's schools and colleges."[25]

To help bring about civic involvement in an "age of self-interest," *Higher Education and the American Resurgence* recommended, among other initiatives, a revamping of student-aid programs to foster community service. Specifically, the report advocated preservice scholarships based on the ROTC model to encourage better students to enter the teaching professions, and postservice educational benefits modeled on the GI Bill to provide student aid in return for community service. Never before had any part of the higher education establishment come out so forthrightly on the side of national service for college students. In 1987, yet another Carnegie Foundation report, *College,* by Ernest L. Boyer (a follow-up to his earlier *High School*), repeated the earlier argument for student service, this time for college undergraduates.[26] Despite the increasing interest in national service, no educationist has yet argued that *only* students who perform national service should be eligible for educational benefits. Until that Rubicon is crossed, proposals for connecting aid and service will remain pallid.

Around the time the Carnegie reports were released, several colleges were coming together to form Campus Compact, a national clearinghouse for university-based service programs. Based at Brown University, the organization works with government officials and community leaders to create service opportunities for students.[27] The co-chairs were Howard Swearer, Timothy Healy, and Donald Kennedy, presidents of Brown, Georgetown, and Stanford universities, respectively, and Frank Newman. By 1987, Campus Compact had organized an active coalition of 125 universities that wanted "to equip their students to be the committed, compassionate citizens upon which this nation depends."[28]

That Campus Compact found a home at Brown was not coincidental. President Swearer had a long interest in national service. In 1982, with funding from the C. V. Starr Foundation, Brown began awarding scholarships to students who had devoted time away from college to full-time public service. Similar scholarships were started at Stanford and Harvard in 1985, and equivalent programs began to take hold on a handful of other campuses throughout the country.

While university administrators were taking up the national-service ideal, a similar movement was gaining steam among undergraduates. It was started by Wayne Meisel, who, while an undergraduate at Harvard, worked with handicapped children. In the process, he became interested in involving more students in community work. Harvard invited him to stay on campus for a year after his graduation in 1982, during which time he developed a program pairing each of Harvard's thirteen residential houses with different neighborhoods in Cambridge. After that, Meisel received a traveling fellowship and used it to make a walking tour of seventy colleges from Maine to Washington, D.C. At each, he consulted with campus leaders on how to set up student-run community projects.

In the fall of 1984, Meisel, with modest foundation support, formed the Campus Outreach Opportunity League (COOL) at Yale University (relocated to Washington, D.C., in 1987). COOL representatives acted as Johnny Appleseed-style "rovers," traveling to campuses to plant seeds of interest in service programs. Meisel consciously distinguishes his work from what he calls "big National Service with a capital N and a capital S." Rather than concentrate on a full-blown national youth corps, COOL uses part-time volunteers in very localized programs—tutoring, meals on wheels, food drives for the indigent—a kind of national service in a minor key. By 1987, COOL's growing network included over 350 campuses and 150 nonprofit voluntary associations. Through its campus workshops, COOL has quietly become a major force in reviving the service ethic among college students.[29] Perhaps COOL's most impressive feature is its ability to match the individual talents of its volunteers with the particular needs of localities—a possible model for future national-service programs.

Although the top-down initiatives of Campus Compact and the bottom-up movement of COOL start from different directions, the programs are organizational complements. Both developments, moreover, are clearly within the William James variant of national service, with an almost exclusive focus on civilian service and an emphasis on what privileged youth ought to do for the broader community.

THE EMERGING CIVIC EDUCATION

The revival of interest in national service among American educators and students is rooted in two concurrent developments. The first is the sense that students should be required to give something back in return for aid. Lessons have been learned from the experience of the GI bills, ROTC scholarships, civilian-service student aid, and the 1984 Supreme Court decision linking federal aid to draft registration. Popular support for the idea that educational benefits and youth service ought be linked is clear. In a 1983 New York State survey, respondents agreed by a three-to-one margin that students who receive financial aid should be *required* to repay that aid through some type of public service. A 1984 Gallup poll reported that two of every three Americans support a year of mandatory national service for young adults in return for GI Bill-type benefits. The public at large seems well advanced in the belief that civic obligations for youth ought be tied to public funding of postsecondary school education.

The second development feeding the renewed interest in national service is the rising belief that formal education needs to be complemented with real-world civic activity. This follows a thread that weaves through the pedagogical theories of John Dewey, through the 1972 report of the Panel on Youth of the President's Science Advisory Committee and the 1980 report of the National Commission on Youth, through the implementation of community-service requirements at certain high schools and scholarships for youth service at selected colleges, to the Carnegie Foundation report of 1985, where "education for citizenship" becomes the "most significant responsibility" of the nation's schools and national service is recommended as the way to meet this responsibility. Clearly, something important is happening in education philosophy.

One major philosophical hurdle remains. Virtually all of the recent developments in the world of education define national service in civilian terms. The Achilles' heel in any emerging national-service consensus remains the disjuncture in political support between those who favor military over civilian service and vice versa. Until this conflict between the tough-minded and the high-minded is resolved, or at least reconciled, national-service proponents are their own worst enemies. This opposition within national-service thought is what we look at next.

SEVEN

The Comparable Worth of Military and Civilian Service

Support for national service divides into two very distinct schools. One is concerned primarily with military manpower. Though acknowledging that civilian participants can perform valuable tasks, this group generally advocates national service as a means of making conscription more politically palatable. The second school, inspired by William James and his "moral equivalent of war," defines national service in exclusively civilian terms. Indeed, it seems to believe that any connection with the military can only taint the service ideal.

The fundamental philosophical question is whether military and civilian service are close together or poles apart. The short answer is that they are both. My argument is that the opposition between the tough-minded and high-minded approaches of national service is resolvable and is even mutually reinforcing once they are both joined by the banner of civic duty.

A civic view of national service seeks a common denominator between military and civilian service, knowing well that a precise standard of comparable worth is as elusive as a will-o'-the-wisp. If types of youth service were simply activities that could be quantified on a unidimensional scale, the only problems remaining would be computational ones. It would certainly be nice if we could come up with a yardstick for different kinds of service.

How convenient if we could arrive at formulations like: one unit of military service equals two units of hospital work equals three units of conservation work, or, alternatively, one unit of hospital work equals two units of conservation work equals three units of military service. But such a mathematical reduction is misleading because it directs attention away from the civic content that must be common to any kind of national service. Once acknowledging that all forms of national service have their source in a concept of shared citizen duty, we need not split hairs over moral or practical equivalences.

Still, the opposition between military and civilian service confounds the national-service debate. Until very recently, the different concepts of military service and civilian service have been like repelling magnets, pushing away from each other and deflecting each national-service initiative as it comes closer to realization. While far from absolute, this contrast—between the "conservative" and "liberal" sides of national service, as one tends somewhat inaccurately to say—is a real one in political terms. Thus, before looking at the conundrum of comparable worth in national service, we need to understand how the political antinomies and similarities of military and civilian service shape policy and legal discussion.

THE POLICY DEBATE

Congressional Initiatives

National-service bills have never fared well in Congress; only a few have been voted out of committee, and none has been passed into law. One main reason is that support has usually fragmented along lines dividing proponents of military and civilian service. An overview of congressional initiatives shows, however, a discernible trend in the recent past toward linking or making some sort of equivalency between military and civilian service, a trend that augurs a fundamental reshaping of the national-service constituency.

The first comprehensive national-service legislation was introduced in 1969 by Republican Senator Mark Hatfield of Oregon. Hatfield proposed establishing a National Youth Service Founda-

tion to provide service and learning opportunities to young people. A majority of the trustees would be appointed by the
president, with the remainder comprising the directors of the
Peace Corps, Job Corps, and other youth service agencies. Acting
during the height of the Vietnam War, Hatfield was insistent
and clear that there was no linkage whatsoever with military
service in his proposal. While Hatfield's bill never left committee,
it did anticipate a spate of national-service proposals seeking
to bring about forms of national service in the civilian sphere.

One set of initiatives dealt with setting up a blue-ribbon panel
to examine the feasibility of a national-service program. In 1979,
Paul E. Tsongas, a Democratic senator from Massachusetts and
a former Peace Corps volunteer, sponsored a bill that would
create a Presidential Commission to study national service. The
commission would be required to hold hearings across the country and, within two years of its creation, report its findings.
The bill passed the Senate in 1980 by a 46-to-41 vote, enjoying
support from most Democrats and a few moderate Republicans.
A companion bill introduced in the House by Leon E. Panetta,
Democrat of California, passed the Education and Labor Committee but failed to reach the House floor. Even if the bill had passed
both houses, it was unclear whether President Carter would have
signed it. The Department of Labor was opposed to the national-
service concept, which it saw as competition for its CETA jobs
programs in the public sector.

Undeterred, Tsongas and Panetta reintroduced similar bills
in 1982 and 1983. The main modification in the new Tsongas-
Panetta bills was the specification that the commission would
study only voluntary service; this provision was an attempt to
disarm critics who saw compulsory service lurking behind the
proposed commission. This time the Senate bill never made it
out of committee; the Panetta bill did make it to the House floor,
but it was voted down by an almost three-to-one margin. One
reason was that the bill was poorly managed on the House floor.
But there was substantive opposition as well. On one side, the
Armed Services Committee was annoyed that it had not been
allowed to examine the bill before it reached the floor; on the
other, some liberals viewed the bill as a stalking-horse for a
military draft. The combined opposition delivered a defeat so
decisive as to brake the momentum that had been building in
Congress for a close look at national service.

By 1985, though, proposals for a national-service commission resurfaced, this time with new Democratic sponsorship. Senator Gary Hart of Colorado and Representative Robert Torricelli of New Jersey introduced identical bills to create a Select Commission on National Service Opportunities. This body would analyze the relative costs and benefits of establishing new national-service programs as well as expanding old ones. The authors seemed less shy about final goals than previous commission sponsors. The commission, Hart and Torricelli stated, would "explore the potential of a system of universal national service. It is our hope that appointment of such a Commission would generate the adoption of such a system."[1] (In 1987, Torricelli reintroduced the bill in the 100th Congress.) Although the bills did not specifically mention military options, Hart and Torricelli did not preclude them, either. Indeed, in accompanying arguments for the bills, both Hart and Torricelli held that any reinstitution of military conscription should be placed in the context of a broader program of national service, one in which both military and civilian service coexisted.

Panetta broke new ground in national-service legislation by proposing the Voluntary National Service Act in 1984 (reintroduced in 1987). He had a very decentralized notion in mind, calling on the federal government to provide grants on a 50/50 matching basis to state and local governments. In turn, the state and local governments would disburse funds to community-based nonprofit associations, social service organizations, and government agencies. These local units would undertake the actual enrollment and management of participants. Enrollees would receive a stipend, which, in necessary cases, would include housing and food. State and local governments could also provide postservice educational benefits to youths who completed their term of service. The idea was to enable localities to tailor programs to fit local needs, in the manner of the old Seattle Program for Local Service.

While these civilian-oriented measures were being considered, Congress was also taking up various national-service proposals with primary emphasis on military recruitment. In 1970, Representative Jonathan B. Bingham, Democrat of New York, submitted a bill titled the National Service Act. The bill called for all male citizens to register at age seventeen with a National Service Agency, which would offer them three options: (1) enlistment in the military, (2) enrollment in civilian service, or (3) registration for a lottery-based draft. Although Bingham's bill never left committee, it did set an important precedent in national-service legislation by subsuming military and civilian service within a single bill.

Another proposal with military overtones was introduced in 1979 by Republican Representative Paul N. McCloskey, Jr., of California. McCloskey's energetic campaigning for the bill, together with his impressive credentials—Korean War hero and anti-Vietnam War presidential candidate in 1972—gained his bill more attention than any other contemporary national-service proposal. The measure would require all young Americans, men and women, to register with a National Service System and select one of the following: (1) two years of military service coupled with GI Bill-style benefits, (2) six months of military training followed by a reserve obligation, (3) one year of civilian service, or (4) a military lottery pool with liability for the draft if it were reinstituted. (The bill was unclear whether women were also to be put in the draft-liable category.) The McCloskey bill mandated reduced salaries for recruits, thus departing from the market orientation of the all-volunteer force (AVF). Indeed, it was McCloskey's uneasiness over the lack of civic content in the AVF, together with his long-time interest in youth service, that led to his national-service proposal.

Also in 1979, Representative John Cavanaugh, Democrat of Nebraska, introduced the Public Service System Act. Its key features were similar to the McCloskey proposal, except that wages for military recruits would not be reduced, while civilian servers would receive only subsistence wages. One innovation of the Cavanaugh bill was its requirement that all federal agencies set aside 5 percent of their employment positions for civilian youth servers.

At bottom, the Bingham, McCloskey, and Cavanaugh bills sought to use the stick of a possible draft to prod young people, men especially, into joining the military, or, secondarily, both men and women, into choosing civilian service. All three measures sprang from a desire to reinstitute the citizen-soldier norm and attain a cross section of youth in the armed forces. Precisely because these bills were seen as facilitating a return to conscription, however, they went nowhere. Also, as the recruiting difficulties of the all-volunteer force during the 1970s gave way to improved recruitment in the early 1980s, the tendency to view national service as a solution to military manpower needs abated. In any event, the retirement of Cavanaugh in 1980 and Bingham in 1982, together with McCloskey's defeat in a 1982 senatorial race, removed from the House of Representatives three principal champions of military-oriented service programs.

Another important proponent of military-oriented programs has been Democratic Senator Sam Nunn of Georgia, Capitol Hill's most influential voice on national defense. A long-time skeptic regarding the viability of a voluntary force and strong believer in the citizen-soldier concept, Nunn commissioned several studies analyzing the potential of national-service programs for solving military recruitment needs. The first of these studies, *Achieving America's Goals: National Service or the All-Volunteer Armed Force?*, written in 1977 by William R. King, a University of Pittsburgh professor, concluded that national service would be a boon to military recruitment and beneficial to the nation as a whole.[2] It recommended the phased implementation of a "minimally coercive" service plan, that is, mandatory registration of all youth with standby draft mechanisms, plus a major expansion of voluntary civilian programs. The tone and direction of the King Report were very much counter to the prevailing marketplace philosophy of the AVF.

Nunn followed up by asking the Congressional Budget Office (CBO) for an analysis of various national-service proposals. The CBO study, issued in 1978, focused on the effect of service programs on military recruitment and youth unemployment programs on military recruitment and youth unemployment.[3] Starting from the narrow perspective of national service as a jobs program in competition with the armed forces, the report's conclusion was predictable: national service would hurt military recruitment. The CBO study neglected to consider noneconomic motivations for civilian service, much less the concept of the citizen soldier. By coming down hard against national service, the CBO study pretty much neutralized the findings of the King report.

Nunn, who took over the chairmanship of the Senate Armed Services Committee in 1987, maintained an interest in the linkage between national service and military manpower. Nunn was worried not only that the abandonment of the draft undermined our conventional forces, but that this vulnerability would be aggravated by the move toward a nonnuclear defense in Western Europe. That the citizen-soldier concept has such a powerful advocate on Capitol Hill insures that legislation pertaining to civilian national service will almost surely be linked in some way to military recruitment concerns. At the least, any downturn in the armed forces would certainly revive the debate about the military manpower aspects of national service.

Finally, in the 100th Congress, another significant step was taken. In early 1987, Senator Claiborne Pell introduced a bill that would offer educational assistance to young people completing two years of either civilian or military service. At the same time, Democratic Representative David McCurdy of Oklahoma introduced legislation that would replace the federal government's current student loan-and-grant programs with a system of educational benefits limited to those who complete a period of national service, indicating that the long-standing military/civilian division was slowly beginning to break down.

Executive Branch and Defense Department Reports

Over the years, the executive branch has undertaken several studies of national-service programs. In contrast to Congress, however, the executive has shown little interest in such programs. In fact, the Office of the Secretary of Defense (OSD) has been actively hostile to any concept of national service.

The first major executive-branch study was issued in 1966, with the Vietnam antidraft movement still in its infancy. By executive order, President Lyndon Johnson appointed a National Advisory Commission on Selective Service, chaired by Burke Marshall, and directed it to analyze a host of draft-related issues, including national service. Its report, *In Pursuit of Equity: Who Serves When Not All Serve?* (1967), devoted only three pages to national service, but at the time any attention to the concept represented a breakthrough of sorts.[4] The Marshall Commission concluded that since there was no fair way, "at least at present" to equate civilian with military service, national service could not be considered a realistic alternative to the draft. However, the commission did recommend that "intensive research" be conducted on such national-service issues as costs, federal involvement, social needs to be served, and the impact on poverty, education, and the labor supply.[5]

The tepid reaction of the Marshall Commission to national service was enthusiastic compared to later reports coming out of the Defense Department. In 1978, in response to growing congressional and public alarm over the recruitment difficulties of the AVF, OSD issued its first white paper on the all-volunteer military, called *America's Volunteers*.[6] Despite clear evidence that educational levels and test scores of AVF recruits were far below those of entrants during the conscription era, the OSD staff perversely concluded that enlistees were of a "quality equal to or superior to that achieved under the draft."[7] Describing national service as a "Federal youth jobs program" in direct competition with military recruiters, the OSD white paper concluded that a broad-based voluntary national-service scheme would "seriously threaten military capability."[8]

The next executive-branch report was generated by an amendment to the 1979 Defense Authorization Act, proposed by Representatives Patricia Schroeder, Democrat of Colorado, Paul McCloskey, and Leon Panetta. In the course of listing possible ways of making the draft more equitable, the amendment requested the president to report on "the desirability, in the interest of preserving discipline and morale in the Armed Forces of establishing a national youth service program permitting volunteer work, for either public or private public service agencies, as an alternative to military service."[9] President Carter's report was prepared by the staffers in the OSD manpower office and issued in 1980. Despite the fact that the AVF was at its nadir at the time the report was written, the authors gamely maintained that the armed forces were meeting their manpower needs in a satisfactory manner. About the effects of civilian national service, the report stated that such a program must "be viewed as deleterious in its impact on the morale and discipline as well as on the force levels of the Armed Forces."[10] Again, the conception of national service was of minimum-wage workers siphoned from those who would otherwise be volunteers for the marketplace military.

The anti-national-service findings of the 1978 and 1980 OSD reports issued during the Carter presidency were repeated in the Reagan administration. A 1982 OSD study on military manpower was, if anything, more adamant than the earlier studies in dismissing national service. The task force asserted that it "was not impressed by the potential of any national service option as an aid to manning a capable military force."[11] Failings in military recruitment, according to the study, reflect insufficient compensation for recruits. Defenders of the AVF in the OSD resolutely resist intimations that military manpower should be recruited by other than marketplace mechanisms. In sum, although national service is often raised on Capitol Hill by those seeking to solve military recruitment problems, military manpower planners have repeatedly opposed any notion of mixing national service with military recruitment.

Constitutionality

Curiously, the Supreme Court has never directly addressed even the legality of a peacetime draft, much less that of national service. Yet the Court, in the draft-law cases of World War I, upheld with sweeping language the constitutionality of conscription, based on the federal government's power "to raise and support armies" under Article I of the Constitution. And the tradition of the peacetime draft, established in 1940 and continued in the years after World War II and during times of undeclared war in Korea and Vietnam, makes it hard to imagine that the Court would now have any reservations about peacetime conscription. The requirement that conscientious objectors perform civilian work in lieu of military service, moreover, has also been consistently upheld by the courts.

We are left with the question: Would compulsory civilian service be constitutional? There is no consensus on the matter. All legal discussions of the issue revolve around the operative sentence in the Thirteenth Amendment to the U.S. Constitution: "Neither slavery nor involuntary servitude, except as punishment for the crime whereof the party shall have been duly convicted, shall exist within the United States, or any place subject to their jurisdiction."

The first serious assessment of the constitutionality of civilian national service was provided in 1967 by Charles L. Black, Jr., a distinguished constitutional lawyer and professor at Yale University.[12] Black held that the Thirteenth Amendment prohibition on involuntary servitude probably includes any form of involuntary labor. He did note the existence of some exceptions, such as jury duty. In addition, he cited a 1915 Supreme Court decision that the Thirteenth Amendment did not prevent a state's requiring a few days' work on its roads each year from able-bodied citizens. Moreover and importantly, Black acknowledged that military conscription constitutes a "striking, even startling exception" to this bar on involuntary servitude.[13] Still, Black concluded that mandatory civilian service (and the disciplinary control it implies) would be "foreign to our tradition and to our Constitution."[14]

The most comprehensive treatment of the constitutionality of mandatory civilian service was completed in 1985 by the Association of the Bar of the City of New York.[15] Its report provides a concise review of court cases dealing with the issue. The bar association found that no form of public service—from jury duty to road work—has ever been struck down as a violation of the Thirteenth Amendment. Granted, such activities fall short of a full-blown national-service program. Nonetheless, the bar report, citing the precedents of conscientious-objection cases, concluded that a national program, conceived as an alternative to military service, would be permissible under the Thirteenth Amendment. It follows that a government empowered to obligate its citizens to perform military service could give citizens the option of performing civilian tasks instead. If, however, the draft were primarily a means to produce civilian servers, then it would violate the Thirteenth Amendment's prohibition against involuntary servitude.

The survey of the legal front thus affords conflicting views. Charles Black and others view mandatory national service as probably, though not definitely, unconstitutional. The New York City Bar Association concludes that such service is probably constitutional, but only as an alternative to military service. Overall, this country's lack of a tradition of national service suggests that a purely civilian compulsory program would almost surely incur serious constitutional problems.

Ironically, if the supporters of a compulsory national program were confidently to assert its constitutionality, they might actually harm, rather than help, their chances of instituting such a program. For one of the most effective arguments used by opponents of *voluntary* service programs is that they represent the start of a slide down the slippery slope toward *compulsory* service. If the fears about mandatory service could be assuaged, the opposition to comprehensive voluntary programs would surely diminish.

THE "DOUBLE HELIX" OF MILITARY
AND CIVILIAN SERVICE

The common thread in the welter of legislative, executive, and legal controversies surrounding national service is the question of the comparable worth of different kinds of national service. The reality is that there is no simple or elegant way to measure comparable worth of citizen soldiers and civilian servers in national service. The argument for an algebraic formula of national-service equivalencies fails for a deep reason: it relies on the mistaken assumption that ultimately there is no contradiction between military and civilian service. It is a matter of some inconvenience to my argument that the military and civilian conceptions of service do in fact appear to contradict one another—and this apparent contradiction does not, on closer inspection, dissolve effortlessly. Rather, we need a commonsense compromise, trading off a little theoretical consistency for the advantages of a broad and undogmatic view.

To assert as I do that civic content underpins all forms of national service does not mean that all require equal sacrifice. Although there is no adequate criterion for measuring the motives of self-sacrifice among national servers, we can weigh the consequences. Soldiers, unlike civilian servers, risk losing their lives. Even short of loss of life or limb, combat soldiers sustain extremes of adversity—including killing others—rarely experienced by civilian servers. I think it can be safely said that military service is inherently more dangerous than almost all civilian service and therefore deserves greater weight in any assessment of duties. This almost surely corresponds to the folk understanding of the relative onerousness of military and civilian service.

As soon as one tries to become more concrete, however, the task grows more difficult. The terrain becomes treacherous indeed when we try to make one-on-one comparisons between certain military members and certain civilian servers. It would no doubt be foolish to maintain that serving as a tutor to inner-city boys and girls, however worthy, is somehow equal to serving as an infantryman in war. (Though the pacifist would rejoin that the tutor is performing a humane service while the soldier is doing harm.) It would be equally foolish to equate a soldier in a staff assignment with a conscientious objector undergoing a medical experiment or with a Peace Corps volunteer enduring physical hardship in a remote Third World village. (But the military proponent might assert, the soldier is nevertheless liable for combat, and the national defense function supersedes that of nonmilitary service.) At the same time, some people would certainly prefer the risk of being sent into combat (though rarely the certainty of combat) to many types of civilian work. Many young Americans would find, say, cleaning and caring for the infirm or aged much more distasteful than undertaking routine military training and duties. Just as advocates of civilian programs must concede that military service as a whole is more onerous, so backers of the military service must grant that civilian servers are not free riders.

We are back at the central point: military and civilian service may have incommensurate worth, but they both entail the performance of civic duties. From this perspective, the citizen soldier has more in common with the conscientious objector performing alternative service than with the vocal patriot who has managed legally to avoid the draft. The Peace Corps volunteer shares more with the draftee than with the political radical who views all service for the American state as an exercise in imperialism. Both citizen soldiers and civilian servers display a commitment to undertaking the duties of citizenship: both have agreed to spend a period of their lives for a civic purpose that is not going to be a lifetime career; both, for the common good, have temporarily stepped outside the cash-work nexus of the marketplace.

In sum, while it is worth acknowledging the differences between military and civilian service, we ought not to press the point too hard. To argue as I have, that both have a shared civic content can take us only so far: a long way to be sure, but not the whole distance. Ultimately, we must be a little inconsistent. While we cannot be unaware of the differences between military and civilian service, we need not always recognize them; better to keep our eye on the civic commonalities.

No metaphor provides a perfect picture of the case at hand, but one that comes close to describing the components of national service is that of the double helix: a spiral consisting of the two strands of military and civilian service, each coiling separately around the axis of citizenship duty.

EIGHT

Reconstruction of the Citizen Soldier

Beginning in 1973, the United States sought to accomplish something it had never before attempted—maintaining a huge active-duty and reserve military force on a strictly voluntary basis. The effort has met with mixed reviews. Since its creation, the all-volunteer force (AVF) has been analyzed, dissected, and critiqued in an endless stream of books, reports, articles, and congressional hearings.[1] While there is little dispute about the basic manpower facts of the AVF, there has been sharp disagreement regarding its effectiveness as a tool of national defense. One party extols the AVF as a great success in need of only minor adjustments, primarily pay increases, to operate at peak efficiency. Another school derides the AVF as a costly failure that has weakened our fighting capacity, and it sees little prospect of a viable defense without some form of compulsory military service.

I place myself in neither camp. In contrast to both AVF boosters and bring-back-the-draft traditionalists, I support retaining the AVF but reconstituting it along the lines of national service and the citizen soldier. My view is based not only on a moral preference for a socially representative military—which a marketplace AVF cannot deliver—but also on a practical desire for a more effective recruitment program. A citizen soldier approach, combined with a voluntary civilian service program (outlined in the next chapter) could help resolve the military's manpower problems—and produce considerable savings in the process. By the citizen soldier I refer to young people who serve short terms in the military at less than market wages. Introducing such a citizen-soldier component would reverse the military's growing tendency to become a career force isolated from the society it is designed to protect. Most important of all, a revived citizen soldiery is a necessity to bolster our nation's more conventional forces. If we are truly concerned about strengthening our military deterrence capability while moving away from a reliance on nuclear weapons, this means coming up with an inexpensive and large supply of manpower. Only by a reconstruction of the citizen soldier can America provide for a credible military deterrent without holding mankind at risk.

CITIZEN SOLDIER VERSUS ECONOMIC MAN

The 1970 Gates Commission, appointed by President Nixon, established the basis of the current AVF.[2] A political decision was made to end the draft. A commission was established, with appropriate representation of distinguished names, that stated the draft was unfair, the volunteer would be a more committed soldier than the draftee, and social representation would improve. The tacit role of contract social researchers was to confirm the political decision. Then the Office of the Secretary of Defense (OSD) acquired a vested interest in this confirmation and spent much of its energy inventing defenses of the AVF.

The AVF is an extreme but real example of the ascendancy of economic thinking in policymaking. In the Pentagon an "economist" means not so much an expert on the economy as someone equipped to use cost-benefit concepts and mathematical tools to analyze proposals in any policy area. "Systems analyst" is a close synonym. The seeds of the economic approach were planted in the early 1960s, when Robert McNamara, as secretary of defense, employed systems analysts to take control of military planning, especially that dealing with weaponry, from the armed services. In the early 1970s, the economic approach was applied full force to end the draft and later to examine military manpower issues in general. This mode of thinking has dominated the staffs of Pentagon study groups, think tanks, and contractors, the nerve centers of military personnel planning.

The mind-set of Pentagon manpower analysts is unable to assess noneconomic factors in military recruitment, retention, and performance. A subtler effect of economic analysis is to downplay the less tangible attitudinal and normative dimensions of military effectiveness. Most analysts prefer to deal with the material dimensions, because these are the only ones that can be easily measured in the quantitative analyses econometricians prefer. The econometric model is a mite too simplistic, however, for it ignores the fact that the armed forces—as other forms of national service—are not just fluid collections of self-maximizing individuals, but sets of social relations and institutional arrangements. Also ignored is that an effective military requires forms of commitment that extend beyond the narrow confines of self. It does not augur well for the republic when Pentagon policymakers (in private, to be sure) look favorably on rising youth unemployment as a way to improve the climate for recruitment.

Large pay raises for lower enlisted personnel, a central Gates Commission recommendation, were envisioned as the principal means to induce persons to join the AVF. The real income of recruits is now double what it was during the peacetime draft. By 1987, a private first class earned the equivalent of $16,000— a salary approximating the average starting wage for a teacher in America.[3] Such generosity for recruits has had the effect of dramatically compressing the pay scale for the enlisted ranks. In the 1960s, the basic pay of a first sergeant with twenty years' service was better than five times that of a private first class. In the AVF that same first sergeant makes only two-and-a-half times the pay of the PFC. Noncommissioned officers (NCOs) could once measure their incomes and perquisites against those of the soldiers they led and feel rewarded; now they see a relative decline of their status within the service and compare their earnings against civilians, and feel deprived.

A look at some dollar figures (presented in constant 1986 values) gives us a sense of the change in military compensation since the peacetime-draft years. In 1964, the average compensation costs for each active-duty soldier were $16,000 compared with $22,000 in 1986.[4] If one factors in other costs, such as housing, medical care, and education for military family members, the figures come to $18,900 and $28,700.[5] The contrast in overall manpower costs is enormous. In 1964, the total bill came to not quite $84 billion; in 1986, the total was $117 billion. In other words, we are now spending $33 billion more a year for manpower costs than during the draft, even though we have far fewer soldiers on active duty. Indeed, it may be its economic costs as much as its sociology that will bring the AVF into question.

The AVF: A Brief Overview

Perhaps the most significant, if least noted, consequence of the creation of the AVF has been a sharp decline in the size of the military. From the early 1960s, when 2.6 million people served on active duty, only 2.1 million are in uniform today. To make up the difference, the AVF adopted a "Total Force" concept, where reserve units would be quickly mobilized to fight side by side with active components in the event of war.[6] Reserve forces are made up of two main categories: state-based guard units (army and air force) and federal reserve units (all services). Members of these reserve units typically meet one weekend a month and train for two weeks in the summer. A third category is the individual ready reserve, consisting of pretrained individuals who have completed active-duty or reserve obligation but no longer attend drill meetings.

Meeting the manpower requirements of the military is no easy task. Each year the armed forces must recruit approximately 320,000 people for the active force and 100,000 more for reserve units. Another 30,000 enter as officers through various commissioning programs. All told, then, the military must bring in some 450,000 recruits a year. Since only one in ten recruits is female, about 400,000 males must be attracted annually. In the mid-1980s, about 1.9 million males were reaching their nineteenth birthdays each year; by the early 1990s, the available pool will decrease to 1.6 million. Applying the rule of thumb that about one-third of all males are ineligible—for medical, mental, or moral reasons—the armed forces will have to recruit one in three eligible males to maintain current manpower strength levels.

Of course, assumptions on the proportion of males that must be recruited and their propensity to join can change dramatically. Raising military pay, spending more money on recruitment, increasing the number of women in the military, lowering standards for males, using civilians to do work now done by uniformed personnel, keeping more people in the military, bringing more prior service back into the armed forces, all are variables that separately or in combination make a big difference in what can be done to maintain an all-volunteer military.[7]

To move beyond end-strength and recruitment numbers, we must examine as well the social composition of service members since the end of conscription. We will focus on the army, the largest of the services, the one that most directly relied on the draft, and the bellwether of the AVF. Over the course of the all-volunteer era, the educational levels—a prime indicator of quality—of army male recruits have fluctuated widely. During the 1970s, entrants with high school diplomas accounted for one in three of all male entrants. In terms of entrance test scores, the average army recruit moved from the bottom of the third quartile in the late 1970s to the middle of the second quartile by the mid-1980s, no mean achievement. This upturn in recruitment had direct effects on life in the rank and file. Desertion and other indiscipline rates plummeted, and company commanders and NCOs were unanimous in reporting the improvement in the morale and trainability of the troops they were leading.

The most significant demographic change in the AVF has been the rise in females. Women today make up 10 percent of the armed forces, compared to only 1 percent in the draft era. The rise in the number of females in the military reflects two main trends. One is an outcome of changing cultural and economic patterns as more women enter the labor force, some number of whom seek nontraditional employment. The other results from the inability of the AVF to recruit the required number of qualified males, thereby opening up avenues for women in the armed forces. Indeed, the new numbers of women in the armed forces, virtually all of whom have high school diplomas or better, have been the saving margin between the success and the failure of the AVF.[8]

Another important, though rarely noted development, has been the change in the marital composition of the AVF. Since the end of the draft, the proportion of married soldiers in the junior enlisted grades has approximately doubled. This change is all the more remarkable in that it runs directly counter to national trends, which show the median age for first marriage has *risen* by two years since 1970. The high incidence of young marrieds is an entirely new phenomenon in the American military, one that has brought with it attendant problems of deployment and morale.[9]

No subject has raised as much interest as the racial and ethnic composition of the AVF.[10] Blacks accounted for 17 percent of army enlisted members in 1972, 33 percent in 1980, and 30 percent in 1987. Today, all minorities (blacks, Hispanics, and others) make up 38 percent of the army's enlisted ranks. A 1982 study by the Brookings Institution showed that an astonishing 42 percent of all qualified black youth entered the active-duty military, compared to only 14 percent of whites.[11] Interestingly, since the end of the draft, the proportion of blacks with high school diplomas entering the army has consistently exceeded the level for whites, although the gap narrowed in the 1980s with the overall improvement in recruiting. Still, in 1986, 96 percent of black men joining the army had high school diplomas, in comparison with 87 percent of whites. In fact, the army's enlisted ranks are the only significant American social arena in which black educational levels surpass those of whites. It is also the case that black achievement in occupying leadership positions in the armed forces exceeds that of any other major American institution.

The military has always recruited large numbers of young men, of all races, who had no real alternative job prospects; it will always continue to do so. But trends toward labeling the army a recourse for America's underclasses are self-defeating for the youth involved, because they contradict the premise that military participation is a form of broadly based national service. Whatever success the military has had as a remedial organization for deprived youth derives largely from its association with non-market values, such as national defense, patriotism, citizenship obligation, even manly honor. If, on the other hand, the military comes to be seen as little more than a welfare agency or an employer of last resort, it will lose its potential for resocializing dead-end youth.[12] The more the army is seen as a truly national institution encompassing a cross section of American youth, the more it can achieve desirable social goals.

But a representative military is needed for much more than accomplishing worthy social ends. Broadening the AVF's membership directly improves military effectiveness. Consider early-attrition rates, a key performance category. High school graduates are twice as likely as high school dropouts to complete their enlistments successfully.[13] Studies indicate that the more schooling soldiers have, and the more stable their family backgrounds, the less prone they are to unauthorized absences and desertions.[14]

The evidence is clear, moreover, that on measures of military productivity, more-educated service members do better not only in highly skilled technical jobs, as might be expected, but also in low-skill ones.[15] But most important is the correlation between soldier quality and combat performance. Here the data is quite convincing. Soldiers with higher educational levels and higher intelligence are generally rated better fighters by peers and immediate superiors.[16]

Of course, being middle class or educated does not make one braver or more able; there are many outstanding soldiers who come from the most impoverished backgrounds. But our concern must also be with the chemistry of unit cohesion, which requires an optimum blend of talents and backgrounds. Research evidence serves to confirm the observations of commanders and NCOs who remember the draft period: the presence of middle-class, upwardly mobile men immeasurably boosts the morale of military units in peacetime as well as in war.

The improved recruiting picture that started in the early 1980s resulted from the convergence of several key developments—a high youth unemployment rate, a significant rise in military pay, and, more intangibly, a waning of the antimilitary sentiments generated by the Vietnam War. But the army's successful enlistment record also owed something to a thorough overhaul of its recruitment machinery undertaken by General Maxwell R. Thurman, head of the recruiting command in the early 1980s. Using social science research, Thurman discerned a "dual market" among potential recruits. One market consisted of economically motivated individuals interested in cash, job security, or technical training. The other market, one not anticipated in econometric models, consisted of individuals who were seeking a hiatus in their life paths or simply a change in environment. This latter group was thus amenable to an army tour, if short enlistments were available, along with deferred rewards in the form of postservice educational benefits. The existence of this group, predominantly college-bound youth influenced by nonmarket motivations, is the starting point for the concept of the citizen soldier in the AVF.

To Draft or Not to Draft

Despite the turnaround in AVF recruitment that began in 1981, the talk of restoring conscription never died down. The long-term appeal of the AVF to draw a cross section of American youth continues to be in doubt. Where close to one in five draftees in the pre-Vietnam era had some college, the corresponding figure has been around one in twenty in the volunteer army. Even in the mid-1980s, the best years of the AVF, the proportion of army recruits scoring in the highest mental category was still lower than in any draft year. Whatever the political considerations affecting the AVF, it seems clear that until the armed forces establish a citizen-soldier component, children of the better-off classes will be absent from the enlisted ranks of the armed forces. This is not to argue that the makeup of the enlisted ranks should be perfectly calibrated to the social composition of the larger society, but to ask what kind of society excuses its privileged from serving in its military.

Beyond broad philosophical questions, supporters for the draft were bound to become more vocal when it appeared that 1987 signaled the end of the good years of recruiting in the AVF. For the first time since 1980, the army and navy stated they were having difficulty meeting their quotas. Also in 1987, a spate of local scandals broke out in which recruiters falsified records or otherwise illegally enabled individuals to enter the armed forces.[17] If these episodes were harbingers of renewed difficulties in AVF recruitment, then calls to bring back the draft will surely become louder.

Yet the prospect of reviving conscription raises many serious questions. Enacting a workable draft requires, first and foremost, a national consensus as to its need, especially within the affected youth population. Such a consensus does not now exist, nor does it seem imminent. A renewed draft could cause turmoil on the nation's campuses and once again make ROTC units the target of attack. If compulsion is used, moreover, many will attempt to avoid induction, and a host of additional problems will arise. Even under a lottery system, decisions about exemptions would inevitably give rise to charges of inequities and favoritism.

If a draft were to come back, which kind would be most desirable? A 1982 OSD report addressed this question. It recommended a "minimal active force draft," that is, conscripting only the number of men necessary to make up the difference between manpower requirements and the number of volunteers.[18] Such a system in a peacetime environment might mean drafting no more than 30,000 to 40,000 people a year. A lottery system would be used to adjust upward or downward the number of draftees needed to make up recruiting shortfalls. Such a limited draft, of course, downplays civic content with its focus on end-strength numbers and thus is quite consistent with the general OSD policy toward military manpower. It is possible, moreover, that a draft based solely on chance might well sow more dissension among young people, especially those in college, than would a more universal system that offered civilian alternatives. Such a draft would almost surely spur discontent among those unlucky enough to be called. In any event, a limited draft that conscripts only the number needed to meet immediate manpower goals would pose anew the question of who will serve when most do not.

Many of the problems posed by the so-called tag-on draft preferred by the OSD could be avoided by reinstituting a version of universal military training (UMT). Under the most likely model of UMT, virtually all eligible males would receive six months of military training followed by some kind of reserve assignment. UMT could also be linked with limited liability, that is, UMT conscripts could not be sent outside U.S. territory without a declaration of war or explicit congressional authorization.[19] While UMT does link military conscription with citizen obligation, it raises its own questions. One can make strong social-equity arguments for drafting women, but the military arguments are much less compelling, especially if the combat-exclusion rule for females remains in effect. In addition, in an era of increasing tolerance for sexual preference, declarations of homosexuality would likely become an increasingly common recourse (unless the armed forces dropped the ban on homosexuals, which would cause other problems). Finally, in light of contemporary Supreme Court rulings, any kind of draft would surely cause a flood of applications from conscientious objectors.

Taken together, these considerations make any return to conscription unlikely, at least in the foreseeable future. Although I am one of those former draftees who looks back upon his military service with some amount of civic pride, I do not presently favor reviving the draft because a bungled draft would leave us worse off than the undesirable status quo. Barring general war, we are unlikely to see the end of the AVF. Rather than become embroiled in a debilitating debate over reviving the draft, it is better to make the AVF over along civic lines.

CITIZEN SOLDIERS IN THE
ALL-VOLUNTEER FORCE

What follows is a set of policy options, both specific and general, intended to make the AVF more effective and to do so at less cost. The recommendations all spring from one basic notion—the resurrection of the citizen soldier.[20] The AVF needs to create a new citizen-soldier track that would offer enlistees postservice educational benefits along the lines of the World War II GI Bill. Such a track would attract many of the same types of individuals normally pulled in by a draft.

Citizen Soldier and Professional Soldier: Complementary Roles

The ways in which the AVF defines military service need change as much as the particulars of its personnel system. As a start, the armed forces need to recognize the difference between those who might see the military as a way station in their lives and those who might make a long-term career commitment to the armed forces. The army can set up a two-track system accommodating both the citizen soldier and the professional soldier.

Potential professional soldiers would be required to enlist for at least three years but preferably for four or more. They would receive entitlements and compensation much in the manner of the current system, but their pay would be significantly increased at the time of their first reenlistment, with the prospect of further significant raises through the senior NCO grades. This would rectify the problem of compressed salaries resulting from the high pay that the marketplace AVF has set aside for recruits. Many career members would receive technical training, with special bonuses provided for those in skill areas suffering extreme shortages. The career force should also receive improved housing and family medical care, as well as adequate reimbursement for reassignments entailing family moves. Such steps would go a long way toward retaining the professional and experienced personnel to operate a complex, high-technology military force.

In contrast to the professional soldier, the citizen soldier would serve a short term, two years maximum (the term of the old draftee) or a six-month term of training followed by a reserve obligation. Citizen soldiers would generally be given assignments, such as in the combat arms, that were formerly filled by draftees. These are the areas in today's military where recruitment shortfalls, premature attrition, and desertion are most likely to occur. Active-duty pay for the citizen soldier would be lower—say, by one-third, or roughly $250 less per month—than that received by the professional soldier of the same rank. Aside from the GI Bill benefits described below, these soldiers would receive no special entitlements, such as off-base housing or food allowances. This would help lower the proportion of married or single-parent soldiers at junior enlisted levels, thereby helping restore unit cohesion in the barracks.

The army recruitment experience convincingly demonstrates that a combination of short enlistments and GI Bill-type benefits is by far the best incentive to reach into the college-bound youth population, youth least likely to be interested in a military career.[21] In 1983, the army began offering a limited two-year enlistment option, along with educational benefits, that was quickly oversubscribed by high-quality recruits. By 1987, about 15,000 soldiers a year were being accepted under this option. Two-thirds of the two-year enlistees scored in the army's top test categories, a proportion double that of the three- and four-year enlistees. Predictably, OSD wanted to eliminate this successful program on the grounds that longer enlistments were more cost-effective.

Compared to the army, the air force and navy rely far more on technicians, so the proportion of career-oriented personnel in those services will necessarily be higher than in the ground forces. The success of a citizen-soldier track in the army, however, might cause the air force and navy to consider the suitability of a short enlistment option as well. In the air force, problems of recruitment, attrition, and morale are most pronounced in such labor-intensive tasks as security guards and munition loaders. The same is true in the navy for "non-rated" sailors, those who perform the manual labor aboard ships. "Citizen airmen" and "citizen sailors" could well perform essential tasks in the less technical military specialties of their respective services.

A somewhat frivolous argument against the citizen soldier

raised by some military manpower policymakers is that introducing a lower-paid soldier into the army would cause discontent in the enlisted force. Invidious comparisons, they claim, would be made between those receiving less pay and others performing the same kind of work and holding the same rank for higher pay. Yet, if the lower-paid citizen soldier does feel put out, he has an easy solution at hand—joining the professional corps. Almost every army in NATO other than the United States already has a two-track system much like the one described here. In West Germany, for instance, a first-term volunteer makes three times the salary of his drafted counterpart. Yet, only about one in ten *Bundeswehr* draftees shifts to the regular soldier track. Interestingly enough, this is the same ratio of draftees in the American peacetime army who chose to become regular soldiers. Our peacetime draft experience shows that many young men accepted short tours in the combat arms over the technical-training advantages of a long enlistment, and even accepted a short tour as a lowly enlisted man over the compensation and privileges of a longer-term officer.

A more substantial argument against the citizen-soldier concept is the assertion that longer enlistments are always preferable to short ones. Why lose soldiers once they have been trained? Although possessing a certain surface plausibility, there are several fallacies in this argument. First, long-term enlistees are less likely to complete their enlistments than short-term servers. It is startling to find that even during the best AVF years about three in ten of those who entered the army failed to complete a three-year enlistment. Second, in a citizen-soldier system, those leaving active duty would automatically enter reserve duty, thus building upon the concept of the "Total Force." Third, short-term servers constantly exercise the military's training system, thus allowing for rapid mobilization in the event of war. That is to say that if circumstances ever warranted a quick return to the draft, the citizen-soldier mechanism would already be in place.

One of the most pernicious effects of the AVF has been its damage to the federal budget. Much more serious than high recruit pay are the costs associated with the growing share of military personnel in the career force. In the draft era, 16 percent of enlisted members were senior NCOs (paygrade E-6 and above); by 1987, the figure was 24 percent. This shift has inflated the military payroll by billions of dollars. Introducing a citizen-soldier component will shrink the career force (not actual manpower strength) and thereby substantially reduce aggregate salaries. Anything that can shave a few percentage points off the $50 billion payroll of the active-duty military will save a lot. A smaller career force will also bring about attendant savings in housing, medical, and school expenses required for military family members.[22]

But can the armed forces cut back on their career personnel? Is not the military much more dependent on highly trained technicians than it was a generation ago? Yes, but it is hard to argue that military readiness would suffer by having somewhat fewer career soldiers, whose work could be done by an equivalent proportion of citizen soldiers, which would most likely improve morale and efficiency in all services by affording greater responsibilities to service personnel all down the ranks.

Of the approximately 420,000 enlisted positions that the AVF must recruit annually, at least a quarter could be adequately filled by citizen soldiers. About half of these could enter the active force with the other half going into reserve units. Although all the branches could benefit from such short-term servers, the citizen-soldier concept makes most sense for what has always been its traditional home—the army and reserve forces. The entry of such large numbers of citizen soldiers into the military every year would bring about a qualitative change in the civic orientation of the volunteer force.

The citizen-soldier concept is directly opposed to the marketplace premise that every member of the military deserves a decent wage comparable to what he or she could expect in civilian life. Rather, the principle set forth here is that short-term enlistees are performing a civic duty that has no real equivalent in the civilian world and thus cannot be calculated in market terms. Citizen soldiers would infuse the military with a degree of civic content that has not been present since the end of the draft.

The two-track system outlined here has advantages beyond immediate manpower considerations. It would be a beginning toward resolving the "benefits/burdens" issue of military service. Broadly speaking, the burdens—service at low pay in combat units and in tasks with low civilian transferability—would become much more a middle-class responsibility than under the marketplace AVF. The benefits—career progression, technical training, and decent compensation—would still be most attractive to youth with limited opportunities in civilian life.

A Citizen Soldier GI Bill

Cost estimates of a GI Bill vary widely, depending on entitlement levels and other variables. In 1982, for instance, the Congressional Budget Office, in a study opposing a proposed GI Bill, based its cost estimates on how much the military would have to offer to attract high-quality entrants—bearers of high school diplomas who fall in the upper half of the armed forces' entrance tests—who would not otherwise join the service. The costs of gaining such "additive recruits" were put at $120,000 per recruit![23] Though vastly exaggerated, this figure does show that any across-the-board GI Bill, by rewarding large numbers who would have joined the military in any event, incurs unnecessary costs. Another disadvantage is that in order to contain such costs and rationalize the outlays, across-the-board GI proposals typically offer low levels of individual benefits and require long enlistments for maximum reward.

The new GI Bill enacted in 1985 was a significant development because it instituted a deferred benefit, thus moving away from the straight bonus-and-high-recruit-pay approach favored by the OSD in AVF recruitment. But the new legislation does not escape the defects of an across-the-board GI Bill. For a GI Bill to be truly cost-effective and attract really "new" recruits into the armed forces, it must be linked to a low-pay, short-enlistment option, the citizen-soldier track described above. Connecting GI Bill eligibility with short-term enlistments would help attract those youth for whom high recruit pay or enlistment bonuses are not sufficient inducements; moreover, the low-pay feature would minimize the siphoning off of those already predisposed to join the military. Such an approach allows for a GI Bill that is generous to the recipient without constituting an exorbitant drain on the treasury.

Let us posit a relatively generous citizen-soldier GI Bill that offers a maximum benefit of $24,000 (that is, up to $6,000 for each of four academic years) for a two-year enlistment. Such a postservice benefit would be about double that of the current GI Bill. (A corollary would be a "Reserve GI Bill," whereby a young person who enlisted in a reserve unit would be eligible for half the benefits of the basic GI Bill.) Still, because only citizen soldiers would be eligible, total costs of such a targeted GI Bill would be less than for an across-the-board bill. Furthermore, the type of soldier attracted by a citizen-soldier bill would provide reductions in net costs, thanks to lower attrition rates, reduced absences and desertions, and, probably, fewer lower-ranking service members with families. Reducing the career share in the manpower balance will also brake skyrocketing military retirement costs—$23 billion annually by 1990.

A GI Bill cannot simultaneously serve the purpose of both recruitment and retention. Recruitment must be the only and the overriding intent of any GI Bill. It may help clarify matters to think of a citizen-soldier GI Bill as a kind of substitute for conscription; for even with a draft, retention problems would persist—especially in the technical branches—and have to be dealt with on their own terms. Although the professional soldier would not receive GI Bill benefits, certain NCOs ought to be allowed to take a "sabbatical" involving an engineering curriculum for future technical work in the military. Retention, however, basically requires well-constructed compensation packages for career military members. The principle to be kept in mind is that a GI Bill aimed at both recruiting volunteers and retaining career soldiers will result in a muddled program that will do neither well.

MILITARY SERVICE
AND NATIONAL SERVICE

Debate about the AVF too often takes the easy path of presenting the options as tinkering with the status quo or bringing back the draft. This is far too simple. The AVF's problems stem not so much from the absence of conscription; the crucial flaw is that the architects of the present AVF view military service primarily as a job like any other job. For all the use of sophisticated economic techniques, the AVF relies excessively on a crude market incentive of cash inducements. It is this perspective we must address in order to reconstitute the AVF.

Now it may well be that recruitment and retention can formally fit into an economic framework. It is no trick to restate all behavior in terms of "costs" and "benefits." The power of the economic model is that, in appropriate kinds of situations, it enables us, operating on simple premises of rational behavior, to deduce by logic and statistics interesting conclusions about what will happen. But the prior question is to what degree noneconomic factors can or ought to be ignored in certain contexts. If we are truly going to have armed forces based on cost-effective grounds—ignoring moral sentiments and civic dimensions—then we should simply hire Third World nationals to man our military and be done with it.

Arthur Hadley in *The Straw Giant* offers an incisive diagnosis of what is really ailing the American military.[24] "The Great Divorce," he calls it—the isolation of the armed forces from the nation's business, political, and especially intellectual elite.[25] Heightened appeals to economic man will not overcome the chief barrier to recruitment—the disdain of the well-to-do for those in the enlisted ranks. What kind of society asks people to risk their lives for those who would look down on them for doing so? The AVF must shift its focus from simply trying to fill empty slots, as is now the case, to seeking a representative cross section of American youth, including the children of the elite. The ideal that the defense of the country is properly a widely shared citizen experience ought to overlay reliance on the cash-work nexus for recruitment.

The challenge facing the AVF is to find an equivalent of the peacetime draftee. Rather than looking backward toward conscription, we ought look forward to a state of affairs where the model of the citizen soldier can be subsumed within a broader concept of comprehensive citizenship obligation. A growing expectation of national service among youth generally will improve the climate of military recruitment without resort to ever-higher compensation for recruits or ever-higher reliance on career soldiers. If the AVF is to survive, it must reach the largely untapped pool of talented and upwardly mobile youth who would find a temporary diversion from the world of work or school tolerable, and perhaps even welcome.

A Practical Proposal
for National Service

National-service proposals have failed to attract sustained policy attention to date for two seemingly contradictory reasons. On the one hand, many of the proposals come across as vague and incomplete; they omit any serious discussion of such crucial matters as administration and budget. Other proposals suffer from just the opposite: too formal and detailed, they tend to ignore both political realities and the historical experience of actual youth service programs.

In order to reach a higher plane, the debate requires new types of proposals that are neither too grand nor too rigid. While surveys have indicated a broad approval among Americans for some form of national service, long-term support will inevitably depend on the particulars of any plan that is actually enacted. Nothing would more rapidly undermine public support than a scheme that ignores real-world problems. Poorly framed proposals by enthusiasts can inadvertently lead to public disillusionment, even cynicism, about national service. This is all to say that the program itself becomes a defining factor in the course of general debate on national service.

To start, any practical service proposal must take into account some basic features of the national mood. Many Americans seem convinced that our society is rapidly losing its civic underpinnings and that, as a result, important social needs are going unmet. At the same time, the public does not seem prepared to support any program that would be compulsory in nature or would require the creation of a huge bureaucracy. Building on such sentiments, a successful national-service program would have to be both voluntary and comprehensive; it should be neither federal nor local but something of both.

A concrete proposal must begin with some numbers. Some 4 million Americans per year turned age eighteen in the 1970s. This figure declined to 3.6 million in the 1980s and is projected to reach a low of 3.2 million in 1992. The number is then expected to begin climbing again, approaching 4 million by the end of the century. But the proportion of youth aged eighteen to twenty-four years will steadily decline as a percentage of the total population, from 12 percent in 1985 to 10 percent in 1990 to 9 percent in the year 2000.

The proposal outlined here would involve about one million young people a year; about 600,000 would enter civilian service and about 400,000 would join the military. One million young people doing national service is a tremendous number, but, because the program would be noncompulsory, this would still be only one-quarter to one-third of the total youth cohort. The focus here will be entirely on civilian service, the most novel component of any comprehensive program. But the point to be kept in mind is that the reconstructed citizen soldier, described in the previous chapter, and the civilian server presented here are each fulfilling a civic responsibility.

MEETING SOCIETY'S NEEDS

For any national-service program to work, it must perform tasks that neither the marketplace nor government can provide. There is work to be done that remains undone because there is no profit in it for the private sector and the public sector cannot afford it. The focus in national service must always be on the services provided. If a national-service program cannot provide services more effectively or more cheaply than private enterprise or employees of public agencies, then there is no basis for it.

The most detailed estimates on the number of tasks that could be performed by short-term volunteers with no specialized training is found in a 1986 Ford Foundation report on national service.

Based on the informed analyses of specialists in various fields, the report concluded that nearly 3.5 million positions could be filled by unskilled young people.[1] Most of these slots are located in education, the health sector, and child care, but several hundred thousand youth could be employed in such fields as conservation, criminal justice, and libraries and museums.

A partial listing of specific tasks within the general categories given above are: education—tutors, teachers' aides; health care—aides for inpatient care in hospitals, nursing homes, hospices, mental institutions, ambulatory care in outpatient facilities, also providers of home care, including meals on wheels, and transportation services; child care—workers for home care, center-based care, and care in work sites; conservation—forestry planting, soil conservation, construction and maintenance in recreation areas; criminal justice—police reserves, civilian patrols, police staff support; libraries and museums—preservers of library and museum collections, makers of braille and talking books, deliveries to homebound and institutionalized borrowers. This list could be extended almost indefinitely by incorporating the many, many services undertaken by nonprofit organizations across the country.

The paradox is that even as society becomes more interdependent, more and more people somehow seem to fall between the cracks. The coming together of social needs and national service can be illustrated by looking at three different kinds of service possibilities: one in tending for young children of employed mothers, a much-needed service in an age when day care is lacking in both quality and quantity; another in correctional facilities, an institution remote from the life experiences of most Americans; and a third in caring for the needs of the infirm elderly and those with chronic disabilities, an experience that for most of us, either through recognition of our own inevitable aging or through the awareness of the advancing infirmities of elderly parents and relatives, has a personal immediacy.

Day Care

National service opens new horizons in providing day care to American families. By 1990, there will be more than ten million children under six years of age with mothers in the labor force.

We find American mothers coping without an extended family system and with the least adequate family-support system in the industrialized world. As Deborah Fallows points out in her book *A Mother's Work*, day care represents a "market failure," a situation in which supply and demand reach a balance that most people find unsatisfactory. Day-care centers exist in an atmosphere where staff members feel they earn too little and parents believe they spend too much.[2] And the situation seems likely to get worse as the day-care field becomes increasingly dominated by large chains of for-profit centers that will seek to keep costs down with low-paid employees. This, sadly, is the exact opposite of what children need, which is plenty of attention from capable adults.

National service could help change all this. Making day-care work part of national service, Fallows points out, would have many benefits. For young people it would offer experience and training in a core societal function. For day-care centers, it would provide a ready pool of competent youth servers for entry-level work who would complement a much smaller but well-paid professional staff. Even if they served for only a year, such a commitment by national servers would exceed the transient terms of most current low-level workers. For day care as an institution, national service would lend dignity to the enterprise of caring for our nation's children.

Corrections

Few Americans realize how important a social institution our correctional facilities have become. In 1986 there were more than 600,000 people in jail, about 60,000 in juvenile facilities, and close to 1.5 million on parole or probation. Maintaining such a large population requires a lot of manpower at considerable cost. According to James B. Jacobs, a leading penologist and sociologist of law, 50,000 national servers could readily be absorbed in correctional facilities nationwide.[3]

The likelihood that national servers would not have specialized job skills need not be a disadvantage. Prisons are highly labor-intensive organizations; almost all could usefully employ more personnel. Such mundane procedures as record keeping and responding to prisoners' requests about parole and release dates could be expedited. Visiting procedures could be improved if there were more personnel to sign visitors in and to conduct routine searches. National servers could prove especially valuable as tutors. Penal institutions are so shorthanded that vocational and recreational programs are increasingly cut; added service personnel could help retain them.

National servers could even act as guards. Jacobs notes that in many states eighteen-year-olds are already eligible to become state prison guards. Several prison systems have employed college students as guards in summer internship programs. Furthermore, since state eligibility requirements are generally low, national servers would probably have higher educational—and better personal—qualities than the regular guard force. This is not to say that anyone can handle such a job. Stress is high. Prisons are dangerous, and inevitably some national servers would be injured. Clearly, any program would allow correction officials to end the participation of servers who are not up to the job.

Incarceration is a severe penalty. It is best that this punishment be administered fairly and that corrections work be viewed as civic duty, to the extent that this is practical. The experience of working in prisons will certainly not be uniform, but it should profoundly enrich the later education and personal development of the servers. It is not inconceivable, moreover, that prisoners would benefit from contact with a cross section of American youth. National service in correctional facilities could thus tie both prisoners and servers to the larger society.

Service to the Aged and Infirm

America is aging quickly. By 2010, one in every seven people will be older than sixty-five years, compared with only one in nine in 1980. Americans over eighty-five years of age make up the fastest-growing segment of all, increasing from 600,000 in 1950 to 1.5 million in 1980 to more than 4 million in 2010. Four out of ten of these "old old" people need some kind of help from another person. The nursing home population is about 1.4 million, and about the same number of people receive health-care services at home.[4]

Such figures portend an escalating financial burden for the

American family. Only the rich can indefinitely afford the long-term costs of a nursing home. Many middle-aged people are already simultaneously putting their children through college, saving for retirement, and providing for an elderly parent. One possible solution—having the elderly parent move in with his or her children—seems unlikely, owing to such distinctive features of American society as the wide geographical dispersion of family members and a rather common absence of close familial ties between generations, among others. As a result, many of today's families, after much soul-searching, decide that a nursing home is the only alternative. That course, however, entails tremendous costs. As more and more Americans confront this situation, the government may feel growing pressure to increase its spending on long-term health care. But how much can the public treasury bear? Already, at current payout rates, entitlements and programs for the elderly will by the mid-1990s absorb up to half of the federal budget. It is very doubtful that the government is going to be able to afford the immense costs of caring for the aged in the coming decades without some major departures from present policies.

All of which adds to the appeal of a national-service program. Consider, for instance, the problems that frail senior citizens have in getting around. In most areas public transportation is not readily available, and even when it is, there are disabled people who cannot use it anyway. A cheap, convenient alternative is needed. One possible prototype is Easyride, a transit system set up by the Vera Institute in 1981 to serve lower Manhattan. Easyride's experience shows that a neighborhood operation can promote flexible scheduling, ride pooling, reliable pickups, and cooperation among employers, churches, hospitals, and senior citizen centers. Such a transit service helps the handicapped and the old maintain a decent quality of life, reduces the demands for institutional care, and does away with expensive wheelchair lifts on buses. With the participation of national servers, an Easyride-style system could become a nationwide reality.

More generally, national service could play a significant role in providing in-home services. Perhaps as many as a third of all nursing home residents could live at home if someone were around to help them get outside the house, to run errands, to do some housekeeping. Historically, female family members have performed such tasks, but this is becoming less the case as more and more of them work outside the home. Increasingly, elderly people needing in-home service are having to contract with profit-making firms. Short-term national servers could perform these functions with greater efficiency at much less cost. Otherwise, by the end of this century, Americans will be spending vastly greater sums to support a nationwide corporate caretaking system for the aged—a prospect that almost everyone regards with dread.

ADMINISTRATIVE ORGANIZATION

National service emphasizes the ethic of citizenship duty rather than employment. National servers would receive a stipend, say $100 weekly, along with health and life insurance; room and board would be provided if need be with corresponding reductions in the stipend. The normal workweek would be forty hours. The basic length of service would be one year, though certain specialized programs would involve longer terms and some local programs might possibly require less. Although in-service compensation would be minimal, generous postservice educational and job-training benefits would be available to those who completed their term of service. The long-term goal is that only national servers would be eligible for such benefits.

Administering the overall program would be a Corporation for National Youth Service.[5] It would function as a public corporation in the mold of the Corporation for Public Broadcasting. The president and Congress would jointly appoint the board, taking due care to make sure that major interest groups are represented (given concerns that national servers might displace workers, union representation would be essential). Congress would appropriate funds for the corporation, which would then award grants to state and local youth corps. The corporation would establish guidelines for acceptable levels of expenditures per enrollee and also would set standards to preclude exploitation of youth servers. The corporation would also coordinate programs administered by federal agencies, serve as a clearinghouse for national-service initiatives, and have a small research staff. The corporation itself would not directly supervise national servers or carry out national-service functions.

The corporation would have no control over the Peace Corps

(to be moderately expanded, with perhaps some cultural-ex-
change programs with industrialized countries) or VISTA (to
be greatly expanded), both of which would retain their current
structure.[6] However, the corporation would be responsible for
newly created "signature" programs, each with a specific mission. Such programs might involve working with the United
States Border Patrol or civil-defense programs. A signature program could be matched to the needs of those afflicted with a
particular disease, Alzheimer's and AIDS being preeminent examples. By meeting clear needs not served by the marketplace,
signature programs would help dramatize the civic content of
national service.

The great majority of civilian youth servers, however, would
not be in federal programs. Most activity would occur at the
state and local levels. By awarding block grants, the corporation
would afford local units considerable autonomy in planning their
programs. The rule of thumb ought to be that larger and higher
agencies should not deliver services that can be performed by
smaller and lower agencies. National responsibility would be
limited to insuring that fund recipients meet certain basic standards pertaining to such matters as compensation, the kind of
work performed, the terms of agreement between enrollees and
employers, the prevention of job displacements, and the screen-
ing out of sectarian and political advocacy.

FIGURE 9.1 Model of Administrative Organization for National Service

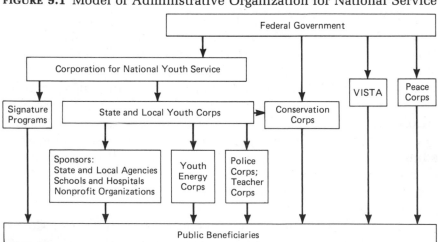

Once funded, state and local units would set up their own corps. They would also be free to choose their own organizational format—panels appointed by the governor or mayor, an add-on to a government youth office, a new office agency entirely, or a single individual. In some instances, servers would enroll directly in state and local youth corps, as is now the case with the California Conservation Corps and the New York City Volunteer Corps. In other (and probably the majority of) cases, state and local youth corps enrollees would be assigned to "sponsors" and live at home. The sponsors—public agencies, schools, hospitals, and nonprofit organizations—would be the backbone of the delivery of human services. The sponsor system would be modeled after the old Seattle Program for Local Service and its successor, the state of Washington Service Corps.

Inasmuch as nonprofit service organizations will play a critical role in any comprehensive national-service program, a word of explanation is in order. Today the number of nonprofit organizations is more than 100,000 (counting local branches of national organizations). The human-service deliveries of nonprofits have long been overshadowed by the dominating presence of the government. National service fits well into the needs of nonprofit associations providing human services because such organizations are typically labor-intensive and have a constant problem affording nonspecialized help. Because of the vagaries of finding funds, the service functions of voluntary agencies are often overwhelmed by grantsmanship, budget-justification research, and accountability rituals. If the nonprofit sector is to come out of the shadows it will be through national service.

The delivery of human services through nonprofit associations supported by public funds presents an alternative between the profit-making sector and government bureaucracy. Precisely because they are close to the ground, nonprofit organizations are attuned to local currents. Few regulations drawn in Washington, D.C., will cover all cases, and even fewer will allow exceptions. The greater potential flexibility of community-based programs would almost surely be a more effective provider of services than a centralized system directed from a national center.

The Netherlands provides a good example of the dominant role that voluntary agencies can play in a nation's social-service system. Owing to historical reasons, Dutch society in the nineteenth century divided into distinct *zuilen* or pillars—Protestant, Catholic, Liberal, and Socialist. Today these *zuilen* provide the administrative structures through which the Dutch government delivers many services, apparently with very good results. This is why the Dutch government employs less than half of the work force of the Swedish government, though the welfare systems of the countries are comparable in size. The government, that is, acts mainly as a funder rather than a deliverer of social services.[7]

With our own tradition of voluntary organizations—a kind of equivalent to the Dutch *zuilen*—coupled with comprehensive national service, we could set our country on an entirely new course of effective yet affordable delivery of human services.[8] Religious or ethnic groups with broad constituencies—the Federation of Protestant Welfare Agencies, Catholic charities, the United Jewish Appeal, the National Urban League, and so on— would be eminently suitable as sponsors. The same is true of the many nonprofit agencies that serve youth. Twelve of them already cooperate through an umbrella group called the National Collaboration for Youth. (Members include the Boys' Clubs of America, the Girls' Clubs of America, the Boy Scouts of America, the Girl Scouts, the Camp Fire Girls, Future Homemakers of America, the National Board of YWCAs, the National Board of YMCAs, the National Federation of Settlements and Neighborhood Centers, the National Jewish Welfare Board, the 4-H Clubs, and the Red Cross Youth Service Programs.) The Guardian Angels could also fit the criteria of a deserving sponsor. In addition to units of state and local governments, these and lesser-known nonprofits could easily become the sponsors of community-based national-service programs.

A national program could also set aside funds for staff-intensive (and therefore expensive) programs that would seek to involve disadvantaged youth who might not otherwise enroll. The prototype is the Youth Energy Corps in New York City, where enrollees receive basic education and hands-on training while undertaking such tasks as weatherizing tenements and rehabilitating public facilities. Such projects are consistent with the civic content of national service because, unlike the Job Corps, enrollees not only acquire training but also serve a community need.

Rounding out the national-service program would be that old stand-by, conservation work. Building on the model of the Young Adult Conservation Corps of the 1970s and the proposed American Conservation Corps, the federal government would distribute funds among three administrative entities: the Forest Service of the Department of Agriculture, the Department of the Interior, and the individual states. Because this table of organization has proven itself in modern conservation history, there is no reason for the National Service Corporation to become involved. The federal programs would be mainly residential, as would most of the state programs. But a sizable amount of conservation work in or near metropolitan areas could also be nonresidential.

It is impossible to predict the exact shape a national-service program would take in practice. America does not stand still, and no such program can be cast in finite detail. But the plan outlined here has several distinct advantages. One is that because it is based on programs already in place, national service could be implemented in a relatively short period of time. Within a year, it could accommodate 100,000 people. Positions for another 100,000 could be added each year, with the final goal of 600,000 being reached in five years or so. Another advantage is that a minimal administrative structure overlays existing and expandable organizations. Yet with its decentralized structure, the proposed national service has an overreaching civic content that will give local programs a chance to feel a part of the whole.

COSTS

It is difficult to be precise about the costs of a national-service program. But from the record of past and present youth-service projects at federal, state, and local levels, there is a reasonable consensus on the factors affecting costs. The key variables are the amount of compensation per enrollee, the level of staffing, the ratio of residential to nonresidential participants, administration, expenditures for capital goods, and postservice benefits. We will assume, unless otherwise noted, that all enrollees serve a one-year term in their national-service program (knowing full well that all programs will have some degree of unplanned attrition).

Let us first turn to the level of compensation. The enrollee in a nonresidential program must earn enough money to buy food and transportation (if these are not otherwise provided) and have a modest amount left over for personal needs. Figuring a $100 weekly stipend plus health and life insurance, the basic annual compensation for a national server would come to about $6,500. An enrollee living in a residential program would require another $4,500 for room and board (with, say, a $1,000 annual reduction in stipend), or approximately $10,000 per year (about the costs of maintaining each individual enrolled in a Job Corps residential center).

Staff costs come in two basic varieties: those required for residential living and those needed for work and training supervision. Residential programs require cooks, maintenance persons, and barracks/dormitory monitors. While some of these jobs can be performed by the national servers themselves, residential programs will always need some regularly paid staff. Costs of work and training staff are another matter. At one extreme, staff-intensive programs include specially hired team leaders, counselors, vocational and basic education teachers; at the other extreme are programs where enrollees are supervised by persons already employed in the sponsoring organization.

Calculating basic compensation and staff costs together, we come to benchmark estimates of $9,000 per slot in a nonresidential program (the average cost per VISTA volunteer) to about $16,000 for a residential program (the per-enrollee cost of the spartan Ohio Conservation Corps). Using these figures, Table 9.1 attempts to estimate the annual budget for a national-service program with 600,000 volunteers.

Let us examine each of the table's components. Conservation work consists of three categories: federal residential, state residential, and state and local nonresidential. Assuming 60,000 servers in each category and the benchmark figures, the two residential programs together would cost $1.92 billion, and the nonresidential programs, $600 million.

Regarding human services, most participants would be assigned to sponsoring agencies—nonprofit organizations, schools, hospitals, local governments—where they would work under the direction of regularly employed staff. The annual cost for each enrollee is calculated at the $9,000 rate for nonresidential programs (about the same as outlays in the Washington Service Corps). Accordingly, the cost for the 160,000 serving in nonprofit organizations would come to $1.44 billion; for the 120,000 employed in schools and hospitals, $1.08 billion; and for the 50,000 working in state and local agencies, $450 million.

TABLE 9.1 ESTIMATED ANNUAL COSTS OF A NATIONAL SERVICE PROGRAM

Type of Program	Number of Enrollees	Per-Slot Costs	Costs (millions of dollars)		
			Total Costs	State/Local Cost Sharing	Federal Outlays*
Conservation Corps:					
Federal residential	60,000	$16,000	$ 960	—	$ 960
State residential	60,000	16,000	960	$ 240	720
State/local nonresidential	60,000	10,000	600	150	450
Federal Programs:					
Peace Corps	10,000	20,000	200	—	200
VISTA (residential & nonresidential)	25,000	13,000	325	—	325
Signature programs (residential)	20,000	16,000	320	—	320
Human Services:					
Nonprofit organization sponsors	160,000	9,000	1,440	360 (160)**	1,080
School and hospital sponsors	120,000	9,000	1,080	270 (120)**	810
State and local agency sponsors	50,000	9,000	450	112	338
Special Programs:					
Police/Teacher Corps	10,000	20,300	200	100	100
Youth Energy Corps (nonresidential)	25,000	18,000	450	112	338
Advertising			30	—	30
Federal Administration			30	—	30
Total	600,000		$7,045	$1,344	$5,701

* does not include postservice benefits diverted from current federal aid to college students and job-training programs

** nonprofit organization, school, and hospital sponsors contribute $1,000 per enrollee

Small federal programs such as the Peace Corps, VISTA, and the new signature programs have variable costs because of their different natures. The annual costs of a Peace Corps volunteer (who serves two years) would come to about $20,000 per year, the highest of any existing civilian national-service program. (By comparison, it costs an estimated $35,000 a year to pay, feed, clothe, and supervise each soldier in today's army, and the costs of keeping an inmate in jail are $40,000 a year.) Assuming an enrollment of 10,000 (double the current level), the Peace Corps budget would come to $200 million. VISTA would be rescued from its current moribund state and expanded into a 25,000-member program. Assuming that the VISTA volunteers are equally divided between residential and nonresidential programs, the per-slot cost would average $13,000 a year, for a total of $325 million. The federal signature programs are calculated at the basic residential rate; with a total of 20,000 members, these would come to $320 million a year.

The special national-service programs—the Police Corps and the Teacher Corps—are relatively expensive. The concept is based on scholarships offered to college students who will then be committed to designated duties following graduation. A good reference point is provided by the military ROTC programs, which spend $20,000 per student, or $5,000 a year calculated over the course of a college education. With 10,000 students a year entering the specialized corps, the total cost would come to $200 million.

Completing the roster is what I have called the Youth Energy Corps—a staff-intensive program with a strong vocational and educational component—based on the existing pilot program of the same name. Unlike the other programs, the energy corps would be targeted to very disadvantaged youth. Though the program would be nonresidential, its special staffing needs would make it relatively expensive. Judging from the New York City program, the energy corps would cost $18,000 per slot. With 25,000 enrollees, total annual costs would come to $450 million.

Federal administration would absorb another $30 million a year. About half this sum would be spent at the headquarters office and half devoted to, say, fifteen regional offices. Finally, we include $30 million for commercial advertising. (By comparison, the 1987 advertising budget for military recruitment was $218 million.)

Overall, the direct costs of the national-service program would come to about $7 billion. With 600,000 enrollees, this works out to a per-slot annual cost of about $11,700. This does not take into account, however, cost sharing by state and local governments. These would be expected to assume 25 percent of the costs of all nonfederal projects. (The exception would be the Police and Teacher Corps, for which cost sharing would be on a 50/50 basis, on the presumption of special arrangements being made with public universities and colleges.) Overall, the state and local governments would contribute an estimated $1.3 billion and the federal government $5.7 billion. The annual costs to the federal government would thus come to about $9,500 per enrollee (not counting postservice educational benefits described below).

Furthermore, the nonprofit sponsors responsible for the delivery of human services would contribute $1,000 a year for each young person they enrolled. As Seattle's Public Local Service program demonstrated in the 1970s, this arrangement is both effective and enforceable. The purpose is not only to help defray expenses but also to insure that young enrollees are not simply treated as free labor. Requiring sponsors to pay enrollees would also make them less reluctant to discharge those who do not perform up to standard.

Although prediction of exact dollar figures in such a large and untried program is a risky business, the general principles of cost accounting of national service are clear. Costs are higher to the degree that programs are more residential, managed by public agencies, directed toward high-risk youth, and staff-intensive. Correspondingly, costs are lower to the degree that national service is nonresidential, managed by nonprofit organizations, untargeted, and low on staff. The spreadsheet given in Table 9.1 can be varied by changing the weights given to each of these factors.

To be really complete, a budgeting exercise on national service must include the value of the work performed. What is the final value of preserving our physical resources, cleaning up the environment, caring for the elderly and handicapped, rescuing our research collections, staffing our public institutions with citizen servers, and opening new avenues for dead-end youth? There is no ready answer. Even though evaluation studies on service programs indicate that for every dollar expended at least one dollar of value is gained, such studies can go only so far. By focusing either on short-term impacts on program participants or economic analyses of specific services delivered, evaluation researchers typically fail to include the more general societal benefits that a national-service program would provide. The gains in civic culture and social consensus, though difficult to measure, would surely be sizable.[9]

Any large-scale national-service program will cost money, and it is best to say so up front. Even the costs presented in Table 9.1 do not include capital expenditures or purchases of equipment, although in many cases these will already be taken care of because most national servers will be working in existing organizations. But we should also place the financial outlays of a national-service program in context. For instance, the program outlined here would (in constant dollars) cost the federal government about two-thirds of the annual funds expended on the unlamented CETA.[10] That a comprehensive national-service program could be had at such a price should make the idea all the more appealing.

POSTSECONDARY-SCHOOL AID AND NATIONAL SERVICE

Educational benefits for youth who complete a term of duty is a keystone of any national-service program. In return for one year of civilian service at subsistence wages, postservice benefits are a proper response to an accomplishment of civic duty. The GI Bill following World War II was a nation's way of expressing its gratitude for those who served in its military. It is time to extend this principle to those who perform civilian service as well.[11] When I first proposed this linkage a decade ago, I was virtually alone. Increasingly, however, the notion of a "GI Bill" for civilian national service is attracting serious attention. I stress that connecting student aid to national service is not adding another expenditure on the federal treasury; rather, the proposal is to shift present appropriations to national service.

In its initial stages, a national-service program should guarantee all enrollees postsecondary school benefits that feature much more favorable terms than those available to nonservers. Student loan forgiveness for national service is one obvious and easily implemented policy. In time, participation in national service would become a prerequisite for federal educational and vocational training assistance. Such an approach would fit nicely with the recommendations of the 1985 Newman report issued by the Carnegie Foundation for the Advancement of Teaching. That report urged that federal student aid move away from loan programs toward outright grants and work-study arrangements.

Imagine if the $8 billion that Congress authorized for federal educational assistance in 1986 were divided equally among 600,000 national servers; each enrollee would receive a $14,000 scholarship! Even if only half that amount were disbursed, each individual would receive $7,000. Think of it still another way: generous scholarship aid could be offered to national servers simply by paying them out of the $4 billion that the taxpayer now spends for bank subsidies and loan defaults in the present student-aid program.

The principal argument raised against linking national service and federal educational aid is that it would have a regressive effect. According to this line of reasoning, students from wealthy families who do not need aid would be unaffected, while poor students would have to enter national service in order to get aid. Without assistance, poor students intent on staying in college would be forced to take more part-time jobs, rely on family and other personal sources, and attend less expensive (mainly public) colleges.

Such a line of reasoning has a certain surface plausibility, but really cannot stand up to scrutiny. The fact of the matter is that the present shift away from grants toward loans in student aid heightens the class division between those who can afford to pay for college and those who cannot. From 1980 to 1986, the proportion of students from working-class families who enrolled in college dropped by one-fifth.[12] The percentage of black high-school graduates entering college dropped from 34 in 1976 to 25 in 1985; for Hispanics the decline was from 36 to 27 percent.[13] The prospect of student-incurred debt is undoubtedly a major factor in the declining number of poor youth entering and completing college.[14] Thus replacing the present student-aid program with one that links national service to a GI Bill-type grant would most likely widen rather than restrict access to higher education.[15] Also important, a movement toward a service-based rather than a needs-based aid program would almost surely strengthen public support for the whole concept of federal assistance to college students.[16]

The argument that linking student aid to national service is regressive also misses on a deeper point. Student aid by its very nature is regressive. Only about half of all young people even enter college, so at the very outset aid goes to those students with the best career prospects.[17] A national service that has special programs for poor youth facing otherwise dead-end prospects is infinitely more progressive than the status quo. Finally, the grossest inequities in our society are found in the differential treatment one can expect in terms of day care for children, primary and secondary school education, and how the aged, sick, and infirm are handled. Youth participation in delivery of human services would reduce such inequities more than any other feasible policy.

We are still left, however, with the question of how a nonmandatory system can bring the most privileged youth into national service. In the end, there is no voluntary scheme that can insure the participation of the very rich in national service.[18] We must acknowledge we are a capitalist society, with all that implies in terms of class advantages. But a comprehensive national-service program linked with student aid would at least introduce the concept of civic responsibility to a very large portion of American youth, thereby helping raise the nation's standards of citizenship. We should not lose sight of the fact that educational costs are a heavy burden for almost all American families. Few readers of these pages look lightly upon college expenses, either their own or their children's. Regarding those who choose not to serve because they are both rich enough to dismiss student aid and unaffected by civic considerations, one feels regret for them and the country.

RECRUITMENT

Most of the debate about national service focuses on the mechanics of the program: placement, compensation, and administration of enrollees. This is, in effect, the demand side of the equation. But what about the supply side? Enter a troubling thought: what if we had a national service and nobody came?

The question is far from facetious. In its fledgling years, even the modest-sized Peace Corps had difficulty meeting its quotas. Not until Sargent Shriver began beating the bushes for volunteers and finding money to pay for advertising did enough recruits enter the new corps. More recently, the New York City Volunteer Corps found itself unable to recruit middle-class youth. The prospect of filling a 600,000-member youth program each year seems daunting indeed.

Civilian national service can work only if it enjoys genuine backing from national leaders and enough publicity to make it a viable option. Sophisticated, admittedly expensive, advertising of the type, if not the scale, used for military recruitment will be required. Once in operation, however, the program should develop its own recruitment momentum through word of mouth and peer example. Moreover, under the decentralized program described here, much local recruitment would fall to community-based organizations.

Two general principles should be kept in mind when appraising national-service recruitment. First, national service must be sold to the public at large in terms of services performed. From the start, everything possible should be done to avoid connotations of make-work, and tendencies to recruit from targeted populations must be resisted. Second, and at the same time, messages can be given to potential enrollees about the personal advantages of a one-year stint beyond the service experience itself. Without compulsion, national service must rely heavily on some notion of postservice rewards. This is why linking national service with postsecondary school benefits is so crucial.

Recruitment could also resort to those old stand-bys, guilt and shame. Without getting cruel about it, society could encourage the notion that those who choose not to serve are shirking their civic duty. In a more positive vein, in the manner older military veterans used to convey the richness of their service experience to impressionable boys, veterans of civilian service might do likewise to both boys and girls.

Throughout this discussion, I have steadfastly focused on that which is practicable. To be successful, a national-service system should build on present trends rather than take a great leap into the unknown. Organizational structures must remain flexible, because they will surely be affected by the social circumstances and political compromises of the real world. As with all programs of this scope, we can expect incidents of fraud and abuse. There will probably be national-service "horror stories." But the program will avoid a negative image largely to the degree it attracts a cross section of American youth early on. Such youth in turn will become the "alumni" supporters of national service for their juniors.

It is within our reach to establish a comprehensive youth program to serve national needs without compulsion, without a Brobdingnagian bureaucracy, and without massive costs. The real key is to link governmental subsidies of higher education and postsecondary job training to voluntary service. The goal is nothing less than making civic duty an intrinsic part of growing up in America.

TEN

The Politics of
National Service

In some ways these are the worst of times for national service.
But they may also be the best of times. Let us start with the
worst. The attack on the state, and particularly on its welfare
functions, has struck a chord. Even in the face of a troubled
economy, the conservative critique has taken its toll on old-fashioned liberalism. It is not, then, an especially propitious time
to be contemplating the creation of an ambitious new public
program. If national service is perceived as a program that creates
a new class of social administrators and a dependent class of
welfare-like beneficiaries, it is doomed—and quite properly so.

Yet the laissez-faire view that the market can do all is ultimately
as utopian as the managed utopias it so effectively derides. Conservative theorists and politicians tend to overlook the fact that
it was the failure of the market to deliver necessary social services
that originally led the state to assume them. Yet in a time of
budgetary deficits, it may be too expensive to maintain social
services at past levels, much less move on to higher levels of
public outlays. At the same time, it is increasingly apparent
that provision of most such services by the private sector is
prohibitively expensive for those who need them.

This brings us to the best-of-times side. The practical argument
for national service is that it can be a means of providing services
that the government cannot afford and in which the private sector
finds no profit. Those deciding whether or not the United States

165

should embark on any national-service program should always try to answer a simple question first. Are the means employed more likely to achieve the purpose, and at less cost, than some other means? If the answer is no, then the activity is not suitable for national service. If it is yes, then national service is the practical means to meet societal needs that would otherwise go unmet.

But beyond this, there is a visionary argument for national service; namely, it is the way to foster and to express civic solidarity. A new tendency in political discourse to speak of the need for citizen responsibility is clearly evident. Thus, in two books released within weeks of each other in 1987, liberal economist Robert Kuttner upholds "citizenship values" over "market values" as a way for the Democratic party to rediscover its progressive roots, and conservative thinker Paul M. Weyrich bemoans the "me first" ethic and the absence of the "concept of the common good."[1] Politics, the new civic mood seems to say, ought to be more than the "something for nothing" or the "every man for himself" that has come to caricature recent liberalism and conservatism.

PUBLIC OPINION AND NATIONAL SERVICE

When it comes to public views on national service, there is a seeming paradox. Gallup and Harris polls over a twenty-year period consistently show high levels of agreement with the idea of youth performing national service, both military and civilian.[2] A slight majority of respondents favor mandatory service (either military or civilian), while support for a voluntary program of national service is in the 80 percent range. Despite such widespread support, though, no national-service program—even a voluntary one—has come close to being enacted.

What accounts for this apparent discrepancy? The main factor is the difficulty polls have in indicating the saliency of an issue. The responses garnered by opinion surveys tend to be spur-of-the-moment answers on issues that are far from uppermost in most people's minds. Surveys generally fail to distinguish superficial from deeply held opinions, peripheral from central concerns. On most matters, there exists no such thing as "public opinion" until an issue becomes politically controversial or is picked up by prominent political figures. At present, national service is in what might be called a "pre-public opinion" phase.

These limitations notwithstanding, there exists an excellent source of data on public attitudes toward national service. This is the General Social Survey (GSS) of the National Opinion Research Center, an annual survey in which a representative sample of 1,500 Americans is interviewed on a wide variety of issues. In 1984, the GSS included a supplemental set of questions on both military and national service.[3] The findings constitute the most comprehensive set of data yet compiled on the subject of national service.

Twenty-five percent of those interviewed supported a peacetime draft—an all-time low. At the same time, 84 percent said they would approve of a return to conscription in case of a national emergency. Support for a draft is generally strongest among veterans and older whites, weakest among young adults, nonveterans, and blacks. Despite the meager support for the draft, military service is regarded as a worthwhile activity; a remarkable 89 percent of all respondents agreed that military service is a "good experience" for men, and a surprisingly high 73 percent said the same for women.

On national service, GSS asked three questions. The first was: "How would you feel about a program that required all young men to give one year of service to the nation—either in the military or in non-military work such as in hospitals or with elderly people?" The second question asked the same thing, but about women rather than men. The third—critical to measuring levels of practical support—asked those respondents who favored national service if they would be willing to pay a 5 percent tax increase to finance it.

Based on these questions, I have constructed a threefold typology of national-service support. *Strong supporters* are those who favor mandatory national service for both sexes and who, in addition, are willing to pay higher taxes for such a program. *Conditional supporters* favor national service for one sex only (almost always males) or favor it but are not willing to pay extra taxes for it. *Opponents* are those who are flat-out against national service or had no opinion. The distribution of these groups is shown in Table 10.1. Overall, 40 percent were strong supporters, and 28 percent were opponents (including the 12 percent with no opinion). Considering the high standards set for the strong-supporter category, the number of convinced backers of mandatory national service is impressively large.

It is risky to draw firm conclusions from such gross numbers. Fortunately, however, the GSS also collects data on the attitudes of various subgroups based on sex, race, age, class identification, and political beliefs. These figures are also set out in Table 10.1. Not surprisingly, the greatest variation occurs according to age. Only among respondents under thirty years of age do opponents outnumber strong supporters. Otherwise, attitudes toward national service remain relatively constant. Sex, class, race, politics—none of these variables predicts views toward national service. If there is another issue with such uniformity across social groupings, I cannot name it. Stated another way, support for national service ranges across the full social and political spectrum. This is a striking finding, indicating that national service may be uniquely suited to promoting a sense of civic consen-

TABLE **10.1** ATTITUDES TOWARD MANDATORY NATIONAL SERVICE BY SOCIAL BACKGROUND VARIABLES (percentages)

Variable	Strong Sup-porters	Condi-tional Sup-porters	Opponents or No Opinion	Total	(N)
Total	40	32	28	100	(1,429)
Sex:					
Female	39	34	27	100	(851)
Male	41	30	29	100	(578)
Class:					
Working & lower	39	32	29	100	(728)
Middle & upper	40	32	28	100	(692)
Race:					
Black	35	41	24	100	(165)
White	39	35	26	100	(1,264)
Politics:					
Liberal	41	30	29	100	(329)
Moderate	38	32	30	100	(555)
Conservative	43	34	23	100	(488)
Age:					
18–29	29	30	41	100	(388)
30–49	43	33	24	100	(539)
50 and over	44	35	21	100	(499)

SOURCE: 1984 General Social Survey, National Opinion Research Center

sus in America, a quality that has been sorely lacking in recent years.

THE POLITICS OF NATIONAL SERVICE

It is one thing to plumb opinion surveys for indications of public support for national service. It is quite another to forge a consensus on the shape such a program should take. To start, consider the stances of the two major political parties. Although neither party directly discussed national service in its 1984 platform, each did touch on the issue, with somewhat different emphasis. The Republican platform expressed a clear preference for volunteer participation, with a stress on "state and local control" in the delivery of human services. The Democrats expressed their intention of expanding such federal programs as VISTA and the Young Adult Conservation Corps. Interestingly, both parties praised the Peace Corps, an indication that the agency has become more or less invulnerable. Both platforms also came out against a peacetime draft, though the Democrats went a step further and opposed peacetime draft registration as well. (The Republicans were silent on the issue.)

Despite this overlap, the two parties have some clear differences on national service, portending difficulties for any effort to incorporate the issue into the political mainstream. The major political obstacle to national service becoming a reality is the laissez-faire bent of many conservatives—a stance that estranges them from national service and makes the idea seem an exclusively liberal concern. Republican opposition is in part due to the increased federal outlays that any such program would entail. But the real nub of the matter is ideology. Congressman Jack Kemp, Republican of New York and 1988 presidential hopeful, belittled the whole idea by asserting: "At the age of eighteen, you should be focusing on your dreams and ambitions, not picking up beer cans in Yellowstone."[4] A similar sentiment was reflected in the comment of Donald T. Regan, when he was secretary of the treasury, who said the question of national service had to be answered in terms of whether the nation needs youth "picking up trash rather than earning their first million."[5] Both remarks were directed at mandatory national service, but the philosophy that underlies them, with its exaltation of the market, is clearly hostile to national service of any sort. The old American homily, "If you're so smart, why ain't you rich?" has been twisted to "if you're so patriotic, why ain't you rich?"

Whatever the validity of laissez-faire critiques of national service, liberals are sometimes their own worst enemies in presenting the case for it. During hearings held in 1982 on a bill proposing the establishment of a commission on voluntary national service, Senator Paul E. Tsongas spoke in behalf of his own bill as follows:

> My commitment to this concept [of national service] is a result of my having served in the Peace Corps, which I consider the formative experience of my life and that—Well, to prove the point, I went to the Peace Corps as a Republican and came out as a liberal Democrat. [Laughter][6]

Tsongas's jocularity should not obscure what could become a real problem for the cause of national service. There is no better way to insure that national service is a nonstarter than to hint that it is part of a not-so-hidden liberal agenda. Survey data indicate that national service presently enjoys broad political support, with no particular social group strongly opposed. Supporters of national service should try to insure that it stays this way.

The best way to prevent national service from becoming the exclusive property of a narrow political band is to link its civilian and military components under a common standard of civic duty. Incorporating the military would dilute tough-minded complaints that national service is nothing but do-gooding; maintaining a civilian program would allay high-minded concerns that national service is only a Trojan horse for reinstating the draft.

Indeed, national service promises to be a policy that will work against ideological polarization—Republicans veering right, Democrats drifting left. In practice, national service would afford each party an opportunity to draw on powerful undercurrents of public opinion. There is overwhelming support for some kind of intervention on behalf of the handicapped, the infirm elderly, or the deserving needy. Most Americans also look favorably on measures aimed to preserve the physical environment. At the same time, there are deep concerns that the market cannot meet such pressing social needs and that government bureaucracy is not the way to do so either. Clearly, then, the political base for national service is present. The key is to prevent the idea from becoming the property of either liberals or conservatives before it comes to the attention of the public at large.

To better understand the political dynamics of national service, it might help to consider Nelson Polsby's *Political Innovation in America*, a pioneer study of the political science field known as "policy initiation."[7] Building on post-World War II case studies, Polsby analyzes the various ways in which new policies are enacted in America. According to one model, the adoption of a policy requires a preliminary period of "incubation." During this phase, which can last for many years, policy innovation takes place slowly, with specific proposals developed by thinkers and proponents of issues who are not the ultimate decision makers.[8] To become part of the political discourse, however, these ideas must be adapted to the needs of the nation as a whole. The passage of an idea from the pet cause of a few to the active agenda of the nation is immeasurably eased if the proposed policy is taken up and adapted to the electoral needs of political leaders.

National service seems to fit nicely with this scheme. It has already experienced an incubation period of considerable duration and is now ready to move into the national political arena. National-service-type ideas have been picked up by such past and potential Democratic presidential hopefuls as Bruce Babbitt, Bill Bradley, Alan Cranston, John Glenn, Gary Hart, Sam Nunn, Paul Simon, and Charles Robb. As this list indicates, interest has not been limited to one or another segment of the party. That two Democratic groups—the Democratic Leadership Council and the Coalition for a Democratic Majority—trying to steer the party away from the left have put forward national service proposals, however, indicates that national-service support is probably strongest in the "moderate" wing of the party.

This seeming monopoly of interest among the Democrats probably reflects less the party's ideology than its having been out of power since 1980, for out-groups are generally much more willing than incumbents to entertain innovative policies. To the extent that pragmatic Republicans can also be considered an out-group within their own party, we can expect national service initiatives to come from that side of the party rather than from the laissez-faire wing. And, in fact, it has been precisely such Republican senators as Mark Hatfield of Oregon, John McCain of Arizona, Ted Stevens of Alaska, and former congressman Paul McCloskey of California, who have pushed for national service within the GOP.

Leaving aside partisan proclivities, national service could come to prominence for another reason—the broad cyclical changes that characterize American politics. Historian Arthur M. Schlesinger, Jr., has discerned alternating thirty-year periods of conservatism and liberalism, dominated by what he calls "Private Interest" and "Public Purpose."[9] Schlesinger sees the current period of concern with private matters coming to an end and a new era of public concern on the horizon. Schlesinger's thesis fits quite nicely with an ascendancy of civic participation consistent with placing youth service on the national agenda.

Complementing Schlesinger's macropolitical theory is the social psychological analysis of political cycles by Albert O. Hirschman of the Institute for Advanced Study at Princeton. In *Shifting Involvements*, Hirschman presents a persuasive explanation of why individuals oscillate between intense interest in public issues and almost total concentration on private happiness.[10] The private sphere is based on consumerism, the ultimate disappointments of which deflate an ideology based on the quest for private happiness. Money grubbing becomes boring, leading in turn to action directed toward public goals. But in time the frustrations of public action, along with inordinate emotional and time commitments, lead to an eventual recoil from that sphere. Private pursuits become attractive once again, and the cycle begins anew.

Hirschman's theory provides a good framework for analyzing the long-term political dynamics of national service. As the 1980s draw toward a close, the absorption in individual happiness seems to be fading. The image of the "yuppie," once celebrated, has been growing increasingly threadbare. But are we destined to enter another cycle of heady activism, whose inevitable excesses will almost surely have a corrosive effect on the body politic, only to be followed by a return to private pursuits? National service is an especially appropriate form of civic participation precisely because it does not rely on overinvolvement of the few and the underinvolvement of the many. Distinctively, national service calls for the moderate civic involvement of the many. This is not to say that national service will do away with predicted cycles of private hedonism versus political activism, but it does promise to flatten the curves, thus helping to avoid the exaggerations of the recent past and contemporary period.

Even if the general mood shifts in a direction favorable to national service, there remain considerable obstacles to its actual adoption. I see three scenarios, not in any way exclusive of one another, by which national service can come into being. One is through the return of a military draft—a development that would surely create pressures for creating some form of alternative civilian service. A second scenario would be for an energetic president to come forward and make the cause of national service his own. Just as the Civilian Conservation Corps was inaugurated by Franklin D. Roosevelt and the Peace Corps by John F. Kennedy, so national service awaits a president who is convinced that such a program is both good politics and good for the country.

The third scenario is the most problematic but also the most desirable, in that it would provide national service with its securest foundation. It would involve fostering a public sensibility to meeting societal needs in national-service terms. The public is already accustomed to thinking in such terms when it comes to military manpower needs, as is clear from the resilience of the citizen-soldier concept. To date, however, the public is less inclined to entertain such an approach with regard to civilian service (with the partial exception of conservation corps). The debate over the delivery of human services pits those who favor a market approach (including the awarding of government contracts to private firms) against those who support the expansion of government agencies to deliver such services. To break out of this typical "conservative versus liberal" mind-set means no less than a paradigmatic shift in American policy thought.

Yet such a shift is essential if we are to meet the challenges that currently confront American society. A few examples should help indicate the range of problems that national service would deal with:

- National service could help families cope with Alzheimer's disease. An incurable mental disorder that causes deterioration of the memory and reasoning abilities, Alzheimer's afflicts about 5 percent of Americans over sixty-five years old and 20 percent of those over eighty. Some two million Americans have the disease. Its direct costs are estimated at $20 billion. The indirect costs may be even greater. The need for constant care places severe emotional burdens on relatives. Just to give family members a temporary break from caring for an Alzheimer's victim—either through home visits or adult day-care centers—would be a major help. Even a small corps of servers specializing in Alzheimer's care would provide immeasurable relief to weary and depressed families.

• In recent years, the cities of America have been inundated with the "deinstitutionalized" mentally ill. From 1965 to 1980, patients in mental hospitals fell from 475,000 to 137,000, with many of those released ending up on the street.[11] There is agreement that many of these would be better off back in institutions, but current staff costs make this financially infeasible. National service, by providing low-level personnel for work in mental hospitals, would offer a way out. The alternative is to allow cities to become increasingly crowded with people incapable of taking care of themselves—and to make Americans increasingly callous toward the plight of the mentally ill on their doorstep.

• Throughout the country, policies seeking to place long-term welfare clients in job-training or work programs are clearly in the ascendancy. To be effective, these programs require a steady supply of day care. For instance, Massachusetts, whose program has received national attention as a model for getting people off welfare into stable jobs, spends more than half of its "employment-training" money on day care. Without a national youth program, there seems no way of absorbing the day-care costs that would be incurred if workfare programs were to be adopted nationwide.

• Every year, some 70,000 books in the Library of Congress crumble between their covers. At least 40 percent of the books in major research collections in the United States will soon be too fragile to handle. Preservation or microfilming of these collections is tedious and extremely labor intensive. Unless a national-service program soon comes to the rescue, we are destined to lose a large portion of our cultural and intellectual heritage.

The point of all this is simply that we the citizenry and our political leadership must be attuned to thinking of how national needs might be met through youth serving their country and community. National service must be understood as something different and apart from either market arrangements or conventional government delivery of services.

FOR AND AGAINST NATIONAL SERVICE

Many arguments have been advanced against national service. Here are a half-dozen of the most serious, in ascending order of difficulty:

- National service would displace gainfully employed workers.
- It would be difficult to find useful work for national servers.
- National-service work could be better performed by the market.
- National service would merely be a cover for a compulsory youth program or a military draft.
- Costs for a national-service system would be astronomical and its administration hopelessly complex.
- Unless national service is universal, it would aggravate already existing divisions in American society.

In responding to these objections, my intention is not to defend all types of national service but rather to keep the argument focused on the program presented in this book, a comprehensive, noncompulsory program embracing both civilian services and a citizen soldiery.

On the issue of job displacement, there is only one acceptable rejoinder: national service must be restricted to work that otherwise would not be performed. The whole rationale for national service is that it meets needs currently being filled by neither the marketplace nor the government. As noted, the Ford Foundation study calculated that there exist 3.5 million jobs not now being performed that nonspecialized one-year servers could fill.[12] Surely, then, a program involving 600,000 civilian slots could be managed so as to have a minimal effect on the regular workforce. We should also keep in mind that less than a tenth of the civilian servers would be assigned to state and local government agencies; large numbers would be placed in conservation work, nonprofit organizations, schools, and hospitals.

At bottom, the labor-substitution issue is more a political problem than anything else. For this reason, it is essential that organized labor be represented on administrative boards at the national, state, and local levels. Much as Franklin D. Roosevelt defused labor opposition to the Civilian Conservation Corps by appointing a labor leader to head it, labor must be allotted a substantial policymaking role in a national-service program. In an important sense, a national-service system could even help labor, for, by reducing unemployment, it would tighten the labor market, thereby enhancing union bargaining power in the long term.

A second argument against national service is, ironically, a partial contradiction of the first. Many detractors maintain that work in national service does not lead to "real" jobs. Such a complaint reflects a basic misconception about national service. It is not a jobs program and should never be defined as such. National service is rather performance of work as a citizenship duty, work of a high priority that otherwise would not get done. As I have tried to show, national service benefits its participants most when it is not defined as a jobs program. Work discipline, personal maturity, self-reliance, participation in a common civic enterprise—these are the qualities that help an individual find a job, and national service can play an important role in inculcating them. In this sense, civilian service could extend the character-building role often performed by the military.

This same objection sometimes comes repackaged in the laissez-faire view that young persons who could be earning more in gainful employment than in national service are somehow failing themselves. Such a view raises selfishness to a social virtue, allowing no room for such values as civic duty and community obligation. Why should work performed at market wages be considered intrinsically more useful than work undertaken for noneconomic rewards? Those willing to forego material gain in order to perform a civic service deserve to be commended, not reproached.

A third objection is that national service work could be more efficiently performed if left to the labor market. This view grows out of the conservative conviction that even the most well-intentioned intervention in the marketplace usually produces negative results. This is not a frivolous argument. But again, this perspective ignores the purpose of national service, which is to perform work neglected by the marketplace as well as by the government. National service is especially suited for work that can be done by nonspecialized workers. Indeed, to the degree that many human services—care for the infirm, aged, and mentally ill comes quickly to mind—require menial labor combined with compassion, short-term servers are better suited for them than the high-turnover, alienated workers who too often perform these tasks today, if they are performed at all.

A fourth argument against national service is that even a voluntary program would inevitably turn compulsory. This is a natural fear, especially when the system being proposed offers strong inducements—postservice educational and job-training benefits—to national servers that are not available to those youth who have not served (or are much restricted). I find singularly unpersuasive the view that only those who serve without any reward are truly worthy of being called national servers. Only the extraordinarily idealistic (or perhaps neurotic) would serve without any recompense whatsoever. Thus I have unabashedly constructed a program that rewards those who serve their country or community more than those who do not. But the transition from the voluntary system proposed here to a compulsory program would certainly be a momentous step—one that simply could not come about without widespread support. And, needless to say, such support would exist only if the voluntary program were widely viewed as a great success. It seems perverse, then, to argue against a voluntary national scheme on the grounds that it might prove too successful.

More to the point, perhaps, is the objection that a comprehensive national-service program could serve as a cover for reinstating a military draft. Indeed it might. But it is virtually unimaginable that a compulsory civilian program would be legislated (even presuming constitutional obstacles could somehow be overcome) prior to enactment of military conscription. If the draft were to come back, however, the prior existence of a voluntary system would surely create strong pressures to make the program compulsory, for men certainly, for women probably. But it seems silly to argue that any form of national service should be avoided simply because it might make a draft more palatable. Surely, a palatable draft is better than a nonpalatable one. Again, the possible success of a program ought not be used as an argument against it.

A fifth source of opposition to national service is found among critics who concentrate on administrative and budgetary problems. Certainly a mandatory program involving millions of young people could become a bureaucratic and financial nightmare. But the plan discussed here envisions a highly streamlined administration. Citizen soldiers would be absorbed into the existing armed forces with a minimum of organizational adjustment. Most civilian servers, too, would be assigned to existing institutions—nonprofit organizations, schools, hospitals, and government agencies. Of the remainder, nearly all would serve in conservation corps for which there is already extensive organizational experience allowing for ready expansion with economies of scale. The key, as has been emphasized throughout, is decentralization. Any scheme that would seek to impose a uniform system on a country as large and diverse as the United States would probably collapse of its own weight.

Nonetheless, it must be acknowledged that comprehensive national service will not come cheap. A 600,000-person program would cost $6 billion in federal funds—and that is not taking into account the $9 billion in federal student assistance that would eventually be transferred into benefits for civilian servers. Another billion dollars or so would have to come from state and local governments and sponsoring agencies. The outlays are substantial; there is no getting around that fact.

Yet there are some weighty items on the other side of the ledger. The introduction of a citizen-soldier track to the all-volunteer military would produce substantial savings in military personnel costs while strengthening our conventional forces. Anything that gets people out of the American underclass will lead to long-term reductions in costs associated with welfare, unemployment, and crime. National service also means savings in the impending costs of meeting the needs of an increasingly older and infirm population, costs that otherwise would decimate family savings and stagger the federal budget. Beyond such bookkeeping exercises, though, it is important to keep the cost issue in perspective. During the peak years of the World War II GI Bill, annual outlays came to over $40 billion in today's money. Consider, then, that total costs for a national-service program would be less than half of the initial GI Bill.

I have saved for the last the most damaging of all objections to national service. Ironically, it is the one that opponents are least likely to mention, perhaps because they view it less as a drawback than a saving grace. National service could conceivably replicate—if not exacerbate—the class and racial divisions within American society. Whatever the legal and practical questions about compulsory service, there is one powerful argument in its favor—social equity. In the words of a sociologist at a conference in 1971:

A voluntary national service program would probably evolve into a two-track system; a lower one trying to "salvage" poverty-scarred youth, and a higher one offering upper-middle-class youth a channel to resolve identity crises through altruistic endeavors. . . . Those national server programs that would appeal to upper-middle-class college youth on a voluntary basis could easily turn into new forms of institutional elitism. . . . At the same time, national service programs directed toward lower-class youth would be quickly defined for what they are—welfare schemes in new guises. . . . Any effective national service program will necessarily require coercion to insure that all segments of the American class structure will serve.[13]

I am very familiar with this harsh indictment of voluntary national service because those words are my own! I now find myself in the awkward situation of rebutting my own former position. To start with, the comprehensive program that I have outlined here is much more inclusive than any other voluntary program ever put forth. Also, my linchpin proposal to give priority, and eventually sole eligibility, for postsecondary school benefits to national servers is a qualitative leap from any other volunteer scheme. My fear at the time I wrote the words quoted above—that the prevailing youth philosophy would only reinforce the existing split between elite Peace Corps/VISTA participants and poor Job Corps enrollees—anticipated what actually came to pass in the 1970s.

The critical point is that sharing the obligations of citizenship will act as a solvent for most of the differences among the various kinds of national servers. That all participants will be living at subsistence levels and that all will be eligible for postservice benefits underscore the egalitarianism of the national-service program. Precisely because large numbers of youth from across the social spectrum would participate—if not shoulder-to-shoulder, then under one large umbrella—invidious stereotyping would be kept to a minimum, bringing about much the same leveling effect that has traditionally occurred among military members.

NATIONAL SERVICE AND
THE NATIONAL SCHISM

Until now, the discussion has focused on the most tangible consequences of national service: the value of the service per-

formed for society and the benefits to the server. Now as we
approach the conclusion, I would like to advance the argument
by turning to the potential impact of national service on American
society as a whole.

The Vietnam War created a division in America that continues
to haunt us. Research findings on elite attitudes toward domestic
and international affairs present a picture of a divided and confused national leadership.[14] The social and political crises that
began to shake American society in the 1960s destroyed, among
other things, an illusion of civic homogeneity that the American
establishment had once fervently embraced. Historians experi-
encing this national self-doubt began to see in the American
past the same failures and divisions they could see in the present.
Modern American historiography reflects a disintegration of the
civic sense.[15] Little wonder that among the public at large, confidence in American institutions dropped precipitously.[16]

The division and confusion will intensify as the generation
that came of political age in the 1960s completes its march
through America's institutions and becomes our country's leadership, as will happen before the end of this century. The Vietnam
generation takes in not only the three million Americans who
fought in the war but those who vehemently opposed it and
the millions of others for whom the conflict was the formative
experience.[17] It is a generation divided not only by America's
role in Vietnam, nor even by America's foreign policy in general,
but by the very essence of American society.

A consequence of the Vietnam War is a national schism that
has produced a generation with two distinct political cultures,
each with its own heroes and villains, political vocabularies,
and, not least, different assumptions about on what side of history
the American nation is to be found. In short, the Vietnam generation embodies within itself the breakdown of civic consensus
that has afflicted American society since the 1960s. Whatever
the list of prerequisites for a republican democracy to flourish,
a failure to reconcile an emerging leadership generation to itself
augurs ill for the future.

National service can help to reconcile the contending factions
within the Vietnam generation. By joining military and civilian
activities under the single standard of civic duty, the Vietnam
generation can come to terms with itself. The two contending
cultures might never truly acknowledge the legitimacy of each

other's case, but they could at least join forces in creating a system designed to nurture good citizenship in future generations. On one side, the high-minded must be willing to recognize the basic need for military service; on the other, the tough-minded must accept the value of civilian service. The inauguration of national service provides a way for our nation to put the Vietnam War behind us and look instead toward building a common civic framework.

While we must be wary of nostalgia for civic perfections that never existed, we must confront openly the question of how to revive citizenship in a technological and bureaucratic society. Words like fraternity and community are so soaked in sentimentalism as to become almost useless as guides to the real possibility of democratic citizenship in tomorrow's America. Modern life has changed the possible forms of civic solidarity, but not the necessity for it.

The civic philosophy underlying national service takes a unique view of the relationship between rights and duties. In 1961, John F. Kennedy, in a one-sided call for citizen duties, proclaimed, "Ask not what your country can do for you, but what you can do for your country." By the 1970s, the Democratic party had turned this admonition on its head. "Ask what your country can do for you," liberals proclaimed, "but not what you can do for your country." In the 1980s, the age of laissez-faire Republicans, the mood was: "Ask neither what your country can do for you nor what you can do for your country." National service conceives a much more balanced approach to citizenship. "Ask what your country can do for you," it urges, "and what you can do for your country."

Appendix

National Service in Other Countries

Cross-national comparisons are a risky business, but with due caution insights can be gained by examining programs of youth service outside of the United States. This appendix will look briefly at Britain, Canada, and the Federal Republic of Germany, three countries where programs of youth service have features that can enhance understanding of national service in our own country.

Britain. Any discussion of national service in Great Britain begins, and almost ends, with Alec Dickson, probably the world's most forceful proponent of national service with followers in fifteen countries.[1] Dickson's involvement extends back to before World War II, when, as a fledgling journalist, he began doing voluntary work among poor young people in England and among refugees from Nazi Germany on the Continent. During the war, Dickson served as an officer with the British Army helping to establish the East Africa Command Mobile Education Unit, a pioneering use of selected African soldiers to be educators among their own people. In 1950, Dickson founded a citizenship and leadership training center in Nigeria; based on Outward Bound principles of self-reliance, it continues to operate into the present day.

In 1958 Dickson founded and was the first director of the Voluntary Service Overseas (VSO), Britain's equivalent to (and forerunner of) the Peace Corps. Dickson contrasts the low overhead and direct-service structure of VSO with the prevailing model of international agencies with their huge staffs, such as UNESCO (for which Dickson once worked in Iraq). VSO in the 1980s had about 1,000 volunteers serving in twenty or so countries. Volunteers are typically young persons delaying their

183

entry to universities. They are paid subsistence wages by agencies, public or private, in the countries in which they serve; in most cases these agencies are recipients of foreign aid from either the British government or international voluntary associations. Despite its relative success, VSO never made quite the splash in Britain that the Peace Corps did in the United States—a source of continuing disappointment to Dickson.

For youth at home, Dickson in 1962 founded the Community Service Volunteers (CSV). Today, about 2,000 young people are enrolled in CSV at any one time, usually serving six-month or one-year terms on a full-time basis. They receive subsistence wages paid for through government funds. Activities cover a broad range of human services such as teaching the physically handicapped, assisting in shelters for the homeless, working with former mental patients and prisoners, and operating a battered wives' center. Although the service content has been a constant, the CSV has gone through three phases. In the 1960s the CSV was mainly an activity for elite youth. In the 1970s, CSV began to use young offenders in release programs to carry out volunteer activities; this also brought relief to the CSV budget with an infusion of funds from the corrections system. In the 1980s, Dickson was moving the CSV to become more a part of a "Study-Service" program in which students will take time out to do good works as a supplement to their formal education.

The hallmark of CSV is that each volunteer serves in an individually tailored capacity. CSV is nothing more than a small office that matches agencies with an individual volunteer's interests and talents. How much of CSV would survive Dickson's personal involvement is hard to tell, but it is a model of a low-overhead operation that could be a component within a larger program of national service in this country.

Canada. For years, Canada was home to a program closely watched by national-service enthusiasts in the United States.[2] In 1977 the Canadian government inaugurated a national youth service called Katimavik (an Inuit word meaning "meeting place"). Before its termination in 1986, the program was host to some 20,000 participants. The program had a dual purpose: one, to provide community service, and two, to help young Canadians develop a sense of national cultural identity. Volunteers, who had to be single and between the ages of seventeen and twenty-three, served for nine months. The term was divided into trimesters, each spent living in different regions of the country, two English-speaking and one French-speaking. Participants were assigned to twelve-person groups, the members of which were selected by computer to insure a proper mix on the basis of sex, region, and most importantly, language. Volunteers received a dollar a day for pocket money and a $1,000 honorarium at the end of the nine-month program.

The typical volunteer was a recent secondary school graduate, though about one in five had some college or university education.

The groups lived in "Katimavik houses," usually rented dwellings in residential neighborhoods. Responsible for housekeeping and meals, each unit had to live within a set budget. The groups were headed by full-time staff members, but the involvement of these supervisors diminished over the course of the trimester as the volunteers assumed more and more responsibilities. The code of conduct was simple: no drugs or alcohol in violation of the law, no sexual relations with other Katimavik volunteers, and everyone doing a fair share of the workload. Attrition rates were about one in four, very low by youth corps standards.

Service projects were a mixture of physical work, mostly renovating public facilities, and social work performed while on assignment to local agencies. There was some tendency, however, for the social work to be reduced to minor clerical tasks, and for the physical work at social-service agencies to count as social service. Still, all in all, the service experience was favorably described by the volunteers. Also, despite an overall lack of accountability of work performed, the efforts of the volunteers were generally well regarded by the agency sponsors and local people.

One very distinctive feature of Katimavik was a "military option" that 10 percent of the participants were allowed to take. The Katimavik rule of an equal sex ratio applied to the military as well as the civilian options. The sponsor in this case was the Department of National Defense. Under this option one trimester could be spent at a military base where Katimavik participants were housed as a separate group and given an accelerated basic military training. By all accounts, the military option was very popular among those who participated, and the number of applicants always exceeded the available openings.

The Katimavik experience provides a number of important lessons. First, there is the rather obvious one that programs that are basically middle class can operate with less supervision of volunteers than those targeted toward "at-risk" youth. Second, and important for political realities, is that a national-service program with multiple objectives creates a fuzzy public image. Katimavik emphasized, with different weights at different times, personal development, group living, delivery of social services, physical work, and fostering a sense of a common Canadian identity. The vagueness, and maybe the inconsistency, of these goals made Katimavik vulnerable to the budgetary cutbacks that brought it down. Finally, military and civilian expressions of national service need not be exclusive. The Katimavik military option was an original and constructive innovation that emphasized an underlying civic content in both civilian and military service.

The Federal Republic of Germany. The link between civilian and military service as a citizenship obligation is most clear in the Federal Republic of Germany.[3] Since the introduction of conscription in 1957, young Germans have been able to choose civilian service in lieu of military service, even without having to commit to conscientious objection. In place of the normal fifteen-month service of the draftee, a young man can choose instead to serve three years with the police or border patrol, two years with an overseas Peace Corps-type program, or to make a part-time and unpaid commitment to civil defense and disaster relief over a ten-year period.

Even though West Germany allows alternative service without conscientious objection, it has also set up a liberal and unique civilian-service system for objectors as well. A 1983 law established conscientious objection as a largely pro forma matter. In most cases, applicants receive objector status by filling out the appropriate forms and making a written declaration. No longer does an applicant have to appear in person before a board that seeks to "read his heart." Also, the law shifted administration of conscientious objectors from the German army to the Federal Ministry of Youth, Family Affairs and Health. Under the 1983 law, however, objectors must serve in alternative civilian service, *Zivildienst*, for a term one-third longer than that for military service. In 1987, that came to twenty months of service—five more than for the draftee.

The easing of conscience standards under the new law has resulted in a substantial increase in conscientious objectors. The proportion of objectors among those eligible for conscription has gone from 10 percent in 1982 to 15 percent in 1985. In absolute numbers, objectors have grown from 17,000 in 1975 to 34,000 in 1980 to 57,000 in 1985. That *Zivildienst* is longer than military service has been accepted with relatively little dispute. West Germany has seen no serious appearance of absolute noncooperation among conscientious objectors, though this behavior is sometimes advocated by antiwar and antinuclear groups. One idea receiving attention, however, is called *Aktion Koffer packen*—"suitcase-packing action"—in which conscientious objectors would simply leave their alternative assignment at the end of the equivalent of a draftee's term of service.

Zivildienst has come to play an integral role in the delivery of human services in West Germany. Virtually all objectors are assigned to social service work: hospitals and sanitoriums, day care for the mentally and physically incapacitated, the ambulance corps, nursing homes for the aged, and other assignments in welfare, social work, and church agencies. Most conscientious objectors work near their homes in positions arranged with local sponsoring agencies (and approved by the authorities). Compensation is more or less the same as that for the military draftee. Alternative servers in Germany are prohibited from the whole range of work in environmental conservation and pollution control. The official reason is that it would meet with trade union resistance; a cardinal principle of *Zivildienst* is that it must not displace regular workers. But the authorities may also not want to bring together large groups of young people in environmental work, many of whom support the "Greens," the antiestablishment political movement. By scattering civilian servers throughout the country's social agencies, the system can better manage its potential dissidents.

From the organizational standpoint, the sheer size of the *Zivildienst* is impressive. Even so, despite the large increase in conscientious objection, the 69,000 positions open for *Zivildienst* in 1985 exceeded the number of available servers by 12,000. *Zivildienst* is a striking example of providing social services outside either the marketplace or conventional governmental bureaucracies. That so many useful service occupations could be found in a society already seemingly well covered by a welfare system is noteworthy. In the United States, a program of proportionate magnitude would have 280,000 civilian positions in social services.

From the standpoint of civic content, West Germany has succeeded in establishing alternative service as a de facto equivalent to military service, at least in peacetime. Under the 1983 legislation, the credibility of an applicant's decision of conscience shifted from religious beliefs to his readiness to render civilian service. What makes the German case so relevant is that it reflects the farthest extent any nation has come in making formal equivalences between military and civilian forms of national service, a harbinger of what may come to pass in our own country.

Notes

Chapter One

1. A 1985 survey of single-term army veterans (all entered the service in the 1980s) found that 83 percent reported "very positive" or "positive" attitudes toward the army experience. *The 1985 Army Experience Survey: Tabular Descriptions of First-Term Separatees*, Vol. 2. (Rockville, Md.: Westat, Inc., January 1986), p. E108. Somewhat more surprising, the most sophisticated study of veterans who had fought in Vietnam found the veterans were five times more likely to describe their military experience in positive (56 percent) than negative (11 percent) terms. Josefina J. Card, *Lives After Vietnam* (Lexington, Mass.: Lexington Books, 1983), pp. 119–41. Anecdotal evidence from former Peace Corps volunteers indicate the service experience is a life-shaping one. Keven Lowther and C. Payne Lucas, *Keeping Kennedy's Promise* (Boulder, Col.: Westview, 1978); Gerard T. Rice, *The Bold Experiment: JFK's Peace Corps* (Notre Dame, Ind.: University of Notre Dame Press, 1985); Coates Redmon, *Come As You Are: The Peace Corps Story* (New York: Harcourt Brace Jovanovich, 1986).

I cannot prove this hypothesis, but I believe that one serious problem facing many young people in contemporary America is that they start off too high on the materialistic ladder upon leaving school. This means that future progression is deemed too little, leading to an eventual feeling of "topping out" too early. Thus an important though latent benefit of national service for young people might be the sense of upward mobility after a period of deprivation for a good cause. National service, that is, could offer itself as an antidote for the too-much-too-soon quality of contemporary American youth. I am grateful for this insight to John J. Mearsheimer, University of Chicago.

2. Robert Nozick, *Anarchy, State, and Utopia* (New York: Basic Books, 1974); and John Rawls, *A Theory of Justice* (Cambridge, Mass.: Harvard University Press, 1971).

3. Michael J. Sandel, *Liberalism and the Limits of Justice* (New York: Cambridge University Press, 1982).

4. William M. Sullivan, *Reconstruction of Public Philosophy* (Berkeley: University of California Press, 1982).

5. Ibid., p. 158.

6. Sandel, *Liberalism and the Limits of Justice*, p. 179.

7. In addition to Sandel and Sullivan, see Carole Pateman, *The Problem of Political Obligation* (New York: John Wiley, 1979); Jennifer L. Hochschild, *What's Fair? American Beliefs about Distributive Justice* (Cambridge, Mass.: Harvard University Press, 1981); Harold Margolis, *Selfishness, Altruism, and Rationality* (New York: Cambridge University Press, 1982); and Larry R. Churchill, *Rationing Health Care in America: Perceptions and Principles of Justice* (Notre Dame, Ind.: University of Notre Dame Press, 1987). Also relevant is Alisdair MacIntyre, *After Virtue* (Notre Dame, Ind.: University of Notre Dame Press, 1981).

Movement toward a communitarian philosophy is also evident among sociologists. See Morris Janowitz, "Observations on the Sociology of Citizenship: Obligations and Rights," *Social Forces* 59, no. 1 (September 1980), pp. 1–24; Irving Louis Horowitz, "Human Rights, Foreign Policy, and the Social Sciences," in Center for Study of the American Experience, *Rights and Responsibilities* (Los Angeles: University of Southern California Press, 1980), pp. 167–80; Edward Shils, *Tradition* (Chicago: University of Chicago Press, 1981); and Philip Selznick, "The Idea of a Communitarian Morality," *California Law Review* 75, no. 1 (January 1987), pp. 445–63. A direct connection between social cohesion and national service is given in Amitai Etzioni, *An Immodest Agenda: Rebuilding America Before the 21st Century* (New York: McGraw-Hill, 1983); see also Etzioni, *Towards Higher Education in an Active Society* (New York and Washington, D.C.: Center for Policy Research, 1970).

8. Benjamin R. Barber, *Strong Democracy* (Berkeley: University of California Press, 1984).

9. Ibid., p. 298.

10. Michael Walzer, *Spheres of Justice* (New York: Basic Books, 1983).

11. Morris Janowitz, *The Reconstruction of Patriotism* (Chicago: University of Chicago Press, 1983).

12. The absence of religious values in the polity and the consequent decline of community and civic responsibility in America are variously discussed in Richard John Neuhaus, *The Naked Public Square* (Grand Rapids, Mich.: William B. Erdmans, 1984); John P. Diggins, *The Lost Soul of American Politics* (New York: Basic Books, 1985); Robert N. Bellah, Richard Madsen, William M. Sullivan, Ann Swidler, and Steven

M. Tipton, *Habits of the Heart* (Berkeley: University of California Press, 1985). Stanley R. Arzo, Harvard Divinity School, is completing a study on how Christian social ethics can be a basis for national service.

13. On the erosion of support for political institutions and the decline of voting, see Samuel P. Huntington, "The United States," in Michael J. Crozier, Samuel P. Huntington, and Joji Watanuki, *The Crisis of Democracy* (New York: New York University Press, 1985), pp. 59–118; Walter Dean Burnham, *The Current Crisis in American Politics* (New York: Oxford University Press, 1982); and Paul Kleppner, *Who Voted?* (New York: Praeger, 1982).

14. In 1981, for example, the federal government lost an estimated $81 billion in tax cheating. Department of the Treasury, Internal Revenue Service, *Income Tax Compliance Research: Estimates for 1973–1981* (Washington, D.C.: Government Printing Office, 1983).

15. Alexander W. Astin, Kenneth C. Green, and William S. Korn, *The American Freshman: Twenty Year Trends* (Los Angeles: Higher Education Research Institute, University of California, Los Angeles, 1987). See also Frank Newman, *Higher Education and the American Resurgence* (Princeton, N.J.: Carnegie Foundation for the Advancement of Teaching, 1985), pp. 36–40; and Arthur Levine, *When Dreams and Heroes Died: A Portrait of Today's College Student* (San Francisco: Jossey-Bass, 1983). The newsletter, *Character*, issued by Edward A. Wynne, University of Illinois at Chicago, gives continuous coverage on the absence of values in policies affecting American youth.

16. James M. Glass, *Delusion: Internal Dimensions of Political Life* (Chicago: University of Chicago Press, 1982).

17. The most influential work in the school of decline is Paul Kennedy, *The Rise and Fall of the Great Powers* (New York: Random House, 1987). See also David P. Calleo, *Beyond American Hegemony* (New York: Basic Books, 1987); and Walter Russell Mead, *Mortal Splendor: The American Empire in Transition* (Boston: Houghton Mifflin, 1987).

18. Seymour Martin Lipset and William Schneider, *The Confidence Gap* (New York: Free Press, 1983).

19. William James, "The Moral Equivalent of War," in *Essays on Faith and Morals* (New York: Longman, Greens, 1943), pp. 311–28 (originally published in 1910).

20. Ibid., p. 323.

21. For a discussion of James's pacifism, see Gerald E. Myers, *William James* (New Haven, Conn.: Yale University Press, 1986), pp. 435–45.

22. Men of love give pacifism a kind of justification, insofar as the human race cannot survive without the ideal of universal brotherhood,

no matter how impractical, and their effort is not in vain. The practice of pacifism through conscientious objection becomes possible only in a liberal democratic society. The conscientious objector, however, requires, in Philip Gold's valuable term, the conscientious consenter. Such a person decides to bear arms, not out of blind patriotism or obedience, but because he knows that while bloodshed is bad, it is not the ultimate evil. All through history people have accepted bloodshed for good cause. Defining what is good cause is the real problem. That some can decide to avoid bloodshed in all circumstances and at any price is possible only because conscientious consenters value the common good so highly as to risk their own existence on behalf of it. Philip Gold, *Evasions: The American Way of Military Service* (New York: Paragon, 1985).

Chapter Two

1. An excellent history of the American military within a societal context is Allan R. Millett and Peter Maslowski, *For the Common Defense* (New York: Free Press, 1984). See also Richard H. Kohn's insightful "The Social History of the American Soldier," *American Historical Review* 86, no. 3 (June 1981), pp. 553–67; and the essays in Peter Karsten, ed., *The Military in America* (New York: Free Press, 1986). The authoritative history of the army is Russell F. Weigley, *History of the United States Army* (Bloomington, Ind.: Indiana University Press, 1984).

Interestingly, Weigley holds that the history of the American army is a history of two armies—the regulars and reserves. On militia and reserve forces, see William H. Riker, *Soldiers of the States* (Washington, D.C.: Public Affairs Press, 1957); Jim Dan Hill, *The Minute Man in Peace and War* (Harrisburg, Pa.: Stackpole, 1964); Lawrence Delbert Cress, *Citizens in Arms* (Chapel Hill, N.C.: University of North Carolina Press, 1982); John K. Mahon, *History of the Militia and the National Guard* (New York: Macmillan, 1983); Richard B. Crossland and James T. Currie, *Twice the Citizen* (Washington, D.C.: Office of the Chief, Army Reserve, 1984); and Bennie J. Wilson, ed., *The Guard and Reserve in the Total Force* (Washington, D.C.: National Defense University Press, 1985).

For important works on the history and issues surrounding the citizen soldier (or his absence) in American society, see Marcus Cunliffe, *Soldiers and Civilians* (Boston: Little, Brown, 1968); Richard H. Kohn, *Eagle and Sword* (New York: Free Press, 1975); Robert K. Griffith, Jr., *Men Wanted for the U.S. Army* (Westport, Conn.: Greenwood Press, 1982); Elliot A. Cohen, *Citizens and Soldiers* (Ithaca, N.Y.: Cornell University Press, 1985); Philip Gold, *Evasions: The American Way of*

Military Service (New York: Paragon, 1985); and Edward M. Coffman, *The Old Army* (New York: Oxford University Press, 1986). Dated but still useful is Walter Millis, *Arms and Men* (New York: G.P. Putnam's Sons, 1956). The definitive treatment on the draft, and regrettably not yet out when I started this book, is John Whiteclay Chambers II, *To Raise an Army* (New York: Free Press, 1987).

2. *The Exercise of the Militia of the Province of Massachusetts Bay* (Boston, 1758), p. 3, quoted in Mahon, *History of the Militia and the National Guard*, p. 15.

3. Charles Royster, *A Revolutionary People at War* (Chapel Hill, N.C.: University of North Carolina Press, 1979). On how the War of Independence shaped armed forces and American society, see John Shy, *A People Numerous and Armed* (New York: Oxford University Press, 1976); and Don Higginbotham, *George Washington and the American Military Tradition* (Athens, Ga.: University of Georgia Press, 1985). The uniqueness of the citizen soldiery in America as early as the French and Indian War is described in Fred Anderson, *A People's Army* (Chapel Hill, N.C.: University of North Carolina Press, 1985).

4. Quoted in Cress, *Citizens in Arms*, p. 90.

5. On the Civil War draft, see Eugene C. Murdock, *One Million Men* (Westport, Conn.: Greenwood Press, 1980). Early on in the Civil War, the Confederacy instituted a conscription, the likes of which have seldom been seen in any nation. Nearly half of all adult white males went into the southern army. Toward the close of the war, consideration was even given to drafting slaves (who would be granted freedom after the war). Chambers, *To Raise an Army*, p. 46.

6. John McAuley Palmer, *Statesmanship or War* (Garden City, N.Y.: Doubleday, Page & Co., 1927); and *America in Arms* (New York: Arno, 1979; originally published in 1941). I am grateful to William R. Berkman, who gave me a photocopy of his personal copy of *Statesmanship or War*, a collector's item; and Richard B. Crossland, who kindly sent me his personal index of Palmer's unindexed books. The definitive and long-needed biography of Palmer and his impact on American military manpower thought is I. B. Holley, Jr., *General John M. Palmer, Citizen Soldiers, and the Army of a Democracy* (Westport, Conn.: Greenwood Press, 1982). See also Jonathan M. House, "John McAuley Palmer and the Reserve Components," in Wilson, ed., *The Guard and Reserve in the Total Force*, pp. 29–39; and Russell F. Weigley's critique of Palmer, in "Problems of the Thinking Man in Uniform," *Air University Review* (July-August 1984), pp. 93–96.

7. Holley, *General John M. Palmer*, p. 133.

8. Two fine books covering the Plattsburgers and their social milieu are John Garry Clifford, *The Citizen Soldiers* (Lexington, Ky.: University

Press of Kentucky, 1972); Michael Pearlman, *To Make Democracy Safe for America* (Urbana, Ill.: University of Illinois Press, 1984).

9. Clifford, *The Citizen Soldiers,* p. 277.

10. *New Republic* (October 9, 1915), pp. 247–49, as quoted in ibid., p. 195.

11. Gene M. Lyons and John W. Masland, *Education and Military Leadership: A Study of the ROTC* (Princeton, N.J.: Princeton University Press, 1959), p. 48.

12. J. Garry Clifford and Samuel R. Spencer, *The First Peacetime Draft* (Lawrence, Kan.: University Press of Kansas, 1986).

13. The best source for how military manpower was raised in World War II remains Robert R. Palmer, Bell I. Wiley, and William R. Keast, *United States Army in World War II: The Procurement and Training of Ground Combat Troops* (Washington, D.C.: Government Printing Office, 1948). See also: James S. Nanney and Terrence J. Gough, *U.S. Manpower Mobilization for World War II* (Washington, D.C.: U.S. Army Center of Military History, 1982); George Q. Flynn, *Lewis B. Hershey, Mr. Selective Service* (Chapel Hill, N.C.: University of North Carolina Press, 1985); and Lee Kennett, *G.I.* (New York: Charles Scribner's Sons, 1987), pp. 3–41.

14. John Morton Blum, *V Was for Victory* (New York: Harcourt Brace Jovanovich, 1976), pp. 141–43.

15. U.S. Advisory Commission on Universal Training, *Program for National Security* (Washington, D.C.: Government Printing Office, 1947). (Hereafter cited as "Compton Report.")

16. Ibid., p. 42.

17. Harry S. Truman, *Memoirs,* Vol. 1 (New York: Doubleday, 1951), p. 511.

18. Stephen M. Kohn, *Jailed for Peace* (Westport, Conn.: Greenwood Press, 1986), p. 6. For histories of conscientious objection, see also: Peter Brock, *Twentieth-Century Pacifism* (New York: Van Nostrand Reinhold, 1970); Charles DeBenedetti, *The Peace Reform in American History* (Bloomington, Ind.: Indiana University Press, 1980); National Interreligious Service Board for Conscientious Objectors, *Words of Conscience* (Washington, D.C.: NISBCO, 1983); Lawrence S. Wittner, *Rebels Against War* (Philadelphia: Temple University Press, 1984); and Caroline Moorehead, *Troublesome People* (London: Hamish Hamilton, 1987). My account of conscientious objection also relies on discussions with L. William Yolton and Charles Maresca of the National Interreligious Service Board for Conscientious Objectors.

19. Cited in Michael Walzer, *Obligations* (Cambridge, Mass.: Harvard University Press, 1970, p. 125).

20. Jehovah's Witnesses, although not pacifists from a strictly theological standpoint because of their plans to fight at Armageddon, will participate neither in any national military force nor in any form of alternative service.

21. Joseph F. Kett, *Rites of Passage: Adolescence in America 1790 to the Present* (New York: Basic Books, 1977); David I. MacLeod, *Building Character in the American Boy* (Madison, Wis.: University of Wisconsin Press, 1983).

22. Edward Bellamy, *Looking Backward* (New York: Modern American Library, 1951; originally published 1888). The totalitarian implications of Bellamy's vision is described in Warren Sloat, "Looking Back at 'Looking Backward': We have Seen the Future and It Didn't Work," *New York Times Book Review*, January 17, 1988, pp. 3–4.

23. William James, "The Moral Equivalent of War," in *Essays on Faith and Morals* (New York: Longman, Greens, 1943), pp. 311–28 (originally published 1910). James first presented his idea of the moral equivalent of war in a lecture given at Stanford University in 1906.

24. Ibid., p. 325.

25. Clifford, *The Citizen Soldiers*, p. 195.

26. Randolph Bourne, "A Moral Equivalent for Universal Military Service," in Martin Anderson, ed., *The Military Draft* (Stanford, Calif.: Hoover Institution Press, 1982; originally published in 1916), pp. 397–402.

27. Ibid., p. 400. For an early statement on national service that incorporates a feminist perspective, see Prestonia Mann Martin, *Prohibiting Poverty* (New York: Farrar and Rinehart, 1933).

28. Bourne, "A Moral Equivalent for Universal Military Service," p. 401.

29. The discussion on the New Deal youth programs draws from George P. Rawick, "The New Deal and Youth: The Civilian Conservation Corps and the National Youth Administration and the American Youth Congress," unpublished doctoral dissertation, University of Michigan, 1979; and Michael W. Sherraden, "The Civilian Conservation Corps," unpublished doctoral dissertation, University of Michigan, 1979.

30. On Eugen Rosenstock-Huessy and Camp William James, see Jack J. Preiss, *Camp William James* (Norwich, Vt.: Argo, 1978).

31. Eleanor Roosevelt was a keen supporter of civilian national service. In a "My Day" column in 1941, she wrote: "I feel that universal service should not be a question of military service alone. It should be a time when all boys and girls know they are giving a year of their lives to fit themselves better to serve their country." Quoted in ibid., p. 186.

32. Compton Report, p. 391.

33. Lewis L. Lorwin, *Youth Work Programs* (Washington, D.C.: American Council on Education, 1941), pp. 151–53.

34. Compton Report, p. 394.

35. Ibid., p. 396.

Chapter Three

1. Two excellent and recent accounts of the history of conscription in America are John Whiteclay Chambers II, *To Raise an Army* (New York: Free Press, 1987); and George Q. Flynn, *Lewis B. Hershey, Mr. Selective Service* (Chapel Hill, N.C.: University of North Carolina Press, 1985). Dated but still informative are James W. Davis, Jr., and Kenneth M. Dolbeare, *Little Groups of Neighbors: The Selective Service System* (Chicago: Markham, 1968); and Gary L. Wamsley, *Selective Service and a Changing America* (Columbus, Ohio: Ohio University Press, 1969). An annotated bibliography on the draft in American history is Martin Anderson, ed., *Conscription* (Stanford, Calif.: Hoover Institution Press, 1976); see also the compendium in Martin Anderson, ed., *The Military Draft* (Stanford, Calif.: Hoover Institution Press, 1982; orig. publ. 1916). On the draft in the late years of the Vietnam War, see Curtis W. Tarr, *By the Numbers: The Reform of the Selective Service System 1970–1972* (Washington, D.C.: National Defense University, 1981). The shift to the all-volunteer force is covered in Robert K. Griffith, Jr., "About Face? The U.S. Army and the Draft," *Armed Forces and Society* 12, no. 1 (Fall 1985), pp. 108–33. The long-term failure of the United States to come up with a durable policy of military service is insightfully addressed in Eliot A. Cohen, *Citizens and Soldiers* (Ithaca, N.Y.: Cornell University Press, 1985). See also Philip Gold, *Evasions: The American Way of Military Service* (New York: Paragon, 1985).

2. Cohen, *Citizens and Soldiers*, p. 249.

3. National Advisory Commission on Selective Service, *In Pursuit of Equity: Who Serves When Not All Serve?* (Washington, D.C.: Government Printing Office, 1967), p. 23.

4. William A. Strauss, *Chance and Circumstance* (New York: Alfred A. Knopf, 1978), remains the best description of the social differentiation in the Vietnam era between and among those who served and those who did not. For the period between World War II and the Vietnam War, see Albert D. Klassen, Jr., *Military Service in American Life Since World War II: An Overview* (Chicago: National Opinion Research Center, 1966).

5. See Michael Useem, *Conscription, Protest, and Social Conflict*

(New York: Wiley, 1983). G. David Curry, *Sunshine Patriots: Punishment and the Vietnam Offender* (Notre Dame, Ind.: University of Notre Dame Press, 1985), presents an analysis of Vietnam-era draft evaders and military deserters. Surveys of public opinion in 1972 at the height of the disillusionment with the Vietnam War showed that 95 percent believed Vietnam veterans "deserve respect for having served their country," and 83 percent disagreed when asked whether "the real heroes of the Vietnam War are the boys who refused induction and faced the consequences." U.S. Congress, Senate, Committee on Veterans' Affairs, *Source Material on the Vietnam Era Veteran*, 93rd Cong., 2d sess. (Washington, D.C.: Government Printing Office, 1974), pp. 632–34. See also *New York Times*, January 6, 1972, p. 10. In a 1979 poll, on a "respect" scale of 1 to 10, the public rated draft evaders 3.3; war protesters 5.0; TV newsmen 6.1; military medics 7.9; and combat veterans 9.8. Cited in *Christian Science Monitor*, November 10, 1987, p. 1.

6. On June 25, 1981, in *Rostker v. Goldberg*, the Supreme Court upheld male-only registration; the ruling was that the judiciary should defer to Congress on matters of military manpower and national defense. On the legal issues surrounding draft registration, see James B. Jacobs and Jeremy Travis, "Compliance Strategies for Draft Registration," *Arizona Law Review* 27, no. 4 (1985), pp. 837–70; and James B. Jacobs and Dennis McNamara, "Selective Service Without a Draft," in Jacobs, *Socio-Legal Foundations of Civil-Military Relations* (New Brunswick, N.J.: Transaction, 1986), pp. 91–110.

7. The President's Commission on an All-Volunteer Force (Gates Commission), *Report of the President's Commission on an All-Volunteer Force* (Washington, D.C.: Government Printing Office, 1970).

8. The conflict between institutional and occupational conceptions of modern military service are discussed fully in Charles C. Moskos and Frank R. Wood, eds., *The Military—More Than Just a Job?* (Elmsford Park, N.Y.: Pergamon-Brassey's, 1988).

9. The data reported here are gathered from the semiannual reports of the director of selective service from the years 1955 to 1972 (Washington, D.C.: Government Printing Office). For useful treatment of conscientious objection in modern America, see Peter Brock, *Twentieth-Century Pacifism* (New York: Van Nostrand Reinhold, 1970); Charles DeBenedetti, *The Peace Reform in American History* (Bloomington, Ind.: Indiana University Press, 1980); and Stephen M. Kohn, *Jailed for Peace* (Westport, Conn.: Greenwood Press, 1986). Invaluable is the newsletter *The Reporter for Conscience' Sake* issued by the National Interreligious Service Board of Conscientious Objectors (NISBCO).

10. Letter to author from Assistant Judge Advocate General for Civil Law, dated April 25, 1985.

11. A complete description of the alternative service offices and their functions is found in Selective Service System, "Chapter 15: Alternative Service" and "Chapter 18: Alternative Service Worker Travel," *Registrant Information and Management Systems Manual* (Washington, D.C.: Government Printing Office, 1983).

12. For reviews of the legal, theological, and philosophical issues surrounding selective conscientious objection, see Ralph Potter, "Conscientious Objection to Particular Wars," in Donald A. Giannella, ed., *Religions and the Public Order* (Ithaca, N.Y.: Cornell University Press, 1969), pp. 44–99; Kent Greenwalt, "All or Nothing at All: The Defeat of Selective Conscientious Objection," in Philip B. Kurland, ed., *The Supreme Court Review* (Chicago: University of Chicago Press, 1971), pp. 31–197; Eileen P. Flynn, *My Country Right or Wrong? Selective Conscientious Objection in the Nuclear Age* (Chicago: Loyola University Press, 1985).

13. The literature on the Peace Corps is quite voluminous considering the relatively small size of the agency. Most useful are Gerard T. Rice, *Twenty Years of the Peace Corps* (Washington, D.C.: Government Printing Office, 1981); and Gerard T. Rice, *The Bold Experiment: JFK's Peace Corps* (Notre Dame, Ind.: University of Notre Dame Press, 1985). See also Harlan Cleveland, *The Future of the Peace Corps* (Aspen, Col.: Aspen Institute for Humanistic Studies, 1977); Kevin Lowther and C. Payne Lucas, *Keeping Kennedy's Promise* (Boulder, Col.: Westview, 1978); Coates Redmon, *Come as You Are: The Peace Corps Story* (New York: Harcourt Brace Jovanovich, 1986); and Milton Viorst, ed., *Making a Difference: The Peace Corps at Twenty-Five* (New York: Weidenfeld and Nicolson, 1987). A negative view of the Peace Corps philosophy is found in Howard J. Wiarda, "Ethnocentrism and Third World Development," *Society* 24, no. 6 (September-October 1987), pp. 55–64.

14. There is some dispute as to who actually conceived the idea of the Peace Corps. In 1957, Representative Henry Reuss, Democrat of Wisconsin, suggested that a "Youth Corps" be part of the foreign aid program. Democratic Senator Hubert Humphrey of Minnesota came up with a similar idea at about the same time. In 1960, Reuss proposed legislation in the House to finance a study of the "Youth Corps" concept. Also in 1960 Humphrey introduced a Senate bill calling for establishment of a "Peace Corps," the first use of that name in a public forum, of young volunteers who would work in underdeveloped countries. Rice, *The Bold Experiment*, pp. 10–11. Another source, however, credits retired General James M. Gavin with coining the name "Peace Corps" for Kennedy's consideration. Redmon, *Come as You Are*, p. 17.

15. A critical commentary on Sam Brown's term as head of the Peace Corps from a former Peace Corps volunteer and leading Peace Corps supporter is Roger Landrum, "Any Future for the Peace Corps?" *Washington Post*, May 14, 1978, p. 16.

16. That the opposition to Thomas Pauken heading ACTION was in large part generated by "antisoldierism" among youth corps proponents is convincingly argued in James Fallows, "The Vietnam Generation," *Atlantic* (July 1981), pp. 19–23. This is a fascinating account of different political cultures of civilian versus military servers.

17. President's Study Group on a National Service Program, "Information on a Proposed National Service Program," 1962. The study group, chaired by Attorney General Robert Kennedy, made explicit recommendations for the training, administration, and budget of a voluntary youth corps. President Kennedy expressed his appreciation of the report and said that he would take steps to enact legislation establishing a "national service program." Memorandum dated February 18, 1963.

18. The literature on VISTA is relatively sparse, certainly as compared to that of the Peace Corps. The best single source is VISTA, *Volunteers in Service to America, 1980 Report* (Washington, D.C.: Government Printing Office, 1981). See the hilarious but true account of VISTA service given by Jonathan Rowe, "I Was a Spear Carrier in the War on Poverty," *Washington Monthly*, November 1984, pp. 38–42.

19. Sam Brown's tenure as head of ACTION is criticized in Joseph Nocera, "Sam Brown and the Peace Corps: All Talk, No Action," *Washington Monthly*, July-August 1978, pp. 28–40.

20. U.S. Congress, House, Subcommittees of the Committee on Government Operations and the Committee on Education and Labor, *Joint Hearing*, 97th Cong., 2d sess., June 9, 1982, p. 149.

21. Cited in Michael W. Sherraden, "The Civilian Conservation Corps," unpublished doctoral dissertation, University of Michigan, 1979, p. 10.

22. There is no full-scale study of youth conservation corps of the 1970s, but see U.S. Congress, House, Subcommittee on Public Lands and National Parks of the Committee on Interior and Insular Affairs, *Public Land Management Policy*, Hearings, 97th Cong., 1st sess., 1981. Useful are David E. Nye, *The History of the Youth Conservation Corps* (Washington, D.C.: Government Printing Office, 1980); Department of the Interior and Department of Agriculture, *Youth Conservation Corps: Tenth Anniversary Report* (Washington, D.C.: Government Printing Office, 1980).

23. Ibid., p. 46.

24. See Jack McElroy, "History of the Young Adult Conservation Corps," unpublished document, 1980; and P/PV, *Youth Corps Profiles: The Young Adult Conservation Corps* (Philadelphia: Public/Private Ventures, 1986), pp. 7–40.

25. *New York Times*, March 12, 1983, p. 22.

Chapter Four

1. Each of the youth corps discussed in detail in this chapter has been visited by the writer. I am indebted to the courtesies extended and candid information given to me by William C. Basl, Robert Burckhardt, Jr., James Davis, Gregory Farrell, John F. Grix, Elizabeth Halas, Edgar Hinton, W. E. "Cisco" Hunter, Harvey Morrison, Ralph A. Romeo, Kelly Ross, and Carl Weisbrod. Every researcher on this topic is indebted to the annual profiles of conservation and youth service corps issued by the Human Environment Center of Washington, D.C. A series of evaluation studies of state, county, and city youth corps has been undertaken by Public/Private Ventures (P/PV), a Philadelphia policy analysis center concerned with youth employment and training. The P/PV studies form the bedrock of most of our quantitative information about local youth corps. See *The State Youth Initiatives Project: The California Conservation Corps*, December 1982; *Youth Corps Case Studies: The Marin Conservation Corps*, January 1985; *The California Conservation Corps: A Report on Implementation*, October 1985; *The California Conservation Corps: An Analysis of Participant Characteristics*, October 1985; *The California Conservation Corps: Assessing the Dollar Value of Its Work*, October 1985; *Youth Corps Case Studies: The San Francisco Conservation Corps Interim Report*, April 1986; *The California Conservation Corps: A Report on Attrition*, December 1986; *Youth Corps Case Studies: The New York City Volunteer Corps, Interim Report*, October 1986; *Youth Corps Profiles: The Young Adult Conservation Corps, the Wisconsin Conservation Corps, the Michigan Civilian Conservation Corps, the Texas Conservation Corps*, December 1986; *The California Conservation Corps: An Analysis of Short-term Impacts on Participants*, June 1987; *Youth Corps Assessment Project: Sources of Funding*, June 1987 (all Philadelphia: Public/Private Ventures).

2. *Los Angeles Times*, July 23, 1981, as cited in P/PV, *The State Youth Initiatives Project: The California Conservation Corps*, p. 4.

3. Ibid., p. 18.

4. In 1987, owing to budget constraints, the Marin Conservation Corps dropped its specialized work crews.

5. Prepared statement of Edward Koch submitted to U.S. Congress, House Subcommittee on Employment Opportunities of the Committee

on Education and Labor, *The Voluntary National Youth Service Act and the Select Commission on National Service Opportunities Act of 1985,* Hearings, 99th Cong., 1st sess., 1985, p. 32.

6. The account of Seattle's Program for Local Service is based on interviews with Donald J. Eberly, the director of the program during its existence from 1973 to 1977.

7. On Youth Community Service in Syracuse, see the report given in U.S. Congress, House, Subcommittee on Select Education of the Commission on Education and Labor, *Select Commission on Voluntary Service Opportunities Act,* Hearings, 97th Cong., 2d. sess., 1982, pp. 538–608.

8. Ibid., p. 597.

9. The account of the Guardian Angels is based on interviews with Curtis Sliwa, observations and talks with Guardian Angels on patrol, and the insights of sociologist Joseph L. Albini, Wayne State University, who has been a longtime observer of the Guardian Angels.

10. P/PV, *The California Conservation Corps: Assessing the Dollar Value of Its Work,* is a good effort to assess the issues involved in determining the cost/benefit ratio of work performed by conservation corps.

Chapter Five

1. William Julius Wilson, *The Truly Disadvantaged* (Chicago: University of Chicago Press, 1987), is a compelling study of the connection between the underclass and unemployment.

No statistic is more misused than "youth unemployment," however. The often reported press figures mislead because they exclude the half of American teenagers and young adults who are full-time students or in the military. Still, a strikingly high number of young people have dropped out of the mainstream society in the sense that they are not legally working, not in school, and not in the military. Most alarming, the trends, especially among male youth, are in the wrong direction. In 1965, 7 percent of male blacks in the critical age range of twenty to twenty-four years were in the unemployed, nonschool, or nonmilitary category, against 4 percent of their white contemporaries. Twenty years later in 1985, the proportions were much higher for both blacks and whites, while the discrepancy between the races had become greater—22 percent among blacks, 9 percent of whites. And certainly the number is higher among inner-city youth than in the youth population at large. Data in this paragraph from Christopher Winship, Department of Sociology, Northwestern University.

2. General overviews of youth jobs and job-training programs are found in Arvil V. Adams and Garth L. Mangum, *The Lingering Crisis*

of Youth Unemployment (Kalamazoo, Mich.: W. E. Upjohn Institute, 1978); Charles L. Betsey, Robin G. Hollister, Jr., and Mary R. Papageorgiou, eds., *Youth Employment and Training Programs* (Washington, D.C.: National Academy Press, 1985); and Donald C. Baumer and Carl E. Van Horn, *The Politics of Unemployment* (Washington, D.C.: Congressional Quarterly, 1985).

3. No history of the Neighborhood Youth Corps has been written, but useful is Edwin Harwood, "Houston's Out-of-School Neighborhood Youth Corps," unpublished manuscript, Department of Anthropology and Sociology, Rice University, October 1968.

4. On public-service employment as jobs programs, see Robert F. Cook, Charles F. Adams, Jr., V. Lane Rawlins, and associates, *Public Service Employment* (Kalamazoo, Mich.: W. E. Upjohn Institute, 1985); Grace A. Franklin and Randall B. Ripley, *CETA: Politics and Policy, 1973–1982* (Knoxville, Tenn.: University of Tennessee Press, 1984).

5. On the Job Training Partnership Act, see Sar A. Levitan, "A Second Chance: Training for Jobs," *Youth Policy* 9, no. 10 (October 1987), pp. 8–11; Robert Guttman, "Job Training Partnership Act," *Monthly Labor Review* 106, no. 3 (March 1983), pp. 3–10.

6. On the Job Corps, see Sar A. Levitan and Benjamin H. Johnson, *The Job Corps: A Social Experiment That Works* (Baltimore: Johns Hopkins University Press, 1975); William Mirengood, Lester Rindler, Henry Greenspan, and Charles Harris, *CETA: Accomplishments, Problems, Solutions* (Kalamazoo, Mich.: W. E. Upjohn Institute, 1982); and "Job Corps in Brief," information paper of the Department of Labor, FY 1985.

7. Charles Mallar et al., *Evaluation of the Economic Impact of the Job Corps Program* (Princeton, N.J.: Mathematica Policy Research, Inc., 1982).

8. The description of the Youth Energy Corps (YEC) is based on interviews with youth enrollees and information provided by John Whalen and Howard Luckett.

9. The YEC principle of "No Work, No School" derives from the Smokey House Project. Started in 1987 in Vermont and funded by the Taconic Foundation, Smokey House pioneered in linking "hands-on work" in a nonschool setting with classroom instruction. The Smokey House precedent has since been followed by a dozen or so local youth programs aimed toward high school dropouts. No study of Smokey House exists, but useful is Jane Lee J. Eddy, "History of Smokey House Project," unpublished paper, no date (circa 1981).

10. A good analysis of the efforts of the Vera Institute of Justice to rehabilitate felons through service work is Douglas Corry McDonald, *Punishment Without Walls: Community Service Sentences in New York*

City (New Brunswick, N.J.: Rutgers University Press, 1986). See also *Status Report* (New York: Vera Institute of Justice, 1983).

11. Lawrence M. Mead, *Beyond Entitlement: The Social Obligations of Citizenship* (New York: Free Press, 1986).

12. Ibid., p. 43. For an informative exchange between Lawrence Mead and William Wilson, see "The Obligation to Work and the Availability of Jobs," in *Focus* 10, no. 2 (Summer 1987), pp. 11–20. Mead supports welfare legislation but also argues for a link between public benefits and work to maintain welfare programs; Wilson sees the main barriers facing the underclass as social isolation from the better-off and the decline of low-skilled jobs available to them. Wilson's argument is given in detail in his *The Truly Disadvantaged*.

13. Bernard Beck, "The Military as a Welfare Institution," in Charles C. Moskos, ed., *Public Opinion and the Military Establishment* (Beverly Hills, Calif.: Sage, 1971), pp. 137–48.

14. Franklin A. Thomas, *Youth Unemployment and National Service* (New York: Ford Foundation, 1983); and *National Service: An Aspect of Youth Development* (New York: Ford Foundation, 1984).

Chapter Six

1. Michael Pearlman, *To Make Democracy Safe for America* (Champaign, Ill.: University of Illinois Press, 1984), p. 176.

2. On the GI Bill of World War II, the best study remains Keith W. Olson, *The G.I. Bill, the Veterans, and the Colleges* (Lexington, Ky.: University Press of Kentucky, 1974). Precursors to the GI Bill included a World War I rehabilitation law that provided educational assistance for disabled veterans. Also, Wisconsin passed an "Educational Bonus Law" in 1919 that paid veterans $30 a month for four academic or vocational years of education. Ibid., p. 7.

3. Veterans Administration, *Historical Data on the Usage of Educational Benefits, 1944–1980* (Washington, D.C.: Government Printing Office, May 1981), p. 10.

4. Quoted in Diane Ravitch, *The Troubled Crusade: American Education 1945–1980* (New York: Basic Books, 1983), p. 13.

5. *Army Times*, November 22, 1974, p. 13.

6. In 1988, a soldier entering the army could receive $17,000 in postservice educational benefits for two years of service in the combat branches. About half of this was covered by the new GI Bill and half by the Army College Fund.

7. Numbers pertaining to those receiving loan forgiveness under the teaching provisions of the National Defense Student Loan Program

(1958–1972) and National Direct Student Loan program (1972–1987), since renamed Perkins Loans, were obtained from Robert Coates, Department of Education. Present provisions of Perkins Loans also allow up to 70 percent of cancellation for service as a Peace Corps or VISTA volunteer. For those doing military service, the Defense Department can repay a portion of the loan.

8. Adam Walinsky, Jonathan Rubinstein, et al., *The New Police Corps* (New York: Center for Research on Institutions and Social Policy Publication, 1983).

9. For background information on the National Health Service Corps, see "Legislative History of the National Health Service Corps," unpublished paper, no date (circa 1985); and "Program Fact Sheet: The National Health Service Corps," issued by Bureau of Health Care Delivery and Assistance, U.S. Department of Health and Human Services, no date (circa 1985).

10. Statement by Edward D. Martin, director, Bureau of Health Care Delivery and Assistance, before the Subcommittee on Energy, Nuclear Proliferation and Government Processes of the Committee on Governmental Affairs, U.S. Senate, April 12, 1984.

11. Spencer Rich, "Did Hippocrates Mention This?" *Washington Post*, February 4, 1986, p. 11.

12. On federal student aid to college students, the basic sources are the reports issued periodically on "Trends in Student Aid" by the Washington Office of the College Board. See also Susan H. Boren, *Authorizations of Appropriations, Budget Requests, Enacted Appropriations (Budget Authority) and Outlays for Federal Student Financial Aid Programs Administered by the Department of Education FY1965 through FY1988* (Washington, D.C.: Congressional Research Service, 1987). A lucid summary of a complicated system is Denis P. Doyle and Terry W. Hartle, "Student-Aid Muddle," *Atlantic* (February 1986), pp. 30–34.

13. For GSL figures, see Charlotte Jones Fraas, *The Guaranteed Student Loan Program: Current Status, Background, and Issues* (Washington, D.C.: Congressional Research Service, 1987); and Jane S. Hansen, *Student Loans: Are They Overburdening a Generation?*, report prepared for the Joint Economic Committee of the U.S. Congress, December 1986.

14. Ibid., p. 9.

15. On the legal and social ramifications of the Solomon Amendment and *Selective Service System* v. *Minnesota Public Interest Research Group* (1984), the Supreme Court decision that upheld the amendment, see James B. Jacobs and Jeremy Travis, "Compliance Strategies for Draft Registration," *Arizona Law Review* 27, no. 4 (1985), pp. 837–70.

16. Mortimer J. Adler, *The Paideia Proposal* (New York: Macmillan, 1982); Twentieth Century Fund Task Force on Federal Elementary and Secondary Education Policy, *Making the Grade* (New York: Twentieth Century Fund, 1983); National Commission on Excellence in Education, *A Nation at Risk: The Imperative for Educational Reform* (Washington, D.C.: Department of Education, 1983); Task Force on Education for Economic Growth, *Action for Excellence* (Denver: Education Commission for the States, 1983); Business–Higher Education Forum, *America's Competitive Challenge* (Washington, D.C.: Business–Higher Education Forum, 1983); National Science Board Commission on College Education in Mathematics, *Educating Americans for the 21st Century* (Washington, D.C.: National Science Foundation, 1984); John I. Goodlad, *A Place Called School* (New York: McGraw-Hill, 1984).

17. Ernest L. Boyer, *High School* (New York: Harper and Row, 1983).

18. Charles H. Harrison, *Student Service* (Princeton, N.J.: Carnegie Foundation for the Advancement of Teaching, 1987).

19. Panel on Youth for the President's Science Advisory Committee, *Youth: Transition to Adulthood* (Chicago: University of Chicago Press, 1972).

20. Ibid., pp. 171–73.

21. National Commission on Youth, *The Transition of Youth to Adulthood: A Bridge Too Long* (Boulder, Col.: Westview, 1980).

22. Ibid., p. 35.

23. Harrison, *Student Service*, pp. 63–65.

24. Frank Newman, *Higher Education and the American Resurgence* (Princeton, N.J.: Carnegie Foundation for the Advancement of Teaching, 1985).

25. Ibid., p. 31.

26. Ernest L. Boyer, *College* (New York: Harper and Row, 1987).

27. Although based at Brown University, Campus Compact is a project of the Education Commission of the States headquartered in Denver, Colorado.

28. Campus Compact information sheet, 1987. See also *Campus Compact Newsletter*, issued out of Brown University. I am grateful to Susan Stroud, director of Campus Compact, for providing additional information.

29. Wayne Meisel and Robert Hackett, *Building Movement: A Handbook for Students in Community Service* (Washington, D.C.: Campus Outreach Opportunity League, 1986). In 1987 Meisel served as COOL's executive director and Hackett as outreach director. COOL issues a periodic newsletter, *Campus Outreach*.

Chapter Seven

1. Gary Hart and Robert G. Torricelli, "Create a System of Universal National Service," *New York Times,* April 14, 1985, p. E23.

2. William R. King, *Achieving America's Goals: National Service or the All-Volunteer Armed Force?* Report to the Senate Committee on Armed Services, 95th Cong., 1st sess., February 1977.

3. Congressional Budget Office, *National Service Programs and Their Effects on Military Manpower and Civilian Youth Problems* (Washington, D.C.: Government Printing Office, 1978). See also Congressional Budget Office, *Costs of National Service Act (H.R. 2206): A Technical Analysis* (Washington, D.C.: Government Printing Office, 1980).

4. National Advisory Commission on Selective Service, *In Pursuit of Equity: Who Serves When Not All Serve?* (Washington, D.C.: Government Printing Office, 1967).

5. Ibid., pp. 61–63.

6. Office of the Assistant Secretary of Defense (Manpower, Reserve Affairs and Logistics), "America's Volunteers," Washington, D.C., mimeographed, December 31, 1978.

7. Ibid., p. 186.

8. Ibid., p. 169.

9. "Presidential Recommendations for Selective Service Reform," report to Congress prepared pursuant to P.L. 97–107, Washington, D.C., mimeographed, February 11, 1980, p. 62.

10. Ibid., p. 52.

11. Military Manpower Task Force, *A Report to the President on the Status and Prospects of the All-Volunteer Force* (Washington, D.C.: Government Printing Office, 1982), p. A13.

12. Charles L. Black, Jr., "Constitutional Problems in Compulsory National Service," *Yale Law Report* 13, no. 19 (Summer 1967), pp. 9–21. A reply to Black is Thomas J. McGrew, "The Constitutionality of Compulsory National Service," *St. Louis University Public Law Forum* 4 (1984), pp. 259–67. Supporting Black's view that compulsory national service would be unconstitutional is Philip Bobbitt, "National Service: Unwise or Unconstitutional?" in Martin Anderson, ed., *Registration and the Draft* (Stanford, Calif.: Hoover Institution Press, 1982), pp. 299–330. A more general overview of the issues of national service and their legal implications is James B. Jacobs, "Compulsory and Voluntary National Service: Analysis of the McCloskey Bill and Other Proposals," in Jacobs, *Socio-Legal Foundations of Civil-Military Relations* (New Brunswick, N.J.: Transaction, 1986), pp. 111–48.

13. Black, "Constitutional Problems in Compulsory National Service," p. 11.

14. Ibid., p. 20.

15. Committee on Federal Legislation, "The Constitutionality of a Mandatory Non-Military National Service Obligation," *The Record* (of the Association of the Bar of the City of New York) 40, no. 6 (November 1985), pp. 1–29.

Chapter Eight

1. For overviews of the pros and cons of the all-volunteer force, see John Keeley, ed., *The All-Volunteer Force and American Society* (Charlottesville, Va.: University of Virginia Press, 1978); Martin Anderson, ed., *Registration and the Draft* (Stanford, Calif.: Hoover Institution, 1982); Andrew J. Goodpaster, Lloyd H. Elliott, and J. Allan Hovey, Jr., eds., *Toward a Consensus on Military Service* (New York: Pergamon, 1982); Brent Scowcroft, ed., *Military Service in the United States* (Englewood Cliffs, N.J.: Prentice-Hall, 1982); Robert K. Fullinwider, ed., *Conscripts and Volunteers* (Totowa, N.J.: Rowman and Allanheld, 1983); and William Bowman, Roger Little, and G. Thomas Sicilia, eds., *The All-Volunteer Force After a Decade* (Elmsford, N.Y.: Pergamon-Brassey's, 1986).

For focused reviews of military manpower trends in the all-volunteer force, see Martin Binkin, "Manpower," in George E. Hudson and Joseph Kruzel, eds., *American Defense Annual, 1985–1986* (Lexington, Mass.: Lexington Books, 1985), chap. 7; David R. Segal, "Personnel," in Joseph Kruzel, ed., *American Defense Annual, 1986–1987* (1986), chap. 7; and Robert B. Pirie, Jr., "Manpower," in Joseph Kruzel, ed., *American Defense Annual, 1987–1988* (1987). A good summary of soldier attitudes in the immediate postdraft era is Jerald G. Bachman, John D. Blair, and David R. Segal, *The All-Volunteer Force* (Ann Arbor, Mich.: University of Michigan Press, 1977). An insightful essay on the societal ambiguities of staffing the armed forces is Irving Louis Horowitz, "Human Resources and Military Manpower Requirements," *Armed Forces and Society* 12, no. 2 (Winter 1986), pp. 173–92.

2. "The President's Commission on an All-Volunteer Force (Gates Commission)," *Report of the President's Commission on an All-Volunteer Armed Force* (Washington, D.C.: Government Printing Office, 1970). For analysis supporting the Gates Commission, see especially Richard V. L. Cooper, *Military Manpower and the All-Volunteer Force* (Santa Monica, Calif.: Rand, 1977). A comprehensive critique of the tendency to view armed forces in occupational rather than institutional terms is presented in Charles C. Moskos and Frank R. Wood, eds., *The Military—More Than Just a Job?* (Elmsford, N.Y.: Pergamon-Brassey's, 1988). Also see James Fallows, "Employees," in his *National Defense* (New York: Random House, 1984), pp. 107–38.

3. The figure of $16,000 as annual compensation for a private first class includes basic pay ($9,200), housing and food allowances ($3,800), monetary advantage of not having allowance counted as taxable income ($700), medical and life insurance ($2,000), and commissary and post exchange savings ($300). Even these figures understate total compensation, as they do not include enlistment bonuses, postservice educational benefits, and potential pension benefits. If these benefits are included, the total annual compensation for a private in 1985 has been calculated at $23,000! Charles Dale, "Military and Civilian Earnings," Technical Report 733, U.S. Army Research Institute for the Behavioral and Social Sciences, Alexandria, Va., 1987. Similarly, the U.S. General Accounting Office has computed the total annual compensation of a nineteen-year-old soldier with a high school diploma at $22,000 per annum in 1986. See General Accounting Office, *Military Compensation: Comparisons with Civilian Compensation and Related Issues*, NSIAD-86–31BR, June 1986; and *Military Compensation: Comparison with Federal Civil Service Compensation*, NSIAD-88–67BR, November 1987 (both Washington, D.C.: Government Printing Office).

4. Department of Defense, *Manpower Requirements Report for FY1988* (Washington, D.C.: Office of the Assistant Secretary of Defense, February 1987), section VIII. All figures in original tables are given in current dollars, therefore for purposes of this analysis, 1986 dollars are computed as 3.5 of 1964 dollars.

5. Ibid., p. VIII-3.

6. A concise guide to the current structure of reserve forces is Philip Gold, "What the Reserves Can—and Can't Do," *Public Interest* no. 75 (Spring 1984), pp. 47–61.

7. On how varying personnel factors affect military manpower, see Martin Binkin with Herschel Kanter and Rolf H. Clark, *Shaping the Defense Civilian Work Force* (Washington, D.C.: Brookings Institution, 1978); Martin Binkin and Irene Kyriakopoulos, *Youth or Experience? Manning the Modern Military* (Washington, D.C.: Brookings Institution, 1979); and Martin Binkin, *America's Volunteer Military: Progress and Prospects* (Washington, D.C.: Brookings Institution, 1984).

8. Martin Binkin and Shirley Bach, *Women and the Military* (Washington, D.C.: Brookings Institution, 1977); Judith Hicks Stiehm, *Bring Me Men and Women* (Berkeley: University of California Press, 1981); Nancy Loring Goldman, ed., *Female Soldiers—Combatants or Noncombatants?* (Westport, Conn.: Greenwood Press, 1982); and Charles C. Moskos, "Female GIs in the Field," *Society* 22, no. 6 (September-October 1985), pp. 28–33; and Patricia M. Shields, "Sex Roles in the Military," in Moskos and Wood, eds., *The Military*, pp. 109–31.

9. On some of the consequences of changing marital and family patterns in the military, see Charles C. Moskos, "The Enlisted Man in the All-Volunteer Army," in David R. Segal and H. Wallace Sinaiko, eds., *Life in the Rank and File* (Elmsford, N.Y.: Pergamon-Brassey's, 1986), pp. 35–57; and Mady Wechsler Segal, "The Military and the Family as 'Greedy Institutions,' " *Armed Forces and Society* 13, no. 1 (Fall 1986), pp. 9–38.

10. On blacks in the armed forces, see Martin Binkin and Mark J. Eitelberg with Alvin J. Schexnider and Marvin M. Smith, *Blacks and the Military* (Washington, D.C.: Brookings Institution, 1982); Bernard C. Nalty, *Strength for the Fight* (New York: Free Press, 1986); Charles C. Moskos, "Success Story: Blacks in the Army," *Atlantic* (May 1986), pp. 64–72; and John S. Butler, "Race Relations in the Military," in Moskos and Wood, eds., *The Military*, pp. 132–44.

11. Binkin and Eitelberg, *Blacks and the Military*, p. 66.

12. Bernard Beck, "The Military as a Welfare Institution," in Charles C. Moskos, ed., *Public Opinion and the Military Establishment* (Beverly Hills, Calif.: Sage, 1971), pp. 137–48.

13. On military attrition and social background, see H. Wallace Sinaiko et al., *Military Personnel: Attrition and Retention* (Alexandria, Va.: Smithsonian Institution, Manpower Research and Advisory Services, 1981); and Robert M. Baldwin and Thomas V. Daula, "The Cost of High-Quality Recruits," *Armed Forces and Society* 11, no. 1 (Fall 1984), pp. 96–114.

14. General Accounting Office, *AWOL in the Military* (Washington, D.C.: Government Printing Office, 1979); D. Bruce Bell and Thomas J. Houston, "The Vietnam Era Deserter," U.S. Army Research Institute for the Behavioral and Social Sciences, Alexandria, Va., 1976.

15. Cooper, *Military Manpower and the All-Volunteer Force*, p. 139; David J. Armor, Richard L. Fernandez, Kathy Bers, and Donna Schwarzbach, *Recruit Aptitudes and Army Job Performance* (Santa Monica, Calif.: Rand, 1982).

16. For the World War II data, see Samuel A. Stouffer et al., *The American Soldier: Combat and Its Aftermath* (Princeton, N.J.: Princeton University Press, 1949), pp. 36–41. On the Korean War, see Roger L. Egbert et al., *Fighter 1: An Analysis of Combat Fighters and Non-Fighters*, Technical Report 44 (Washington, D.C.: HumRRO, 1957). A valuable summary of the literature dealing with "quality/performance" in the military is Juri Toomepuu, *Soldier Capability-Army Combat Effectiveness—SCACE* (Ft. Benjamin Harrison, Ind.: U.S. Army Soldier Support Center, 1981). For studies completed after Toomepuu's review, see Barry L. Scribner, D. Alton Smith, Robert H. Baldwin, and Robert L.

Philips, "Are Smart Tankers Better?" *Armed Forces and Society* 12, no. 2 (Winter 1986), pp. 193–206; and David K. Horne, "The Impact of Soldier Quality on Army Performance," *Armed Forces and Society* 13, no. 3 (Spring 1987), pp. 443–55. A pathbreaking article relating soldier values to effectiveness is Stephen D. Wesbrook, "Sociopolitical Alienation and Military Efficiency," *Armed Forces and Society* 6, no. 2 (Winter 1980), pp. 170–89.

17. In 1987, major violations of recruitment procedures were reported in California, Illinois, Iowa, Michigan, Minnesota, New Jersey, Puerto Rico, and Tennessee. No major recruitment scandals had appeared in the five previous years.

18. Military Manpower Task Force, *A Report to the President on the Status and Prospects of the All-Volunteer Force* (Washington, D.C.: Government Printing Office, 1982), p. A2.

19. For current proposals to institute universal military training (UMT), see Elliot A. Cohen, *Citizens and Soldiers* (Ithaca, N.Y.: Cornell University Press, 1985); and Philip Gold, *Evasions: The American Way of Military Service* (New York: Paragon, 1985). Cohen and Gold see UMT in terms of "limited liability," that is, soldiers drafted and trained for reserve duty could not be sent overseas without declaration of war.

20. An earlier version of the citizen-soldier concept given here is Charles C. Moskos, "Making the All-Volunteer Force Work: A National Service Approach," *Foreign Affairs* 60 (Fall 1981), pp. 17–34.

21. Robert L. Kaplan and P. T. Harris, "The Measurement of High School Students' Attitudes Towards Recruiting Incentives," SR 82–3–1, U.S. Army Recruiting Command, Fort Sheridan, Ill., May 1983; David F. Burrelli, "Evaluation of the Program to Recruit College Bound Youth into the Army," unpublished doctoral dissertation, University of Chicago, 1986; Paul A. Gade and Timothy W. Elig, "The Citizen Soldier in the All-Volunteer Force: Making the Enlistment Decision," U.S. Army Research Institute for the Behavioral and Social Sciences, Alexandria, Va., 1987.

22. Studies sponsored by the Department of Defense consistently come up with the finding that a draft would likely cost more than the current volunteer force. See, for example, *The Differential Budget Costs of Conscription-Based Alternatives to the All-Volunteer Force,* (Springfield, Va.: Syllogistics, Aug., 1986). The General Accounting Office, however, has concluded that a draft would result in budgetary savings of $1.4 billion in the first year and $7.8 billion annually in the long run. General Accounting Office, *Military Draft: Potential Impacts and Other Issues,* NSIAD-88–102 (Washington, D.C.: Government Printing Office, March, 1988).

23. Congressional Budget Office, *Improving Military Educational Benefits* (Washington, D.C.: Government Printing Office), 1982, p. 50.

24. Arthur T. Hadley, *The Straw Giant* (New York: Random House, 1986).

25. Can it be coincidental that in the fifteen years since the end of the draft not a single novel has been written about the AVF? It appears that no serving member of the AVF has had the initiative and ability to write such a book and that there is little interest in the lives of service members on the part of the reading public.

Chapter Nine

1. Richard Danzig and Peter Szanton, *National Service: What Would It Mean?* (Lexington, Mass.: Lexington Books, 1986), pp. 17–40.

2. Deborah Fallows, *A Mother's Work* (New York: Houghton Mifflin, 1985). A detailed analysis of how at least 500,000 care-giver positions could be effectively filled by national servers is given in Susan Woolsey and S. Gutchess, "Child Care Jobs for National Service Participants," unpublished paper prepared for the National Service Study Project, Ford Foundation, September 1983.

3. James B. Jacobs, "The Implications of National Service for Corrections," in his *New Perspectives on Prisons and Imprisonment* (Ithaca, N.Y.: Cornell University Press, 1983), pp. 202–12.

4. Bruce C. Vladeck, *Unloving Care: The Nursing Home Tragedy* (New York: Basic Books, 1980). One study reported that chronically impaired elderly who are recipients of long-term, nonskilled home care were half as likely to be institutionalized as those not receiving such care. Susan L. Hughes, David S. Cordray, and V. Alan Spiker, "Evaluation of a Long-Term Home Care Program," *Medical Care* 22, no. 5 (1984), pp. 460–75. How the plight of those in nursing homes can be alleviated by heavy use of volunteers is discussed in Lee H. Bowker, *Humanizing Institutions for the Aged* (Lexington, Mass.: Lexington Books, 1982). According to one informed account, 30 percent or so of those even in expensive nursing homes are restrained most of the time. *Wall Street Journal*, January 29, 1988, p. 21.

5. The idea of a public corporation to be the administrative agency of national service originates with Donald J. Eberly. See Eberly, "A Model for Universal Youth Service," unpublished paper prepared for the Eleanor Roosevelt Institute, 1976; also Eberly, "An Administrative Model: National Youth Service (NYS)," in Michael W. Sherraden and Donald J. Eberly, eds., *National Service: Social, Economic and Military Impacts* (New York: Pergamon, 1982), pp. 122–24.

6. The Peace Corps might be revamped to include volunteers serving (most likely as aids to English instructors) in countries where long-term American interests would be advanced by developing a future cadre of Americans with knowledge of the host country's language and culture. Japan, China, the USSR, Israel, and most of the countries of Europe and the Arab world come quickly to mind. In the more industrialized nations, a cost-sharing feature might be introduced.

7. For a concise description of the Dutch system of delivery of human services, see Ralph M. Kramer, *Voluntary Agencies in the Welfare State* (Berkeley: University of California Press, 1981), pp. 19–37.

8. The generally unknown story of nonprofit organizations as deliverers of human service in America is given in Lester M. Salamon, "Nonprofits: The Results are Coming In," *Foundation News* (July/August 1984), pp. 16–23. On the potential of local voluntary associations in this country delivering human services at less cost to the taxpayer, see Nathan Glazer, "Towards a Self-Service Society," *Public Interest* no. 74 (Winter 1983).

9. A penetrating critique of how evaluation studies deal only with short-term and directly quantifiable outcomes is Harold L. Wilensky, "Political Legitimacy and Consensus: Missing Variables in the Assessment of Social Policy," in S. E. Spiro and E. Yuchtman-Yaar, eds., *Evaluating the Welfare State* (New York: Academic Press, 1983), pp. 51–74.

10. On CETA costs, see Grace A. Franklin and Randall B. Ripley, *CETA: Politics and Policy, 1973–1982* (Knoxville, Tenn.: University of Tennessee Press, 1984), p. 24.

11. National servers who choose not to go to college or obtain vocational training should be eligible for GI Bill-type home loans on the post-World War II model and/or some kind of modest bonus upon completion of service.

12. Robert Kuttner, "The Patrimony Society," *The New Republic*, May 11, 1987, p. 20.

13. Edward B. Fiske, "Colleges Open New Minority Drives," *New York Times*, November 18, 1987, p. 18.

14. Kathryn Mohrman, "Unintended Consequences of Federal Student Aid Policies," *Brookings Review* (Fall 1987), pp. 24–30; Jane S. Hansen, *Student Loans: Are They Overburdening a Generation?* Report prepared for the Joint Economic Committee, U.S. Congress, December 1986.

15. The probable effect of limiting college student aid to national servers might go something like the following. Some number of middle-class students who do not presently receive student aid would receive

such aid because of their enrollment in national service. But we also know that poor youth greatly oversubscribe youth corps. Thus some number of poor youth who otherwise would not go on to college will do so because of their newly acquired eligibility for student aid. I am indebted for this formulation to Richard Danzig.

16. On the political implications of means versus non-means tested social programs, see Robert Kuttner, *The Life of the Party* (New York: Elisabeth Sifton/Viking, 1987).

17. *The Forgotten Half: Non-College Youth in America* (Washington, D.C.: William T. Grant Foundation Commission on Work, Family, and Citizenship, 1988).

18. William F. Buckley, Jr., has proposed a voluntary national service in which elite colleges and universities would only accept applicants who had completed "one year in public service." As quoted in Sherraden and Eberly, eds., *National Service*, p. 116.

Chapter Ten

1. Robert Kuttner, *The Life of the Party* (New York: Elisabeth Sifton/Viking, 1987); and Paul M. Weyrich with William S. Lind and William H. Marshner, *Cultural Conservatism* (Washington, D.C.: Free Congress Research and Education Foundation, 1987). Weyrich and his associates join fellow conservative George F. Will, who has also argued that the principle of self-interest is not a suitable basis for government aiming at justice, social cohesion, and material strength. Will, *Statecraft as Soulcraft* (New York: Simon and Schuster, 1983).

2. For a summary of the Gallup and Harris poll data on national service, see U.S. Congress, House, Subcommittee on Select Education of the Committee on Education and Labor, *Select Commission on Voluntary Service Opportunities Act*, Hearings, 97th Cong., 2d sess., 1982, pp. 493–95.

3. James A. Davis and Paul B. Sheatsley, *Americans View the Military: A 1984 Update* (Chicago: National Opinion Research Center, 1985).

4. As quoted in *The New Republic*, March 11, 1985, p. 43.

5. As cited in *Army Times*, October 29, 1986, p. 11.

6. U.S. Congress, House, Subcommittee on Select Education of the Committee on Education and Labor, *Select Commission on Voluntary Service Opportunities Act*, Hearings, 97th Cong., 2d sess., 1982, pp. 31–32.

7. Nelson W. Polsby, *Political Innovation in America* (New Haven, Conn.: Yale University Press, 1983).

8. If the sobriquet "Mr. National Service" fits anyone, that person is Donald J. Eberly. No other individual has played such a key role

over such a long period in the development of national-service policy and thought. Eberly, who served as a draftee in the army in the early 1950s and subsequently did volunteer work in Nigeria, started the National Service Secretariat in 1966, the first, and for many years the only, organization formed to develop a constituency for national service. In 1986, Eberly formed the Coalition for National Service, a kind of lobby of individuals and organizations that subscribed to a common set of principles on a noncompulsory program of youth service.

Roger Landrum, a former Peace Corps volunteer, is another leading exponent of national service. In 1978, Landrum served as director of the Committee for the Study of National Service sponsored by the Potomac Institute. Landrum, like Eberly and most other national-service activists, is very much in the William Jamesian tradition that gives higher priority to civilian over military service. Landrum became codirector (with Frank Slobig) of Youth Service America, founded in 1987. The goals of Youth Service America were to advance nationwide development of local service corps and to develop a public mandate for youth service.

Youth Service America, like many other national-service initiatives, was supported by the Ford Foundation. This in large part reflects the keen interest of Franklin A. Thomas, the foundation's president, who sees national service as a way to improve the long-term employment and earning prospects of jobless youth. The Ford Foundation has been the principal supporter of the evaluation studies of state and local youth corps being carried out by Private/Public Ventures (P/PV), a Philadelphia policy analysis center concerned with youth employment and training.

Organizations with ongoing involvement in the national-service debate include: the Youth Policy Institute, under the directorship of David Hackett; the Human Environment Center, which, under founding director Sidney Howe and current head Margaret Rosenberry, has been the linchpin in the movement to start a national youth conservation corps; and the National Association of Service and Conservation Corps, whose membership represents the forty or so state and local youth corps.

No list can be complete, but the following names some of the major figures in the invisible college of national-service activists: R. Sargent Shriver, Jr., first head of the Peace Corps and Democratic candidate for vice-president in 1972; William Josephson, New York attorney, whose conceptual paper helped shape the Peace Corps and whose subsequent activities have promoted national service in both pragmatic and theoretical ways; Adam Yarmolinsky, lawyer and educator, who held high Defense Department positions in the Kennedy and Johnson administrations and was one of few to see national service in both military and civilian terms; Eddie Williams, head of the Joint Center for Political Studies, a black-oriented research organization and think tank; Anthony Kline, San Francisco juvenile court judge and key figure in the establishment of the San Francisco Conservation Corps; Matthew Cossolotto, former Peace Corps volunteer and present congressional staffer who watches out for national service on the legislative front; Cynthia Parsons, former education editor of the *Christian Science Monitor*, who has stimulated a school-based program of youth service in her home state of Vermont.

Current developments in national service can be followed in the newsletters of the National Service Secretariat (5140 Sherier Pl., NW, Washington, DC 20016), Youth Service America (1319 F Street, NW, Suite 900, Washington, DC 20004), and the Human Environment Center (810 Eighteenth Street, NW, Suite 507, Washington, DC 20006). The literature on national service is not extensive, but for background see Donald J. Eberly, ed., *A Profile of National Service* (New York: Overseas Educational Service, 1966); Donald J. Eberly, ed., *National Service: Report of a Conference* (New York: Russell Sage, 1968); "The Quest for Equity: National Service Options," special issue of *Teachers College Record* 73, no. 1 (September 1971); Potomac Institute, *Youth and the Needs of the Nation* (Washington, D.C.: Potomac Institute, 1979); Potomac Institute, *National Youth Service: What's at Stake* (Washington, D.C.: Potomac Institute, 1979); Youth Policy Institute, *National Service and America's Future* (Washington, D.C.: Youth Policy Institute, 1984). Only two books before this one have been commercially published on the subject: Michael W. Sherraden and Donald J. Eberly, eds., *National Service: Social, Economic and Military Impacts* (New York: Pergamon, 1982); and Richard Danzig and Peter Szanton, *National Service: What Would it Mean?* (Lexington, Mass.: Lexington Books, 1986), in which see especially the bibliography.

Interesting and relevant observations on national service are found in Timothy Noah, "We Need You," *Washington Monthly*, November 1986, pp. 35–41. A successful effort to place the national-service discussion in a broader political and intellectual context is Randall Rothenberg, "National Service," in Rothenberg, *The Neo-Liberals* (New York: Simon and Schuster, 1984), pp. 208–20.

9. Arthur M. Schlesinger, Jr., *The Cycles of American History* (New York: Houghton Mifflin, 1986).

10. Albert O. Hirschman, *Shifting Involvements: Private Interest and Public Action* (Princeton, N.J.: Princeton University Press, 1982).

11. Paul S. Applebaum, "Crazy in the Streets," *Commentary* 83, no. 5 (May 1985), pp. 34–39.

12. Danzig and Szanton, *National Service*, pp. 17–40.

13. Charles C. Moskos, "The Social Equivalent of Military Service," *Teachers College Record* 73, no. 1 (September 1971), p. 10.

14. Ole R. Holsti and James N. Rosenau, *American Leadership in World Affairs: Vietnam and the Breakdown of Consensus* (Winchester, Mass.: George Allen and Unwin, 1984).

15. Thomas Bender, "Making History Whole Again," *New York Times Book Review*, October 6, 1985, pp. 1, 42–43.

16. Seymour Martin Lipset and William Schneider, *The Confidence Gap* (New York: Free Press, 1983).

17. Scott McConnell, "Vietnam and the 60's Generation," *Commentary* 79, no. 6 (June 1985), pp. 40–46.

Appendix

1. The information on national service in Britain is based mainly on two interviews with Alec Dickson during his visits to the United States. See also Alec Dickson, *A Chance to Serve* (London: Dobson Books, 1976).

2. This account of Katimavik in Canada draws heavily from Michael W. Sherraden and Donald J. Eberly, "Reflections on Katimavik, an Innovative Canadian Youth Program," unpublished paper, January 1986; and P/PV, *Youth Corps Case Studies: Katimavik, The Canadian Youth Corps* (Philadelphia: Public/Private Ventures, 1986). I am also indebted to Ken de la Barre, former deputy senior director of Katimavik, for printed and telephoned information on the program.

3. A seminal study of alternative service in West Germany is Jürgen Kuhlman, "Wehrpflicht und alternative zivile Dienste in der Bundesrepublik Deutschland," paper presented at the International Conference of the Inter-University Seminar on Armed Forces and Society, Chicago, October 21–23, 1983. Basic information is found in Bundesamt für den Zivildienst, "Datum und Fakten zur Entwicklung von Kriegsdienstverweigerung und Zivildienst" (February 1986). Current developments are covered in the government magazine *Der Zivildienst*. I am grateful to Bernhard Fleckenstein and his colleagues in the Sozialwissenschaftliches Institut der Bundeswehr (Munich) for their time and generosity in obtaining and sharing data on *Zivildienst*.

Index